Queering the Global Filipina Body

THE ASIAN AMERICAN EXPERIENCE

Series Editors
Eiichiro Azuma
Jigna Desai
Martin F. Manalansan IV
Lisa Sun-Hee Park
David K. Yoo

Roger Daniels, Founding Series Editor

A list of books in the series appears at the end of this book.

Queering the Global Filipina Body

Contested Nationalisms in the Filipina/o Diaspora

GINA K. VELASCO

UNIVERSITY OF ILLINOIS PRESS
Urbana, Chicago, and Springfield

Publication of this book was supported by funding from
Gettysburg College.

Library of Congress Cataloging-in-Publication Data
Names: Velasco, Gina K., 1977– author.
Title: Queering the global Filipina body: contested nationalisms
    in the Filipina/o diaspora/ Gina K. Velasco.
Description: Urbana: University of Illinois Press, 2020. | Series:
    The Asian American experience | Includes bibliographical
    references and index
Identifiers: LCCN 2020025978 (print) | LCCN 2020025979
    (ebook) | ISBN 9780252043475 (cloth) | ISBN 9780252085376
    (paperback) | ISBN 9780252052354 (ebook)
Subjects: LCSH: Women—Philippines—Social conditions. |
    Women household employees—Philippines. | Filipinos—
    United States. | Women in popular culture—Philippines. |
    Women in popular culture—United States. | Feminist
    theory. | Queer theory.
Classification: LCC HQ1757 .V43 2020 (print) | LCC HQ1757
    (ebook) | DDC 305.409599—dc23
LC record available at https://lccn.loc.gov/2020025978
LC ebook record available at https://lccn.loc.gov/2020025979

In memory of my grandmother Lody Chan Kummer (1937–2003),
who was the heart of our family and an inspiration to me always.
Your love, support, and confidence in me have sustained me
throughout the long years of finishing this book.

Contents

Acknowledgments

The seeds of this book began many years ago when I was an undergraduate student activist fighting for Asian American studies at the University of Texas at Austin. Professors Kamala Visweswaran and Asale Angel-Ajani, feminist activists and scholars of color, were the first to encourage me to apply to graduate school. My political analysis was sharpened by my organizing work with fellow student activists in the Asian American Relations Group and the Anti-Racist Organizing Committee. In particular, I thank Yalini Thambynayagam, Andre Lancaster, Jacob Childress, Zafar Shah, Robyn Citizen, and Jamie Munkatchy for their friendship, hard work, and commitment to our collective goals. Andre, may you rest in power. We lost you far too soon, my brother.

I collected the raw materials for this research project while completing my PhD in the History of Consciousness program at the University of California at Santa Cruz. I thank my dissertation committee, Neferti Tadiar, Donna Haraway, James Clifford, and Anjali Arondekar, for their patience, support, and guidance during the early years of my intellectual training. While this project has greatly transformed from its earliest roots in my graduate studies, it would not have been possible without the interdisciplinary theoretical training I received in the History of Consciousness program.

The following grants and fellowships made the writing of this book possible: the Eugene Cota-Robles Fellowship at the University of California at Santa

Cruz, the Davis Putter Scholarship Fund grant, the University of California Office of the President Dissertation Year Fellowship, and the Andrew W. Mellon Foundation Postdoctoral Fellowship in the Humanities at Bryn Mawr College. Publication of this book was supported by funding from Gettysburg College.

My enduring gratitude goes to the artists whose work inspired parts of this book, including the Mail Order Brides/M.O.B. (Jenifer Wofford, Reanne Estrada, and Eliza Barrios) and Gigi Otálvaro-Hormillosa. I also thank the students and faculty at the Philippine Studies Program for your support of this project.

This book is truly the product of the communities that have held me up and sustained me through the long years since I entered academia. My graduate school partner in crime, Andrew Wegley, has had my back since that first day we met while looking for apartments in Santa Cruz almost two decades ago. The Research Cluster for the Study of Women of Color in Collaboration and Conflict, particularly my writing group members Pascha Bueno-Hansen, Elisa Huerta, and Rose Cohen, showed me what peer mentoring, solidarity, and accountability look like in practice. Thank you also to Deb Vargas and Maylei Blackwell, two WOCas who have mentored me since my days at UCSC. I owe a debt of gratitude to the founding advisor to the WOC Cluster, Professor Angela Davis. There are many colleagues, mentors, and friends who have shaped the multiple itera-tions of these pages over the years, including Lázaro Lima, Verónica Martínez-Matsuda, Jin Haritaworn, Jian Neo Chen, Riley Snorton, Aren Aizura, Roderick Ferguson, and Tara Daly. I thank Gayatri Gopinath for her support while I was a visiting scholar at the Center for the Study of Gender and Sexuality at New York University. Thank you to Cathy Schlund-Vials for her invitation to participate in the Asian American Studies Institute workshop at the University of Con-necticut at Storrs. Feedback from the workshop participants, Cathy Schlund-Vials, Jennifer Ho, Asha Nadkarni, Heather Turcotte, Jason Chang, and Brian Locke, helped me to revise chapter 1. Ivette Rivera-Giusti, Roberta Hunte, and Neba Noyan helped brighten my days amid the gray skies of Portland, Oregon. I offer big *abrazos* to Patricia Pedroza, my closest friend during my time in the snowy woods of New Hampshire. My writing accountability partners over the years have kept me on track: Erica Williams, Robin Turner, Sonny Nordmarken, Michelle Hardesty, Caroline Ferraris-Besso, and Pavitra Sundar. Thank you for your consistency. I owe a debt of gratitude to my editor, Dawn Durante, whose patience and steadfast support over the years guided the overdue birth of this book. You are a book doula extraordinaire!

Filipina/o studies has always been an intellectual home for me. I thank the many Filipina/o scholars who read chapter drafts and supported the research that led to this book, including Joi Barrios, Faye Caronan, Kale Fajardo, Verna-dette Gonzalez, Theo Gonzalvez, Allan Isaac, Joyce Mariano, Victor Mendoza, Rhacel Parreñas, Dylan Rodriguez, Robyn Rodriguez, Sarita See, Celine Parreñas Shimizu, Harrod Suarez, and Roland Tolentino. I have been fortunate to be a part of a community of Filipina/o studies scholars who have provided collegial-ity and friendship to me since my days as a graduate student, including Ethel Tungohan, Genevieve Clutario, Tessa Ong Winkelmann, Nerissa Balce, Jeffrey Santa Ana, Robert Diaz, Karen Buenavista Hanna, and Mark Villegas. Martin Manalansan has been a mentor par excellence to me and to an entire genera-tion of Filipina/o studies and queer studies scholars.

Gettysburg College has truly been a wonderful place to work. In particular, I thank my colleagues in the Women, Gender, and Sexuality Studies Program for their support over the years: Nathalie Lebon, Temma Berg, Susan Russell, Lin Myers, Isabel Valiela, Beatriz Trigo, and Stephanie Sellers. Radi Rangelova, Jennifer Bloomquist, Hakim Williams, McKinley Melton, and Megan Adam-son Sijapati have been ideal mentors and friends. Ari and Gia Dimitriou, Amy Young Evrard, Alex Trillo, Veronica Calvillo, Ivanova Reyes, Mónica Vallin, Aarón Lacayo, Nathifa Greene, and David Walsh have given me the experience of camaraderie and community, a rare gift within academia. Provost Chris Zappe has been a supportive advocate for me and my family since our arrival on cam-pus. Thank you also to the Growing Place at Gettysburg College for providing peace of mind and excellent childcare.

My friends and family have kept me grounded through the many changes that an academic life brings. From Oakland to Dallas to Washington, DC, my network of friends and loved ones reminds me of who I am. Thank you to Yalini Thambynayagam, Michelle Rodriguez, and Miranda Shackelford for the multiple decades of friendship, support, and phone calls, despite my five cross-country moves. Savannah Shange, thank you for being my dharma sis through it all. I am grateful to Pascal Emmer, Q Quintero, Allison Joy Faelnar, Connie Yip, Shereen D'Souza, and Xiaojing Wang for making Oakland and New York still feel like home. Tania Lee and Elaine Kamlley, thank you for driving up from DC to see us on a regular basis! To Karon Mershani, Nydia Mershani, Jana Essary, and Sue Cavaco, thank you for welcoming me into your family. Many thanks to my Tito Junior and his family, Tita Vee, Dino, Rico, Karen, Dominic, Trina, and Joy, for their generosity and hospitality during my stays in Manila. The Kummer family in Dallas has always been my heart home. I am grateful to Liza Kummer, Maria Lott, Ted Kummer Jr., Michael Kummer, and Richie Kummer for being the aunts and uncles I could always come home to. Louie Kummer, I wish you could be here to celebrate with me. Thank you to my brother, Jon Velasco, for being the best *tito* to Zayn and Zara and caretaker of Kala. Of course, I owe the largest *utang na loob* to my parents, Ricardo Velasco and Genie Kummer Velasco. I can finally answer "Now!" to your question, "When will you finish your book?" Thank you for everything.

Thank you most of all to Aisha Mershani, who gave me the life and family that I always wanted. I love you. To Zayn and Zara, you are the purest joy of my heart. I am grateful for the gift of your lives every day.

Queering the Global Filipina Body

Introduction

The Global Filipina Body

The second season of the TLC cable television show *90 Day Fiancé* introduced viewers to Daya, a pediatric nurse and a prospective bride from the Philippines who travels to the United States for the first time on a K-1 visa (a "fiancé visa") to visit Brett, a white American man who lives in Washington state. A US-based reality television show, *90 Day Fiancé* offers a glimpse into the lives of couples who meet by correspondence. Replacing the older paper catalogs of international matchmaking services of the 1980s and 1990s, the Internet now serves as the medium through which long-distance couples meet. Each season of *90 Day Fiancé* focuses on a group of these couples, in which one member of the couple arranges to bring his or her fiancé to the United States on a ninety-day visa. The couple has three months to meet in person for the first time, fall in love, and marry. The audience shares in the tears and frustration experienced by Daya as she faces rejection from Brett's overprotective mother, who fears that Daya is only interested in Brett for his US citizenship. Against all obstacles, Daya and Brett proceed to fall in love and get married during the course of her three-month stay in Washington. This drama plays out the familiar tropes of the global Filipina body with which US consumers of popular culture are already familiar. The figure of Daya, who is both a nurse and a prospective "mail-order bride," embodies two tropes of Filipina/o transnationalism for the ninety-five million viewers of the TLC channel: the hardworking Filipina nurse who migrates to work abroad and the mail-order bride who seeks an American man to marry for purposes of immigration.[1] The nurse and the mail-order bride are examples of the "global Filipina body," a term I use to describe the gendered figures of Filipina/o transnationalism that embody the forms of domestic, sexual, and affective labor that Filipina/o workers provide for a global economy. Responding to global capital's need for devalued, flexible labor, the Philippine state has played a significant role in brokering a contemporary global labor diaspora of more than eight million Filipina/o migrant workers.[2] Although they are not all women, Filipina/o workers perform gendered labor, working as nurses, maids, nannies, eldercare providers, housewives, and sex workers. Despite the diversity of the kinds of gendered transnational labor that Filipinas provide—from the domestic labor of maids to the sexual labor of sex workers—these distinct forms of labor are often collapsed in the generalized figure of the global Filipina body within both global popular culture and Filipina/o American cultural production.

The familiarity of US audiences with the figure of the Filipina mail-order bride on the television show *90 Day Fiancé* reflects the circulation of this figure within Global North popular culture from the 1990s onward. For example, on an episode of the popular 1990s US television sitcom *Frasier*, Frasier's father tells him that for "that amount of money, you could buy a Filipino wife."[3] Over two decades later, if one were to Google the term "Filipina," dozens of mail-order bride websites and news articles about migrant Filipina domestic workers in places such as Singapore and Saudi Arabia would appear onscreen. From the widespread representation of Filipinas on internet dating websites and films such as *The Adventures of Priscilla, Queen of the Desert* and *Closer to Home*, to actor Alec Baldwin's controversial quip in 2009 (on the television show *Late Night with David Letterman*) that he would enlarge his family by "looking for a Filipino mail-order bride," it is clear that global Filipina bodies are omnipresent figures within contemporary popular culture in the Global North.[4] These multiple iterations of the global Filipina body circulate within US popular culture, from the figure of the hyperexploited Filipina overseas domestic laborer (maid, nanny, or eldercare provider) to the figure of the Filipina sex worker / trafficked woman—a participant or victim (within the "traffic-in-women" discourse) in the international sex trade. From 1990s films to more recent cable reality shows, these examples demonstrate a dominant capitalist logic in which Filipina bodies are represented as sources of easily available sexual, domestic, and affective labor.

As a Filipina mail-order bride character, Daya is familiar to viewers of *90 Day Fiancé* because of the broader material context of Filipina laboring bodies under neoliberalism. Daya, who is both a nurse and a mail-order bride, is a popular cultural example of the global Filipina body, a figure that embodies the gendered affective and sexual labor that migrant Filipina/o workers provide for a global economy. A figure for the feminized position of the Philippines within a gendered international division of labor, the global Filipina body serves as a "geobody" for the Philippine nation's status under contemporary neoliberal globalization. Philippine film studies scholar Roland Tolentino introduced the term "geobody" to describe how transnational figures such as the Filipina mail-order bride stand in for the Philippine nation itself.[5] Daya is a geobody for the Philippine nation. She corporealizes devalued and feminized Filipina/o transnational labor. Within both global popular culture and Filipina/o diasporic culture, the ubiquitous figure of the global Filipina body signifies the subjection of Filipina/o bodies to the gendered and racialized effects of neoliberal globalization. As such, the global Filipina body indexes broader debates about gendered migrant labor and embodiment in the context of globalization. Whether represented as a mail-order bride, trafficked woman, or overseas contract worker, the figure of the global Filipina body makes evident the ways in which global capitalism naturalizes exploited racialized and gendered labor.[6]

The Global Filipina Body examines several instantiations of the global Filipina body that circulate within Filipina/o American cultural production, including the mail-order bride, the Filipina sex worker / trafficked woman, the *balikbayan*, and the cyborg.[7] Each of these figures embodies the gendered and sexual politics of representing the Philippine nation within the Filipina/o diasporic imagination. My analysis of these gendered figures of Filipina/o transnationalism reveals the essential contradictions that are at the heart of this project; on the one hand, *The Global Filipina Body* critiques the heteronormativity and masculinism of diasporic nationalisms as they are reproduced within Filipina/o American performance, film, video, and heritage language programs. On the other hand, in the context of the Filipina/o diaspora, the Philippine nation continues to function as a sign of sovereignty and liberation from neoimperialism and neoliberal globalization.

The Failure of the Heteropatriarchal Nation

A naked Filipina woman faces backward, gaze downward, with the words "For Export" stamped in red ink on her bare back. The naked figure is facing a bare concrete wall, her face mostly obscured, in what could be assumed to be a cell or space of involuntary confinement. This image accompanied an article in the online news source, GMA News Source, a website that provides Philippine news for Filipinos across the diaspora.[8] The familiarity of this image reflects the ubiquity of images of trafficked women within both US popular culture and Filipina/o diasporic culture. From the *Taken* films, starring Liam Neeson, to the antitrafficking campaigns of the women's philanthropic organization Soroptomists

International, the figure of the trafficked woman is pervasive.[9] The article, written by Lila Ramos Shahani, an assistant secretary during the Aquino Philippine presidential administration and head of communications of the Human Development and Poverty Reduction Cabinet Cluster, was originally delivered as the keynote lecture at a conference held at the University of Washington, Seattle, titled "Human Trafficking in an Era of Globalization: Forced Labor, Involuntary Servitude, and Corporate and Civic Responsibility" in January 2013.[10] The image accompanied a poignant story of a young Filipina girl who was offered a high-paying waitress job abroad and who arrived in Malaysia to find out that she had been deceived. Instead, she was held against her will and forced into sexual slavery. Intended to invoke transnational affects of pity and indignation, the figure of the Filipina trafficked woman is pervasive within Filipina/o diasporic political culture. However, the figure of the Filipina trafficked woman is often collapsed with the migrant sex worker. The traffic-in-women discourse, as it circulates within contemporary Filipina/o American cultural production, makes very little distinction between migrant workers who do domestic work, migrant sex workers who choose to do sex work, and migrant Filipinas who are forced or coerced into sexual labor. The traffic-in-women discourse often conflates distinct forms of gendered labor, such as the domestic labor performed by maids and nannies and the sexual labor of Filipina bar hostesses in Japan.

The fraught politics of the heteropatriarchal nation, transnational labor, and global capitalism coalesce within the constellation of figures of racialized, gendered Filipina/o labor—the trafficked woman, the mail-order bride, the domestic helper—that constitute the global Filipina body. The figure of the global Filipina body circulates within the political-economic context of outward transnational labor migration from the Philippines.[11] While there have been several studies of Filipina/o migration and the gendered transnational labor market, there has been less scholarship on how the global Filipina body circulates as a figure within both global popular culture and Filipina/o diasporic culture, particularly from a cultural studies viewpoint. Sociologists Anna Guevarra and Robyn Rodriguez have described how the Philippine state brokers a contemporary global labor diaspora of more than eight million gendered Filipina/o workers, including nurses, maids, nannies, eldercare providers, housewives, and sex workers.[12] Philippine literary and film studies scholars Neferti Tadiar, Caroline Hau, and Roland Tolentino have argued that Filipina domestic workers, sex workers, and mail-order brides serve as a sign of the Philippine nation, as well as the commodification of gendered Philippine labor within the global economy.[13] Unlike these texts, however, this project combines textual and visual analysis with ethnographic methods to examine both the representation of the global Filipina body within Filipina/o American cultural production and the social worlds in which these discourses circulate. *The Global Filipina Body* introduces an interdisciplinary and transnational feminist cultural studies analysis of the broader discursive terrain of the global Filipina body as a sign of the broader gendered and sexual politics of the Philippine nation within the Filipina/o diaspora.

The identification of the Philippine nation with sex work, both by the international sex industry and by nationalist movements in the Philippines, incites broader nationalist anxieties about transnational capital's threat to the sovereignty of the heteropatriarchal nation.[14] In the diasporic context, the exploitation of the global Filipina body—who provides gendered and sexual labor outside the domestic space of the Philippines—signifies both the failure of the heteropatriarchal nation under global capital and the racialization of an international division of labor. Within the Philippines and its diaspora, the trafficked woman / sex worker embodies the crisis of the Philippine nation under global capitalism. As Tadiar has argued, the figure of the Filipina sex worker signals the shift in the Philippine economy to export-oriented industrialization and tourism, showing how "prostituted women thus became the symptoms of the crisis of the nation."[15] The figure of the Filipina sex worker / trafficked woman exemplifies the subordination of the Philippine nation within an international division of labor, highlighting the Philippine economy's reliance on remittances from Filipina/o workers abroad. Within Filipina/o diasporic culture, the Filipina sex worker / trafficked woman epitomizes the threat of transnational capital to the heteropatriarchy of the nation.[16]

The trope of the sex worker as the sign of the heteronormative nation's failure in the face of capitalist exploitation is not new. Queer theorist Roderick Ferguson discusses a similar trope in the work of Karl Marx in which the sex worker (or prostitute, in Marx's terms) represents the threat of capitalist exploitation. The figure of the sex worker signifies the broader commodified condition of labor, symbolizing human degradation under capitalism. Ferguson specifically addresses the "drag queen" sex worker of color as "the other of heteropatriarchal ideals, an other that is simultaneously the effect of racial, gender, sexual, and class discourses, an other that names the social upheavals of capital as racialized disruptions."[17] Tadiar describes the position of the Philippine nation within a global capitalist economy: "In this misogynist, homophobic, racist worldview, pussy is not only what the Philippines *has*, it is what the Philippines *is*."[18] In this sense, the global Filipina body signifies the failure of the heteropatriarchal family to retain a traditional gendered division of labor (a rupture of traditional forms of gendered domesticity, with women providing domestic and sexual labor only for their husbands, not for clients outside the home), as well as the inability of the heteropatriarchal nation to maintain its sovereignty in the face of global capital. Here, the cohesiveness of the national body as a heteropatriarchal unit is threatened by the "prostitution" of feminized transnational labor migration. Philippine popular discourses echo this anxiety that Filipina women's migration abroad causes the breakdown of the nuclear family; popular and scholarly narratives portray the challenges of transnational parenting and the plight of unemployed men whose wives are working abroad. Within both Philippine popular culture and scholarship on transnational Filipina/o labor—from the popular Philippine film *Anak* to the ethnographic research of sociologist Rhacel Parreñas, who describes the effects of labor migration on the children left behind—the deterioration of the heteronormative nuclear family has been a highly visible discourse.[19] Nationalist anxieties about the maintenance of the heteronormative family unit persist within Philippine popular culture precisely because transnational labor migration destabilizes the gendered and sexual politics of the nation.

If the figure of the global Filipina body reflects nationalist anxieties about the destabilization of the heteropatriarchal nation, then this figure also has the potential to "queer" the Philippine nation-state. By this I mean that the figure of the global Filipina body, as well as the transnational labor that she represents, highlights the impotence of the heteropatriarchal Philippine state to provide for and protect its citizens and reveals the porosity that the diaspora introduces into the boundaries of the nation-state. Here I use the term "queer" to refer to the way in which the diaspora, and transnational labor more specifically, requires a renegotiation of the gendered and sexual politics of the nation.[20] Transnational labor is an essential site in which the heteropatriarchal politics of imagining the Philippine nation within its diaspora are negotiated. The Filipina trafficked woman / sex worker corporealizes the gendered and sexual anxieties of the Philippine nation, as her body signifies the gendered subordination of the Philippines to an international division of labor. Thus, transnational labor functions to "queer" the Philippine nation not only because the diaspora has the potential to disrupt the politics of nationalism but also because transnational labor unsettles the very heteropatriarchy of the nation itself.[21] The crisis of the emasculation of the Philippine nation under global capital is manifested in the global Filipina body. This diasporic anxiety is evident in the pervasiveness of figures such as the mail-order bride and the sex worker / trafficked woman, iterations of the global Filipina body that circulate within Filipina/o American cultural production. Representations of the global Filipina body are always already formed in relation to the overarching fear of the failure of the heteropatriarchal nation. The gendered and sexualized labor provided by the global Filipina body—within the homes, bedrooms, and brothels of the Global North—cannot be contained within the heteronormative family of the Philippine nation.

The queering of the global Filipina body also introduces a shift within the field of queer studies to an analysis of racialized, transnational labor within queer cultural politics. The global Filipina body represents a double and multidirectional queering of both the heteropatriarchal nation and the field of queer studies. More specifically, *The Global Filipina Body* presents a queer analysis of the nationalist politics of diaspora within Filipina/o American cultural production and heritage language programs. This study explores how Filipina/o American tropes of the Philippine nation, which both reproduce and challenge the heteronormativity and masculinism of nationalism, can encompass a queer and feminist imagining of the Filipina/o diaspora. The historical role of the Philippines within the US imperial imagination and the influence of US capital in shaping contemporary notions of Philippine national identity inform this book's focus on Filipina/o American cultural production.[22] *The Global Filipina Body* uses a *queer diasporic* approach to analyze the politics of nationalism in the Filipina/o diaspora from a Filipina/o American feminist and queer perspective. In doing so, this project integrates transnational feminist analyses of globalized gendered labor with a consideration of queer cultural politics. Ultimately, *The Global Filipina Body* uses a queer diasporic analytical framework to ask how we can envision forms of belonging beyond the familial model of the nation, even as we hold on to the liberatory potential of popular nationalist movements as vehicles of struggle against US neoimperialism and capitalist globalization.

A queer diasporic approach to theorizing Filipina/o American culture must foreground how gender and sexuality shape multiple modes of national belonging and citizenship in a transnational context. While much of queer studies scholarship has critiqued or dismissed the nation for its heteronormativity and masculinism, few scholars have focused on queer engagements with nationalism as a form of anticapitalist and anti-imperialist resistance.[23] Despite the turn toward transnationalism in queer studies, this field of study has largely ignored diasporic subjects who participate in anticapitalist and anti-imperialist struggle in the name of national liberation, while simultaneously engaging with feminist and queer critiques of the nation. In contrast, I argue that even as the figure of the global Filipina body signifies the failure of the heteropatriarchal nation under global capitalism, the "queering" of this figure within Filipina/o American diasporic cultural production can destabilize the gendered and sexual politics of diasporic nationalisms. The *queering* of the global Filipina body requires a simultaneous consideration of cultural production by queer Filipina/o Americans as well as a contestation of the gender and sexual politics of the nation in the diasporic context.

Indeed, it could be argued that diasporic nationalisms are an inherently queer—in the unfixed and multivalent sense of the term—phenomenon. James Clifford describes the instability of diasporic nationalisms, arguing that "whatever their ideologies of purity, diasporic cultural forms can never, in practice, be exclusively nationalist. They are deployed in transnational networks built from multiple attachments, and they encode practices of accommodation with, as well as resistance to, host countries and their norms."[24] The global Filipina body is a sign that is invoked in the name of diasporic nationalisms, even as it is reworked and reconfigured through queer Filipina/o American cultural production. The queer diasporic framework of *The Global Filipina Body* builds on the work of queer of color and queer globalization scholars, such as Roderick Ferguson, Jacqui Alexander, and David Eng, who critique the masculinist and heteronormative politics of nationalism, from Ferguson's critique of black revolutionary nationalism to Eng's critique of Asian American cultural nationalism.[25] As scholarship in queer globalization studies has shown, the diaspora presents the possibility of queering the nation, as well as the risk of reifying conservative forms of nationalism.[26] In her discussion of queer South Asian diasporic cultural production, Gayatri Gopinath argues that a "consideration of queerness . . . becomes a way to challenge nationalist ideologies by restoring the impure, the inauthentic, nonreproductive potential to the diaspora."[27] However, unlike much of the previous scholarship within queer of color and queer globalization studies, *The Global Filipina Body* insists on the political potential of nationalism(s) as a form of anti-imperialist struggle, despite the legitimate critiques of the heteronormativity and masculinisms of such formations.

The Global Filipina Body's queer and feminist analysis of nationalism requires a delineation of the distinct political stakes between imperialist forms of nationalism in the Global North and anticolonial, anti-imperialist, and antistate popular nationalist movements in the Global South.[28] The resurgence of white nationalism that characterized the 2016 US presidential election of Donald Trump exemplifies the risks of imperialist forms of nationalism that are backed by white supremacy and state power. Since Trump's assumption of the US presidency in 2017, the administration of Rodrigo Duterte in the Philippines has worked hand in hand with the Trump administration to enact authoritarian state violence.[29] Duterte has focused on a genocidal "war on drugs" that has resulted in over twenty-three thousand deaths, many of them extrajudicial killings, from drug users and drug dealers to judges, attorneys, and progressive activists.[30] Since

2018 Trump has largely focused on the detention of undocumented migrants and their children, leading to family separation and, in some cases, death while in US migrant detention facilities. While both Trump and Duterte have used the rhetoric of the nation to legitimize state violence, popular nationalist movements in the Philippines continue to struggle for national liberation from Philippine state power, US imperialism, and the effects of neoliberal globalization. It is thus crucial to distinguish between the forms of authoritarian state violence enacted in the name of the nation and antistate social movements that organize under the discourse of national liberation. Popular nationalist movements in the Philippines and its diaspora, such as the National Democratic movement, have long harnessed the power of nationalist discourse to combat both ongoing forms of US imperialism and Philippine state oppression.[31]

Ultimately, *The Global Filipina Body* contends that queer Filipina/o American cultural production has the potential to disrupt diasporic discourses of the nation as they are corporealized within the figure of the global Filipina body. *The Global Filipina Body* builds on the burgeoning field of queer Filipina/o American studies, including the work of Martin Manalansan, Kale Fajardo, Allan Isaac, Robert Diaz, Victor Mendoza, and Martin Joseph Ponce.[32] A queer diasporic analysis of the figure of the global Filipina body integrates a queer politic into the discourse of anti-imperialist nationalisms. Far from a static figure, the global Filipina body has been reimagined by queer Filipina/o American artists and cultural workers to destabilize the normative gendered and sexual politics of this figure as a geobody for the Philippine nation. As I discuss in chapter 3, the campy visual and performance art of the Filipina American art group Mail Order Brides/M.O.B. reworks the figure of the Filipina mail-order bride, another instantiation of the global Filipina body. Visual and performance art by Mail Order Brides/M.O.B. *queers* the global Filipina body through their parody of the figure of the mail-order bride. In doing so, they shift from the popular discourse of the mail-order bride as an abject figure of the sexual subjugation of the Philippine nation to a critique of the gendered politics of respectability within Filipina/o American cultural nationalism that are embedded within popular discourses about mail-order brides. In this way, the reconfiguration of the global Filipina body within Filipina/o diasporic cultural production implicitly challenges the heteropatriarchal politics of the nation.

A transnational feminist critique is central to *The Global Filipina Body*'s queer diasporic analysis of Filipina/o American cultural production.[33] In my discussion of the global Filipina body as a sign of gendered labor migration from the Philippines, I draw on Chandra Mohanty's germinal argument that the subjectivity of the "third world woman worker" is crucial to theorizing the racialization and gendering of transnational labor, as well as a starting point for modes of transnational feminist solidarity.[34] The nationalist anxiety incited by the figure of the global Filipina body as a provider of sexual labor also indexes ongoing debates within both transnational feminist theory and social movements on the politics of sex work.[35] Framed within the discourse of the "traffic in women," the global Filipina body is situated between, on the one hand, activist work to end human trafficking and, on the other hand, feminist calls for the rights and protections of sex work as a legitimate form of labor. Like those of other transnational feminist theorists, my analysis of the global Filipina body draws on earlier theorizations of the intersections of race, gender, sexuality, and class by women of color feminist scholars.[36] As a sign of the gendered and sexual politics of representing the Philippine nation, the figure of the global Filipina body also highlights the tension between feminisms and the nation.[37] However, as I discuss in chapter 1, critiques of nationalism within US feminist and queer theory have been challenged by some Filipina/o diasporic feminists, such as Delia Aguilar, who argue for an explicitly nationalist, antistate perspective.[38] This tension between US feminists who argue against nationalism as a form of heteropatriarchy and feminists from the Global South who view national liberation as intertwined with feminist goals must be situated within a critique of historical and contemporary forms of US empire.

The Global Filipina Body builds on Philippine and Filipina/o American studies' emphasis on the past and present imperial relationship of the United States to the Philippines as constitutive of both a Philippine national imagination and the transnational imagination articulated within the diaspora.[39] The archive of *The Global Filipina Body*, found primarily in Filipina/o American diasporic cultural production from the 1990s to the 2010s, must be situated in relation to the history and ongoing presence of US imperialism in the Philippines, the historical impetus for Filipina/o migration to the United States. The centrality of critiques of US imperialism within Filipina/o American studies has complicated its relationship to the broader project of Asian American studies, which has historically focused on a framework of immigration, not US empire. Kandace Chuh describes how the field of Asian American studies has been complicit in the US national "forgetting" of Filipino Americans: "Because . . . Asian American strategic identities have been organized largely through paradigms of inclusion and exclusion most often articulated through the trope of immigration in Asian Americanist discourse, Filipino Americans have been repeatedly cast out into the space of difference that must be forgotten rather than the identity to be sustained."[40] E. San Juan Jr. also notes the distinction between Filipina/o Americans and other Asian Americans: "The chief distinction of Filipinos from other Asians domiciled here is that their country of origin was the object of violent colonization by US finance capital. It is this foundational event, not the fabled presence in Louisiana of Filipino fugitives from the Spanish galleons, that establishes the limit and potential of the Filipino lifeworld."[41] As scholars within Filipina/o American studies and Philippine studies have noted, the invasion and occupation of the Philippines by the United States is the elided historical condition of possibility for the notion of a Filipina/o American identity. Oscar Campomanes contends that the very idea of a Filipina/o American identity relies on the purposeful amnesia of the US colonization of the Philippines, contributing to the notion of American exceptionalism.[42] Indeed, Dylan Rodriguez goes so far as to argue that the pursuit of Filipina/o American studies as an academic discipline entails a disavowal of the genocide enacted by the US military during the Philippine American War.[43] As a body of scholarship, Filipina/o American studies has largely foregrounded US empire as a fundamental locus of analysis; this has not necessarily been the case for Philippine studies or studies of the Filipina/o diaspora outside the United States.[44] Increasingly, Filipina/o American and Filipina/o Canadian studies scholars have explored the relationship of diasporic subjects and diasporic cultural production to US empire and neoliberal globalization more broadly.[45]

Tracking the Global Filipina Body: Archive and Method

The global Filipina body—manifest as the trafficked woman / sex worker, the mail-order bride, or the domestic worker—is ever present within Filipina/o diasporic cultural production. The figure of the global Filipina body stands in for the Philippine nation itself as it is reduced to the gendered and sexual labor that it provides for a global economy. The pervasiveness of the global Filipina body across diverse sites within the Filipina/o diaspora, from websites, film, video and performance art to heritage language programs and Pilipino Cultural Night performances, is evidence of the centrality of this figure to the Filipina/o diasporic imagination. As a result, this project necessitates an examination of a broad archive of both Filipina/o American cultural production and global popular culture.[46] Located within the material context of capitalist globalization, particularly the reliance of the Philippines on transnational labor migration, this project is situated temporally within a contemporary archive of Filipina/o American cultural production and heritage language programs, ranging from the 1990s to the first two decades of the twenty-first century. The diverse forms of cultural production that constitute the archive of this book reflect the ubiquity of the figure of the global Filipina body within both Filipina/o diasporic culture and global popular culture. Not limited to Philippine state rhetoric or Filipina/o American popular culture, a figure such as the Filipina mail-order bride or trafficked woman is invoked within transnational feminist political campaigns, as well as Filipina/o diasporic political organizing. Distinct forms of Philippine gendered and sexual labor coalesce in the figure of the global Filipina body. Within both global popular culture and Filipina/o American activist rhetoric, forms of gendered Filipina/o labor—from bar hostesses in Japan to nannies in Italy—are collapsed within the traffic-in-women discourse. For example, the Filipina trafficked woman is often conflated with the Filipina sex worker, who is represented as a victim of both US empire and the global sex industry within the Filipina American film *Sin City Diary*, as well as antitrafficking political campaigns by Filipina American feminist organizations such as Af3irm.[47] *Sin City Diary* combines a documentary film exposé about the sex industry that developed in tandem with US military bases in the Philippines with the autobiographical narrative of the Filipina American filmmaker's departure from and eventual return to Olongapo, Philippines. Similarly, the Filipina overseas contract worker / domestic helper is often subsumed under the traffic-in-women discourse.[48] The Filipina migrant domestic helper is a central figure in *National Heroes*, a dramatic vignette in ReCreation, a Pilipino Cultural Night (PCN) at the University of California at Berkeley. The title of the vignette, *National Heroes*, echoes Philippine state discourse that narrates Filipina migrant domestic helpers as "heroes of the nation."[49] The invocation of Philippine state discourse within a Filipina/o American PCN demonstrates how the discourse of Filipina domestic helpers as signs of the exploited nation circulates between both Philippine popular culture and Filipina/o American culture. In a similar vein, Filipina women who marry white American men through correspondence services, commonly referred to with the derogatory term "mail-order brides," are equated with sex workers and domestic helpers. For example, I examine the figure of the mail-order bride within both Filipina/o American cultural production in the video art piece *Always a Bridesmaid, Never a Bride* and the website Bagong Pinay, as well as in global popular culture in the Australian film *The Adventures of Priscilla, Queen of the Desert*.[50] The various iterations of the global Filipina body that circulate within Filipina/o American video/film, websites, performance, and heritage language programs highlight the centrality of this figure to the Filipina/o diasporic imagination.

The archive of *The Global Filipina Body* spans multiple national sites and genres, from Filipina/o American film/video, performance, and websites to ethnographic sites such as a heritage language program at the University of the Philippines. As an analysis of the figure of the global Filipina body within the

Filipina/o diasporic imagination, this study necessitates an analysis of visual and performance texts, as well as an ethnographic analysis of the social worlds in which a Filipina/o diasporic imagination is articulated. The figure of the global Filipina body is not only a discursive figure that emerges in performance and visual texts but also a figure that is invoked within Filipina/o diasporic political culture. For example, the figure of the global Filipina body galvanizes transnational political organizing, as well as heritage language programs, both sites in which diasporic nationalisms are articulated through everyday interactions. As such, both ethnographic and discursive analyses are crucial in order to trace the contours of the multifaceted figure of the global Filipina body.

While previous studies of gendered Philippine labor migration have used largely disciplinary approaches, from social scientific ethnographies to textual analyses of literature or film, the diverse archive of *The Global Filipina Body* requires a dynamic mixed methodological approach. The circulation of the figure of the global Filipina body across distinct forms of cultural production requires a dialogical analysis in which visual and performance texts are put into conversation with everyday interactions among Filipina/o Americans. For example, in chapter 1 I analyze the figure of Filipina/o American *balikbayan* within the transnational site of the Philippine Studies Program (PSP), a heritage language program at the University of the Philippines, Diliman, that is targeted toward Filipina/o American college students. I examine the *balikbayan* as both a political actor within transnational political movements and a figure within the Philippine national imagination. Thus, I am interested in both the representation of Filipina/o Americans within Philippine national discourses and the everyday ways in which Filipina/o American subjects participate in diasporic political culture as activists in transnational organizations and students in heritage language programs. This chapter utilizes an ethnographic approach that combines open-ended interviews and participant observation with students and faculty in the program. The depiction of the figure of the Filipina/o American *balikbayan* within national Philippine discourses is situated within the actual social worlds in which these discourses emerge—in transnational spaces such as heritage language programs and activist organizations. I juxtapose the ethnographic site of the University of the Philippines and the surrounding area of Quezon City, Philippines, with sites of cultural production that are visual and textual: film/video, performance, and websites. The multiple sites of cultural production that I examine require not only an interdisciplinary dialogic approach but also an explicitly transnational methodology.

As a multisited interdisciplinary project, *The Global Filipina Body* builds on both ethnographic and cultural studies approaches to examining transnational subjectivities.[51] In her ethnography of Chinese diasporic identity within heritage programs for Chinese Americans in mainland China, anthropologist Andrea Louie notes, "Given the fluid nature of transnational processes, and the fact that identity is always situated, under negotiation, and never complete (Hall 1990), the exploration of identity at specific sites and at specific moments of contact was to become more important to me than delineating a fixed geographical site."[52] Similarly, the global Filipina body is a figure that spans multiple national sites, from heritage language programs in Quezon City, Philippines, to performances that occur in small Filipina/o American theaters in San Francisco, California, requiring a flexible, multisited analytical approach. While I focus primarily on Filipina/o American cultural production, my examination of the global Filipina body is not limited to US articulations of this figure. Instead, I use a broad transnational approach to analyze both global popular culture and Philippine state and popular narratives.

The Global Filipina Body also takes its methodological inspiration from "transnational feminist cultural studies," a term that Caren Kaplan and Inderpal Grewal use to describe scholarship that integrates Marxist, poststructuralist, and feminist approaches. Similarly, following Kaplan and Grewal, The Global Filipina Body employs a "feminist analysis that refuses to choose between economic, cultural, and political concerns."[53] The emergence of the figure of the global Filipina body within the material context of capitalist globalization requires a blending of a political-economic analysis with a consideration of feminist and queer critiques of nationalism. While I foreground the transnational and the diasporic as analytical frameworks, I emphasize the necessity of analyzing nationalism as the "condition of possibility for various forms of feminism."[54] Furthermore, I argue that feminist analyses that foreground a critique of imperialism and a need for decolonization must take nationalism into account.

The Global Filipina Body is a project that is invested in the political potential of diasporic and revolutionary nationalisms, even as it critiques the heteropatriarchy of the nation. This is a "loving" critique of diasporic and revolutionary nationalisms that simultaneously calls for feminist and queer engagements with the nation.[55] As such, this study draws on similar scholarship that is embedded within the social movements that it also critiques. For example, Nadine Naber's ethnography of Arab American activism in the San Francisco Bay Area uses a comparable methodological model. An activist herself, Naber critiques the gendered and sexual politics of national liberation movements even as she realizes the need for an explicitly anti-imperialist feminist framework.[56] Similarly, The Global Filipina Body calls for a specifically anti-imperialist diasporic queer feminist *politics* that resists US empire while critiquing the heteropatriarchal politics that often characterize national liberation and diasporic leftist movements.

The Global Filipina Body builds on an anti-imperialist diasporic feminist framework in its envisioning of a queer diasporic methodology that foregrounds the historical and contemporary condition of US empire. Thus, my approach combines anti-imperialist critique with a queer diasporic framework. I emphasize the political possibility of popular nationalist movements to resist ongoing forms of neoimperialism, even as I consider the ways in which the diaspora can queer the politics of nationalism. More specifically, my *queer diasporic* approach examines how the reimagination of the figure of the global Filipina body challenges the heteropatriarchal politics of representing the nation. *The Global Filipina Body* explores how queer Filipina/o American cultural production contests the heteropatriarchy of the nation—from cultural nationalism to revolutionary nationalism—even as it imagines other forms of belonging beyond the familial trope of the nation. An anti-imperialist queer diasporic approach *queers* not only the nation but also the very notion of a diaspora itself. Simultaneously, an explicitly *anti-imperialist* queer diasporic approach refuses to dismiss the political potential of nationalism(s), as much of US-based feminist and queer studies has done. I come to these questions from the perspective of a queer feminist second-generation Filipina American scholar and activist. As a Filipina American scholar born and raised in the United States, with academic training in the US-dominated fields of feminist and queer studies, my relationship to the politics of nationalisms is multifaceted and at times contradictory. Steeped in the racial politics of the United States, trained in both Asian American studies and US ethnic studies, my intellectual and political commitments are shaped by my position in the US academy. As a feminist and queer studies scholar based in the US academy, a site that has historically been hostile to anticolonial and anti-imperialist forms of nationalism, I bring my critiques of the heteropatriarchy of nationalism together with my deep investments in Filipina/o diasporic nationalist movements struggling against both neoliberal globalization and ongoing forms of US imperialism. Ultimately, I am committed to the political necessity of diasporic nationalisms as a form of anti-imperialist struggle. At the same time, as a transnational feminist and queer studies scholar focused on Filipina/o American cultural production and visual culture, I maintain that the gendered and sexual politics of representation are crucial, indeed essential, to the forms of political struggle that we can imagine and enact in the world. The political stakes are both material and discursive; one cannot be discounted for the other.

The Structure of *The Global Filipina Body*

The organization of this book mirrors the foundational tension from which this project emerges. The first part of this book presents a critique of the heteropatriarchal politics of representing the global Filipina body as a sign of the Philippine nation, while the second half explores how queer iterations of the global Filipina body disrupt the gendered and sexual politics of nationalism, from Filipina/o American cultural nationalism to US homonationalism. Chapters 1 and 2 critique the heteronormativity and masculinism of Filipina/o American diasporic cultural politics, focusing on the figures of the Filipina/o American *balikbayan* and the Filipina sex worker / "trafficked woman." In contrast, chapters 3 and 4 describe how queer Filipina/o American artists refigure the trope of the global Filipina body.

Chapter 1, "Mapping Diasporic Nationalisms: The Filipina/o American *Balikbayan* in the Philippines," introduces the figure of the Filipina/o American *balikbayan*: the return migrant or expatriate. Drawing on ethnographic research conducted at the Philippine Studies Program, this chapter maps the contours of diasporic nationalisms among Filipina/o Americans. I argue that diasporic nationalisms emerge at the juncture of Filipina/o American cultural nationalism and Philippine revolutionary nationalism. This chapter analyzes the gendered and sexualized tropes through which diasporic and national belonging are imagined by juxtaposing the masculinism of the figure of the Filipina/o American *balikbayan* with the exploited and feminized global Filipina body. Chapter 1 ends with a consideration of the relationship of the queer *balikbayan* to both Filipina/o American diasporic nationalisms and US LGBT cultural politics.

Chapter 2, "Imagining the Filipina Trafficked Woman / Sex Worker: The Politics of Filipina/o American Solidarity," examines the politics of representing the Filipina trafficked woman / sex worker within Filipina/o American diasporic political culture. The discourse of the trafficked Filipina woman collapses together women who perform multiple kinds of commodified sexual and domestic labor within a global capitalist economy, including Filipina mail-order brides, domestic helpers / overseas contract workers, and sex workers. The invocation of this figure within Filipina/o American political organizing, film, and performance incites both national and transnational affective structures of belonging. This chapter focuses on the diasporic circulation of the figure of the Filipina trafficked woman / sex worker within three sites of Filipina/o American cultural production: the website for GABRIELA Network's Purple Rose Campaign, the Filipina American documentary film *Sin City Diary*, and the vignette *National Heroes* from ReCreation, the 2006

Pilipino Cultural Night at the University of California at Berkeley. These sites reveal the tension in representing the Filipina trafficked woman / sex worker within Filipina/o diasporic political culture, from her portrayal as a victim to be saved by her Filipina American sisters to her discursive construction by the Philippine state as a "national hero" in the context of transnational labor migration.

While the first half of the book critiques the gendered and sexual politics of representing the global Filipina body as a sign of the Philippine nation and its diaspora, the latter half explores how Filipina/o American video and performance art "queers" this figure. The artists that I discuss in chapters 3 and 4 reconfigure the global Filipina body, transforming her from a sign of the heteropatriarchal nation to a figure that challenges both the homonationalism of US LGBT politics and the heteronormativity of dominant notions of diaspora. Chapter 3, "Performing the Filipina Mail-Order Bride: Queer Neoliberalism, Affective Labor, and Homonationalism," focuses on the video/performance art piece *Always a Bridesmaid, Never a Bride*, by the Filipina American video and performance art ensemble Mail Order Brides/M.O.B. In this analysis, I argue that M.O.B. destabilize the discourse of Filipina mail-order brides as abject figures within Filipina/o American culture. In doing so, M.O.B. undermine the heteronormativity and masculinism of Filipina/o American cultural nationalism while also critiquing the homonationalism of LGBT cultural politics in the United States. As a faux infomercial advertising "bridesmaid services" for LGBT couples and couples getting married for purposes of immigration, *Always a Bridesmaid, Never a Bride* is situated within a broader US political context of queer neoliberalism, in which gay marriage is a sign of homonational belonging. The subjugation of the Third World woman worker within a queer neoliberal logic that commodifies the labor of transnational Filipina bodies reveals the inherent racism of the mainstream LGBT movement, particularly its inability to address issues of race, migration, and labor.

Chapter 4, "The Queer Cyborg in Gigi Otálvaro-Hormillosa's *Cosmic Blood*," uses José Muñoz's canonical text, *Cruising Utopia*, as a theoretical framework for analyzing the cyborg as a utopian figure for queer forms of diaspora beyond the heteronormativity and masculinism of the nation. This chapter focuses on the performance and video art piece *Cosmic Blood*, by the queer Colombian / Filipina American artist Gigi Otálvaro-Hormillosa. *Cosmic Blood* parodies the racialized, gendered, and sexualized codes of reading the mixed-race, ambiguously gendered Filipina body within the contemporary context of the multicultural San Francisco Bay Area, utilizing a science fictional mode to present a retelling of the moment of first contact between the colonizer and the colonized. In doing so, *Cosmic Blood* challenges the taxonomy of racial difference, a legacy of colonization, and the contemporary modes of reading the racialized gendered body within a global capitalist system. In contrast to the commodification of global Filipina bodies under neoliberal globalization, *Cosmic Blood* presents another vision of Filipina subjectivity. The alien/robot hybrid character, a central focus of the piece, functions both as a figure for racial and gender hybridity and as a figure for a queer Filipina/o diaspora beyond the familial ties of blood and kinship.

Envisioning an Anti-imperialist Queer Diasporic Politics

On May 15, 2015, over seventy workers, many of them women, were killed in a fire in a Kentex shoe factory in Valenzuela, Philippines. Stories of the fire spread rapidly through social media as Filipinas/os throughout the diaspora mourned the deaths of the workers, who died a fiery death trapped in a factory with sweatshop-like working conditions. As Biel Pante argued on the popular Philippine news and commentary website Rappler.com, the death of these workers was not so much an accident as a reflection of the "death trap" of the export-oriented Philippine economy, in which companies such as Kentex employ Filipina/o workers, many of them women, as subcontractors without adequate pay, job security, or safe working conditions.[57] Here, the worker in the global sweatshop is another instantiation of the figure of the global Filipina body, whose exploited labor drives the engine of capitalist globalization. Stories of her death within social media remind us diasporic Filipinas/os of how little our lives mean in relation to the immobilizing productivity of capitalism.

Rooted in ongoing forms of US imperialism and neocolonialism, the dehumanization of Filipina bodies under capitalist globalization reflects a longer history in which our bodies have served as gendered and sexual labor for US empire. Months before the Kentex fire, in October 2014, Joseph Scott Pemberton, a US marine serving in Olongapo, Philippines, killed Jennifer Laude, a twenty-six-year-old transgender woman. Laude's murder sparked international outrage, stirring debate about the ongoing presence of the US military in the archipelago, which had halted temporarily after the US military bases were closed in 1991, then resumed after the events of 9/11 under the guise of fighting the War on Terror. These related deaths highlight the twin political stakes of representing the global Filipina body, a figure rooted in the history of US empire and the contemporary violence of neoliberal capitalism. On the one hand, the hyperexploitation of Filipina/o workers under capitalist globalization requires political mobilization both within the Philippine nation and across its diaspora. As the murder of Jennifer Laude makes evident, Filipina women (both cis- and transgender) are the collateral damage of over a century of US imperialism in the Philippine archipelago. These deaths and many more remind us of the urgent need for transnational political movements to combat both ongoing US imperialism and the disastrous effects of neoliberal globalization.

However, political mobilizations under the sign of the global Filipina body as a figure for the exploited nation—whether as the Filipina trafficked woman / sex worker or the mail-order bride—risk the reification of heteropatriarchal forms of nationalism. The figure of the global Filipina body embodies the crisis of the Philippine nation, inciting anxiety about the destabilization of the national family. Within this masculinist discourse, the Philippine nation is unable to maintain its masculine autonomy and sovereignty in the face of capitalist globalization. In spite of this, one of the most powerful forms of resistance to both neoliberal capitalism and ongoing forms of US imperialism has been and continues to be popular nationalist movements in the Philippines and across its diaspora. Ultimately, the politics of representing the global Filipina body—as both a sign of the heteropatriarchal crisis of the Philippine nation and a site of cathection for Filipina/o diasporic politics—indexes a tension between feminist and queer engagements with the nation and the political necessity of national liberation movements against US imperialism and capitalist globalization.

An anti-imperialist queer diasporic politics offers an alternative trajectory, one that resists the heteropatriarchy of Philippine nationalist discourses about the global Filipina body while holding on to the political necessity of diasporic nationalisms. For example, the Filipina/o American political organizing in New York City in response to Jennifer Laude's death exemplified a Filipina/o diasporic politics that is explicitly queer, as well as anti-imperialist. The Filipina American feminist organization GABRIELA NYC, along with the queer Filipina/o American organizations BAYAN's Queer Caucus and Barangay New York, organized a protest at the Philippine Consulate in New York City on October 15, 2014.[58] The event was also endorsed by Trans Justice (a subgroup that is part of the queer people of color organization the Audre Lorde Project) and the New York City Anti-Violence Project (an organization that works against violence against LGBT communities). Here, queer political organizing operates within an anti-imperialist diasporic framework that holds on to the political potential of nationalisms while also forming political alliances with various queer social movements in the United States. An anti-imperialist queer diasporic politics is multidirectional; it not only *queers* anti-imperialist social movements in the Filipina/o diaspora but also expands US queer politics by introducing an *anti-imperialist* framework within US queer social movements. In doing so, a queer diasporic politics connects the concerns of queer and trans people of color organizations, such as the Audre Lorde Project, to transnational movements against US imperialism and capitalist globalization. Ultimately, this study aims to *queer* the global Filipina body—to enact a form of diasporic politics committed to national liberation as a form of freedom against US imperialism, even as it imagines forms of queer belonging beyond the nation.

CHAPTER 1

Mapping Diasporic Nationalisms

The Filipina/o American *Balikbayan* in the Philippines

"**C**ouldn't you just imagine busting out the *tinikling* right here?" asked my new acquaintance, Jeremy, as he gestured toward the vast grounds and Spanish colonial architecture of Intramuros.[1] Jetlagged and unaccustomed to the summer humidity of Manila in the summer, I stared at Jeremy, unsure how to respond to such an incongruous question. It was June, and I had arrived in Manila the night before after over twenty-four hours of travel from Santa Cruz, California, to attend Tagalog on Site (TOS), a heritage language program that was affiliated with the University of California system.[2] Unlike my younger, undergraduate-age classmates, I chose to attend TOS not because of a desire to "find" my Filipina/o identity or culture but to fulfill my language requirement for my PhD program at the University of California at Santa Cruz. While the majority of my classmates were undergraduate students from across the University of California system, I was a graduate student who had been born and raised in Dallas, Texas. My unfamiliarity with US West Coast Filipina/o American cultural nationalism, particularly the performance of cultural dances such as the *tinikling* at Pilipino Cultural Nights (PCN), informed the silence with which I responded to Jeremy's question. I had not spent my undergraduate years rehearsing PCN scenes with Filipina/o American student associations. I lacked the repertoire of images and cultural fantasies of the homeland that shape Filipina/o American cultural nationalist imaginations of the Philippines. That summer, I was both fascinated with and unsettled by the narratives of diasporic "return to the homeland" that structured my classmates' affective journey to the Philippines. Their romanticized notions of the Philippines sparked the development of my research questions, which eventually took the form of this book. I wondered, What forms of diasporic nationalisms emerge in the space of heritage language programs, the site in which revolutionary Philippine nationalism and Filipina/o American cultural nationalism converge? How do these narratives of diasporic belonging draw on gendered and sexual narratives of the Philippine nation? How do Filipina/o American *balikbayans* articulate and participate in forms of diasporic nationalism? I returned to the Philippines a few years later to conduct ethnographic research at the Philippine Studies Program (PSP), a heritage language program at the University of the Philippines at Diliman.

Within the Filipina/o diasporic imagination, the term *balikbayan* brings to mind the many Filipina/o expatriates who make their annual pilgrimage to the Philippines, waiting in customs lines at the Ninoy Aquino International Airport with their oversized "*balikbayan* boxes," filled with everything from televisions and clothes to canned Kraft cheese. *Balikbayan* boxes, the most ubiquitous symbol of a contemporary Filipina/o labor diaspora, represent the affective and material relationships of Filipina/o expatriates to their country of origin, as well as the dependence of the Philippine economy on the remittances of Filipina/o migrant workers. The Philippines is a site of emotional tourism for Filipinas/os from the Global North, including second-generation Filipina/o Americans. Unlike Filipina/o expatriates, second-generation Filipina/o Americans' imagination of the Philippines is largely mediated through their parents' memories and their engagement with Filipina/o American cultural nationalism. Seeking a connection to their imagined homeland, some young Filipina/o Americans choose to study at heritage language programs in the Philippines, becoming *balikbayans* themselves.[3]

Focused on teaching Philippine history and language, heritage language programs for Filipina/o American youth are a crucible in which conflicting discourses of Philippine nationalism emerge: Philippine revolutionary nationalisms, Filipina/o diasporic nationalisms, and Filipina/o American cultural nationalisms. Based on ethnographic research conducted in 2006 at the PSP, this chapter examines the Filipina/o American *balikbayan* as a *figure* within the Philippine national imaginary, as well as a political *actor* within diasporic nationalist political movements, in which discourses of Filipina/o diasporic nationalism are articulated. The figure of the Filipina/o American *balikbayan* is positioned opposite the global Filipina body, a feminized figure that haunts the Filipina/o diasporic imagination. The global Filipina body—the overseas contract worker (OCW), the mail-order bride, the sex worker—circulates within

Filipina/o diasporic cultural production as the corporealization of the Philippine nation, a source of exploited gendered labor for a neoliberal global economy. In contrast, within the Philippine popular imaginary, the Filipina/o American *balikbayan* represents the social and material capital of the United States, as well as the long reach of US imperialism. These twin figures, the figure of the Filipina/o American *balikbayan* and the present absence of the exploited global Filipina body, shape the articulation of diasporic nationalisms.

As a sign of the Filipina/o diaspora, the Filipina/o American *balikbayan* is a fraught figure that simultaneously embodies the failure of the Philippine nation in a context of capitalist globalization and the promise of Filipina/o diasporic political movements. The Filipina/o American *balikbayan* suggests the porousness of Philippine national boundaries in relation to outward labor migration. Simultaneously, Filipina/o American *balikbayans* are actively involved with anti-imperialist nationalist movements in the Philippines. The Filipina/o American *balikbayan* embodies the discursive struggle over the meaning of the Philippine nation, particularly the gendered and sexual politics of imagining a diaspora. Within the diasporic site of Philippine heritage language programs, distinct forms of gendered Philippine nationalisms—state nationalisms, popular nationalisms, and diasporic nationalisms—converge and come into tension.[4] This contact zone of contradictory nationalisms reveals the inherent tensions between feminist and queer critiques of the nation and Philippine antistate, decolonial nationalist feminisms. This chapter considers the political potential of Filipina/o American diasporic nationalisms from a specifically feminist and queer perspective, taking into account both the violence and political possibilities of the nation as an organizing model for anticapitalist and anti-imperialist social movements. As such, the triangulation of the masculinist heterosexual Filipino American *balikbayan* and his supplement, the global Filipina body, with the queer *balikbayan* embodies the innate tension between revolutionary nationalisms and feminist and queer critiques of the nation. On the one hand, within both popular and scholarly discourses in the Global North, the nation has been critiqued as an inherently heteronormative and masculinist social formation. On the other hand, decolonial social movements in the Global South have mobilized the nation as a locus for decolonial, anti-imperialist, and anticapitalist resistance. The figure of the queer Filipina/o American *balikbayan* is positioned between queer diasporic engagements with anti-imperialist and revolutionary Philippine nationalism and mainstream US homonationalism. The triangulation of these three figures reveals the conflicting discourses of the nation in which Filipina/o diasporic nationalisms emerge.

The Figure of the Filipina/o American *Balikbayan*

Serving as a discursive interlocutor between the United States and the Philippines, the Filipina/o American *balikbayan* is an ambivalent figure within the popular Philippine imaginary.[5] The PSP is an especially rich site of analysis for examining the Filipina/o American *balikbayan* as both a figure within the Filipina/o diasporic imagination and an actor in Filipina/o transnational social movements. Most PSP students were born in the United States, and almost all of them identified as Filipina/o American, having spent a large portion of their lives in the United States. As Filipina/o Americans "returning" to the Philippines, they fit within and exist apart from popular discourses about *balikbayans* in the Philippines. S. Lily Mendoza describes young Filipina/o Americans who "return" to the Philippines as a "different breed of Filipina/o *balikbayans*" in which one encounters "the diaspora in reverse." Mendoza asks, "But what of U.S.-born Filipina/o Americans who travel to the Philippines for the first time? Surely, they could not be balikbayans in the same sense of the word? Given that such persons—save perhaps for the color of their skin—would not be marked by a 'native' identity, it isn't likely that their (re-)turn would be imbued with the same 'authenticity' as a native born like me? And yet, on another level, might one not say that a virtual (re-)turn is possible even for Pinoys who have never set foot on Philippine soil?"[6] The enthusiasm with which Mendoza, a self-described "native born" Filipina, responds to the presence of Filipina/o American *balikbayans* contrasts with a more ambivalent popular discourse in the Philippines about US Filipinas/os. The figure of the *balikbayan* reveals the failure of the Philippine nation to maintain its borders in the face of neoliberal globalization, as well as the ongoing neoimperial relationship of the United States to the Philippines. As a figure that invokes both anxiety and envy, the Filipina/o American *balikbayan* occupies an uneasy position within the Filipina/o diasporic imagination. Unlike the Filipina OCW, who is hailed as a national hero within Philippine state discourse, the Filipina/o American *balikbayan* is seen as both a traitor to the nation and a privileged figure to admire and emulate. Vicente Rafael distinguishes between OCWs and *balikbayans*: "Whereas overseas contract workers (OCWs) are seen to return from conditions of near abjection, *balikbayans* are frequently viewed to be steeped in their own sense of superiority, serving only to fill others with a sense of envy."[7] Rafael's statement echoes a comment made by Leah, a PSP language instructor: "I used to say [about Filipina/o Americans], 'I think they're brats. Why would they want to learn the language?' . . . Well, that's the usual impression of Fil Ams."[8] Indeed, the popular Philippine journalist Conrado de Quiros compares Filipina/o *balikbayans* to the

Thomasites: "Balikbayans as Thomasites are thus positioned as neocolonizers whose ambitions lie in setting themselves apart from the rest of the so-called natives rather than affiliating with them."[9] In contrast to Mendoza's laudatory description of Filipina/o American youth's desire to "return" to the Philippines, de Quiros's criticism of *balikbayans* reveals the tensions evoked by the presence of US Filipinos/as in the Philippines.

The figure of the Filipina/o American *balikbayan* in the Philippines reflects the historical development of Philippine state policy to promote return tourism among *balikbayans*, creating a state-initiated form of diasporic nationalism. From expedited immigration lines at the Ninoy Aquino International Airport in Manila to the existence of a tourist industry that caters to the needs of returnees, *balikbayans* are given special treatment by the Philippine state. Eric Pido describes the role of *balikbayans* in the development of the Philippine economy, emphasizing the ambivalent role that *balikbayans* play in the Philippine nation.[10] In 1973 the Marcos administration created the Balikbayan Program to develop the Philippine tourist industry and attract *balikbayans* to the country. The Balikbayan Program provided a means of securing foreign aid and remittances for the foreign debt–ridden Philippine economy. Through the *mabuhay* (welcome) campaign, the Philippine Department of Tourism (DOT) organized training programs to instruct local city and provincial governments in the "culture of tourism" in order to encourage *balikbayan* tourism.[11] According to Pido, the *mabuhay* campaign created a tourist culture that positions *balikbayans* as the privileged elite, drawing on the simultaneous nostalgia of *balikbayans* for their pre-Marcos memory of the Philippines while encouraging their paranoia about the dangers of life in the Philippines.[12] The ambivalence toward the Filipina/o American *balikbayan* is an effect of state initiatives such as the Balikbayan Program and the *mabuhay* campaign, which has positioned *balikbayans* as both privileged elites and traitors to the nation. As Robert Diaz argues, "The creation of a tourist industrial complex during Marcos' time was first and foremost an attempt to 'repair' the human rights abuses and limits to freedom affected by the dictatorship."[13] Thus the Balikbayan Program served the dual purpose of ameliorating the effects of martial law while creating a new form of diasporic nationalist identity among Filipinos abroad. Under President Cory Aquino's administration, the Balikbayan Program became Republic Act (RA) 6768, which provided even more economic incentives for *balikbayans* to visit the homeland.[14]

Filipina/o American *balikbayans* are often positioned as "privileged outsiders whose connections to an imagined 'America'—land of opportunities, consumer goods, middle-class or upper middle-class lifestyles, Hollywood—grant them special access to the Philippine social, literary, and mass-media circles."[15]

Despite the cultural capital granted to Filipina/o Americans, they are often perceived as without culture, inauthentic, privileged versions of authentic Filipinas/os. The presence of Filipina/o Americans in the Philippines evokes mixed responses. Caroline Hau notes: "Filipinos in America by their very presence evoke anxieties and fantasies on the part of the middle classes and intellectuals in Manila. Their departure for greener pastures abroad is characteristically seen by these Filipinos as an act of selfishness, a 'betrayal' of the Philippine nation."[16] This sense of national "betrayal" may or may not transfer to the children of Philippine expatriates. Although viewed with both envy and scorn for their inherent and inherited material and social capital, Filipina/o Americans who were born and/or raised in the United States articulate a counternarrative to the notion of national betrayal through the Filipina/o American discourse of "returning to the motherland." Within the transnational site of heritage language programs, young Filipina/o American *balikbayans* narrate their journey to the Philippines as "coming home," "finding their Filipino culture," and assuming a Philippine national identity that they lacked as racial and ethnic minorities in the United States. One PSP student, Jeremy, commented, "I had never been to the Philippines, and I wanted to come home for the first time. . . . You have all these expectations. You want it to be the best. . . . I wanted to let the country enter me. . . . I wanted to feel at home, and I did."[17] Jeremy's statement illustrates the affective narratives inherent to discourses of diasporic nationalism within heritage language programs. Narratives of return are central to the affective structures of diasporic nationalisms, in which Filipina/o Americans play a central role.[18]

Similarly, discourses of return undergird the participation of PSP students in transnational Filipina/o political organizing. "Exposure programs" such as the PSP serve to galvanize feelings of diasporic nationalism among Filipina/o American youth. Discourses of diasporic nationalism among Filipina/o Americans are shaped by revolutionary nationalist discourses of the Philippine Left, particularly the National Democratic (ND) movement of the Philippines, as well as identity-based Filipina/o American cultural nationalism in the United States. Heritage language programs are a crucible in which disparate discourses of the nation converge in the formation of diasporic nationalisms. The practice of "exposure programs" serves the purpose of politicizing Filipina/o American youth in the hopes that they will become involved with transnational Philippine social movements.[19] In the tradition of exposure programs oriented toward Filipina/o American youth, the PSP blended academic instruction in Philippine history and culture with "exposure trips" geared toward exposing students to the social conditions in the Philippines.

The PSP was established in 2003 and was affiliated with the University of California from 2004 to 2006. The program was a joint project of UP Diliman and Philippine Forum, a US-based nonprofit organization that operated out of the New York City area. Philippine Forum administered the US end of the program, including advertisement of the program, selection of participants, and other logistical matters. The Philippine Forum is an education and advocacy-based organization that works on various Filipino American issues, from organizing Filipino workers to producing cultural events.[20] Filipina/o American participation in the PSP builds on a long history of transnational political movements between the United States and the Philippines.

The Philippine Studies Program website describes the PSP as an intensive Philippine studies and Filipino language program for Filipino American students, as well as international students interested in Philippine studies. Further, it presents testimonials from former students in which they describe how their experience in the PSP gave them a renewed commitment to working toward social justice in the Philippines. According to one testimonial from the PSP website, "As a Filipino American concerned with social justice, attending the Philippine Studies program at UP Diliman was the best thing I could do. Studying the historical perspective of how Philippine society has evolved, coupled with the stories told to us first-hand by various communities, has really opened my eyes to the daily struggles of poverty and hardship experienced by an overwhelming majority of the population. . . . I learned that Filipino-Americans hold enormous power to affect change among our community both here and in the Philippines. And that even the smallest action can make a huge difference."[21] The central narratives of these testimonials present the possibility for both personal and political transformation, as well as the development of an affective connection to the Philippines. Although the PSP website invokes a commitment to social justice in its self-representation through the student testimonials, the website emphasizes the academic nature of the program, listing a number of well-known Philippine scholars as lecturers in the program's Philippine Studies Lecture Series. The PSP website focuses on the proximity of students to established scholars in Philippine studies and other fields and highlights the opportunity for graduate students to conduct research at UP Diliman.

The twenty-five students in the PSP during the summer of my research came from across the United States, ranging from fourth-generation students from large Filipina/o American communities to students who were born in the Philippines but who migrated to the United States in their childhood or adolescence. Students came from a diversity of geographic regions in the United States, from the San Francisco Bay Area and Los Angeles, areas with large Filipina/o

American communities, to parts of the US South and Southeast with relatively small Filipina/o populations, such as Missouri, Texas, and Florida. The students ranged in age from seventeen to twenty-seven years old. While one student was a senior in high school, most participants were undergraduate students. A few were in graduate school or had recently graduated from college. While some students chose the PSP primarily to study Philippine language and history, others came for the independent research component of the trip, which matched students with a faculty mentor. I conducted a total of seventeen open-ended interviews with PSP students and faculty and did participant observation in the classes and social gatherings of participants. I also sought out both interviews and more casual interactions with faculty members in order to understand their relationships with their Filipina/o American students. In order to understand the emergence of diasporic nationalisms within the space of heritage language programs, it was crucial to obtain the perspective of the teachers as the primary political and cultural interlocutors between the students and various discourses of the Philippine nation.

In choosing personal narratives to highlight in this chapter, I decided to foreground interview subjects whose experiences revealed the key differences among the range of students in the PSP. Thus, my methodology is less focused on representing commonalities in perspectives of PSP students. Instead, I examine vignettes and anecdotes that point to the sites of divergence and contestation. The gendered and sexual nature of diasporic nationalisms emerged obliquely, as gender and sexuality were topics that were only minimally addressed in the official curriculum of the program. Instead of describing the PSP student body as a whole, I chose a smaller number of key interactions and occurrences that suggested that, while not the primary focus of discussion, discourses of gender and sexuality shaped the emergence of diasporic nationalisms among the Filipina/o American students in the PSP. It is in the moments of tension and contestation, through that which is not said as much as what is said, that one can catch a glimpse of the subtle ways in which gendered and sexual nationalisms emerge. With this in mind, I chose to emphasize divergent perspectives of specific students within the program—a masculinist militant nationalist, a feminist critic, a queer *balikbayan*—whose commentary revealed crucial nodes of friction and dissent. Throughout this analysis, I include my own self-reflexive positioning as a queer Filipina American researcher and activist with my own political investments and relationship to the politics of nationalism in the Filipina/o diaspora. As a queer Filipina American *balikbayan*, I support Filipina/o diasporic nationalist political movements in the United States, even as I am critical of the heteropatriarchal politics of the nation and the violence of the state. Simultaneously, I maintain that it is crucial to untether the violence of the Philippine state as an extension of US empire from analyses of popular nationalist movements in the Philippines and throughout its diaspora.

UP Diliman, where the PSP is located, has historically been a locus of nationalist activism. As the flagship institution for the national university system, UP Diliman has highly regarded programs in various fields, from medicine to law and business, drawing students from across the Philippine archipelago. Despite a post-9/11 context in which Philippine leftist organizations are often labeled as "terrorists" by the Philippine state and the United States, it is not uncommon for UP Diliman students and faculty to participate in organizations that espouse a national democratic framework. Since the early 1970s, the ND movement has been one of the most consistent and vocal critics of US imperialism and capitalist globalization. As a mass movement, the NDF functions through a multitude of organizations geared toward improving the welfare of various sectors of society, including peasants, workers, women, and youth. The NDF calls for a societal revolution as the solution to the poverty and dispossession that are the result of what it describes as a semifeudal and neocolonial system.[22]

The location of the PSP within the politically engaged environment of UP Diliman's College of Arts and Letters and the program's location within the historically nationalist discipline of Philippine studies speak to the political and academic orientation of the program. However, after affiliating with the University of California's Education Abroad Program, the PSP shifted to a more academic focus with a range of political, ideological, and academic perspectives rather than a singular emphasis on nationalist politics.[23] The PSP was established at UP Diliman in 2003 and was affiliated with the University of California from 2004 to 2006.[24] In the beginning, the program had a more explicitly political agenda, which attracted Filipina/o American student activists supportive of the ND movement. However, the program's institutional affiliation with the University of California resulted in a less explicit emphasis on political education within the program and a more visible focus on academic inquiry. I conducted my research after much of the overt politicization of the PSP had been deemphasized, during the time period when the program was affiliated with the University of California's Education Abroad Program.

Bea, a PSP language instructor, described the institutionalization of the program from one that was originally focused on building links between the people's movement and the academy to one grounded within the institution of the university: "Before, it was intended to give a more comprehensive approach. Later, it was institutionalized. Before, it had more of a framework of the people's movement. [Now,] it has to be patterned within the framework of the academic community, with the idea of an intellectual, an expert, people with PhDs. Now, most of the speakers are known to be academic 'experts' in their fields. [Before,] the immersion programs were basically a National Democratic framework."[25] Despite the depoliticization of the program, many PSP faculty maintained an explicitly nationalist approach to linking language instruction to the development of political consciousness among Filipina/o American students. Bea described her teaching methodology: "I tried to make language instruction more discursive, but I know my limitations. *I'm not in a position to change the program, but I tried to make the discussion in the language class more substantial. The students were asking for more.* It was really different from the last year. At this point, most of the students are more involved with organizations inclined toward the ND [National Democratic] line" (emphasis mine).[26] When I asked Bea about the relationship between social justice and students' search for a Filipina/o identity, she responded: "A commitment to social justice is more important than a Filipino identity."[27] Bea's statement is particularly telling of the disjuncture between a Marxist class-based critique of neocolonialism and feudalism characteristic of a National Democratic analysis and the racial/ethnic identity-based politics of Filipina/o American cultural nationalism. While the approach of the ND movement aims for a social revolution and a more equitable society, Filipina/o American cultural nationalism often invokes the notion of Filipina/o identity and culture in response to the broader systemic racism of US society.

Other PSP language instructors echoed Bea's pedagogical philosophy. Another language instructor, Trina, viewed language instruction as a means of inciting a nationalist consciousness among students:

> Of course, we have to contextualize our experience of colonialism, which I believe is continuously existing, and imperialism. You have to start with something, with symbols, because we're very busy with our desperate lives, so we have to start with something . . . our language, at least for a start . . . from our observations, our consciousness, because there is cultural imperialism, you don't know yourself anymore. . . . We just have to have this culture, this identity, these symbols as a starting-off point for a more comprehensive analysis of the situation and the realities. . . . This nationalism will espouse social justice, identifying yourself with the oppressed, the marginalized, those who cannot go to school, those who are less fortunate. I think it's very important to the academic community, having your knowledge production oriented toward the less fortunate. It's a starting process of social justice in the Philippines.
>
> The use of language is more than sentimental, it's also practical. By using the language of the people, you empower them. You allow them to express themselves. It's an issue of democratization, to be down to earth . . . trying to be part

of them, to reach out. It's more than a political issue of national language. It's a method of getting in touch with the people.[28]

Trina's commentary reflects the connection between nationalist politics and Filipina/o language instruction in the context of Philippine academia. Situated within the historically nationalist discipline of Philippine studies at the University of the Philippines, the Philippine Studies Program sought not only to impart language skills but also, in the tradition of "exposure trips," to expose Filipina/o American students to the social conditions of the Philippines. As Rico, a language instructor, commented, "I still look at the program as providing an opportunity for students—this is how I see my contribution to the program—to get in touch with basic exploited and oppressed sectors, to meet some of the organizations, as a first step in developing nationalist, progressive political consciousness. That's how I see my role."[29]

The development of a nationalist consciousness among PSP students took place within a context in which students were confronted daily with the violence of the Philippine state. The ongoing state violence in the Philippines, which increased with the beginning of the US-led War on Terror, shaped the experiences of both faculty and students in the PSP. Beginning with the Arroyo administration and continuing into the Duterte administration, the Philippine state has adopted the US rhetoric of "fighting terrorism," cracking down on suspected "terrorists." Since 2001, hundreds of activists, journalists, community organizers, and students have been the victims of extrajudicial killings, abduction, and torture.[30] The number of extrajudicial killings has increased exponentially under Duterte's administration, and the violence and harassment of activists and journalists continue.[31] This environment of state violence and political repression fundamentally shaped the academic context of UP Diliman while I was there. In 2006 two UP Diliman students, Sherlyn Cadapan and Karen Empeño, were abducted and killed. Both women were active in nationalist youth organizations at UP Diliman and were doing volunteer work in a rural community at the time of their abduction. The university community responded with outrage and demands for justice, ranging from official statements by the president of the university to mass student protests.[32] Since the PSP is affiliated with one of the more politically progressive colleges at the university, the College of Arts and Letters, PSP students routinely encountered protests, teach-ins, and other acts of resistance to this state violence. At the College of Arts of Letters, intellectual production was often explicitly linked to social justice work. Within this politicized environment, PSP students were exposed to multiple strains of nationalist thought. Although not all PSP students came to the program with a national democratic or anti-imperialist political orientation, their studies were shaped by a context of political resistance to the daily violence of the Philippine state.

The political participation of PSP students in the Philippine ND movement must be situated within a long history of Filipina/o American political organizing against US imperialism in the Philippines since the 1970s and against Marcos's regime of martial law (1972–81). As Helen Toribio notes in her history of the Filipina/o American anti-imperialist organization Katipunan ng Mga Demokratikong Pilipinos (KDP, Union of Democratic Filipina/os), the 1960s labor organizing by Filipina/o American farmworkers such as Philip Vera Cruz was influenced by an awareness of socialism as the only viable alternative to capitalism.[33] Toribio locates the development of anti-imperialist groups such as the KDP within a lineage of anticapitalist, socialist political organizing among Filipina/o Americans and other ethnic groups in the United States that identified with Mao's idea of "third worldism."[34] As an anti-imperialist organization, the KDP worked to support the ND movement in the Philippines, as well as the development of socialism in the United States. During Marcos's regime of martial law in the Philippines, the KDP worked with a coalition of anti-Marcos activists in the United States through the umbrella organization Movement for a Free Philippines (MFP).[35] Catherine Choy describes women's participation in several Filipina/o American anti-imperialist organizations in the 1970s, including the Support Committee for a Democratic Philippines (based in New York), Samahan ng Makabayang Pilipino (SAMAPI, Association of Nationalist Filipina/os, based in Chicago), and the National Committee for the Restoration of Civil Rights in the Philippines.[36] More recently, groups such as Bagong Alyansang Makabayan (BAYAN, New Patriotic Alliance), including BAYAN USA, and Anakbayan (Sons and Daughters of the Nation) have continued Filipina/o American solidarity work with the ND movement in the Philippines.[37]

The "unfinished revolution," a persistent discourse within the Philippine national imagination since the War of 1896, in which anti-Spanish revolutionaries fought the colonial dominance of Spain, is also central to the articulation of diasporic nationalisms within Filipina/o American political organizing. Throughout the US occupation and into the current moment of US neocolonialism, the discourse of revolution persists as a primary mode of imagining anticolonial and anticapitalist resistance; revolution is routinely invoked in the service of national progress and liberation. Calls for national progress often invoke the historical figures of the anti-Spanish revolutionary movement Katipunan. The discourse of revolution as the necessary vehicle for national liberation is mobilized by different sectors of the Left and has at times also been co-opted by official Philippine state discourse.[38] The notion of an unfinished revolution has also been taken up by Filipina/o American activists and has shaped the articulation of a Filipina/o diasporic imagination.

Geobodies of the Nation

The global Filipina body is a figure that haunts the Filipina/o diasporic imagination. The discursive construction of diasporic nationalisms within the transnational context of the PSP relies on the present absence of the Filipina as a sign of the Philippine nation. Although the gendered nature of this discourse was not immediately apparent, several key interactions among the students suggest that the articulation of diasporic nationalisms is inherently gendered and sexualized. I focus much of my analysis on interactions and discussions with three key student types—the masculinist militant nationalist, the feminist critic, and the queer *balikbayan*—not because their experiences can be generalized as the norm but because of the sites of divergence that they represent. The militant nationalist student, Joshua, expressed much of the masculinism and heteronormativity for which nationalist discourse has been critiqued.[39] Joshua was a student who was active in National Democratic organizations in the United States. During a lecture about Philippine history, Joshua critiqued the representation of Jose Rizal as a legitimate national hero because he "wrote his works in Spanish and had a European girlfriend." In expressing this criticism, Joshua invoked Philippine nationalist debates over the rightful revolutionary hero of the Philippine nation, making clear how Filipina/o diasporic nationalisms emerge from the conjuncture of Filipina/o American cultural nationalism and Philippine revolutionary nationalism. Joshua's critique of Jose Rizal's enshrinement as a Philippine national hero versus the more "egalitarian" Andres Bonifacio echoes the nationalist debates in the Philippines in the 1960s, in which many historians argued for an emphasis on the more plebeian Bonifacio as the actual leader of the anti-Spanish revolutionary movement.[40] Joshua was not unique in his concern with legitimate national heroes. Filipina/o American organizations such as Anakbayan Seattle, part of the BAYAN USA network, reproduce Philippine nationalist discourse. On the Anakbayan Seattle website, the mission statement reads: "We hope to improve our conditions by studying and educating others about the rich culture and *proud revolutionary heritage of the Filipina/o people's continuing struggle . . . in the spirit of Andres Bonifacio*" (emphasis mine).[41] Invoking one of the heroes of the 1896 revolution against Spain, Andres Bonifacio, Anakbayan's mission statement mobilizes the language of revolutionary struggle as a common basis for ethnic and national belonging. Anakbayan's choice of Andres Bonifacio, as opposed to the more often cited Jose Rizal, demonstrates how the language of 1960s radical movements in the Philippines, has been incorporated into Filipina/o American cultural nationalist discourse as well.

Joshua's comment is suggestive of a Filipina/o diasporic imagination in which nationalist authenticity relies on the present absence of the Filipina geobody as the sign of the nation.[42] Within the Filipina/o American diasporic imagination articulated by Joshua, the (implicitly masculine) revolutionary nationalist subject's belonging to the Philippine nation is figured through his relationship to the Filipina geobody. Within this version of Filipina/o diasporic nationalism, Rizal is foreclosed from nationalist subjectivity due to his choice of sexual partner—a white European woman, not a Filipina woman. Joshua's statement suggests a discursive terrain of Filipina/o diasporic nationalisms in which the sexualized body of the Filipina is a sign of national belonging, while the male revolutionary is the historical actor who is cited as the inspiration of Filipina/o American diasporic nationalisms. This is not to say that female nationalist figures are not cited by Filipina/o Americans but rather to suggest that the consolidation of an implicitly male diasporic nationalist subjectivity relies on its opposite, the feminized figure of the Filipina geobody.

Joshua's masculinist and heteronormative statements did not go unchallenged among PSP students. In contrast to Joshua, some students expressed feminist critiques of the gendered discourses of diasporic nationalism. One student in particular, Lisa, who identified as a feminist, was particularly critical of gendered discourses of the "motherland." Over the course of the summer, I developed a friendship with Lisa. As an undergraduate student with an academic background in women's studies and Filipina/o American studies, Lisa was particularly cognizant of issues of gender and sexuality within the context of the PSP. One day, Lisa took me aside and described her frustration and anger about an off-campus open mic performance that she had attended with several other Filipina/o American PSP students. At this performance, Joshua had performed a spoken word poem in which he described the Philippine nation as a female body to be sexually claimed by the implicitly male Filipino American *balikbayan*. Angrily, Lisa described the poem's narration of the male Filipino American *balikbayan*, who succeeded in *taking back* the feminized Philippine nation from the hands of white male US imperialists. Lisa expressed her disgust in response to a narrative that she termed "fucking the motherland."[43] The narrative of Joshua's poem implied that the possession of the gendered and sexualized body of the (implicitly) heterosexual Filipina is crucial to the male *balikbayan*'s claims to national authenticity and diasporic belonging. Within this masculinist Filipino American narrative of fucking the motherland, the possession of the global Filipina body by the male *balikbayan* authenticates his identification with the Philippine nation. In this heteronormative fantasy of the homeland, the heterosexual male *balikbayan* triangulates his relationship to the Philippine nation through his possessive investment in the global Filipina body as a geobody for the Philippine nation.

The trope of heterosexual romantic or sexual relationships as a sign of Philippine nationalism was not limited to Filipina/o American students such as Joshua. I attended a Filipina/o language class taught by Trina, a self-described activist with a history of working in trade unions affiliated with the ND movement. Trina had decided to enroll in a master's program at UP Diliman in order to become a more competitive candidate for university teaching positions, but she had maintained her work with NGOs. She had met her husband, another activist, through her work with trade unions. During class, Trina described the history of the *kilusan kaliwa* (the Philippine leftist movement) and asked the students to translate a song popular among activists during the martial law period. She gave a detailed history of the Philippine Left in class and explained that within the context of the song, romantic (and primarily heterosexual) love represents the love for one's country. Within Trina's narrative, romantic love, especially the love between a man and a woman, is synonymous with Philippine nationalism. Trina explained how the song was banned in the New People's Army camps because it was feared that young men would leave the camps to return to their sweethearts in their hometowns after listening to the romantic, melancholy lyrics.[44] In this classroom of Filipina/o American students, language instruction was infused with a pedagogy of the nation. As students were taught to conjugate Filipino verbs, they were simultaneously exposed to heteronormative discourses of revolutionary nationalism. The implicit nationalist narratives of institutionalized spaces such as the classroom were echoed within the everyday interactions of the students. Joshua's spoken word poem and his comments about Rizal's choice of sexual partner occurred within a broader diasporic context in which nationalist sentiment is narrated through the trope of heteronormativity. The affective connection of Filipina/o Americans to the homeland is narrated through the romantic and sexual love for the gendered Filipina as a sign of the nation.

The relationship of the implicitly male Filipina/o American *balikbayan* to the elided yet ever-present global Filipina body suggests the "gender trouble" of the Philippine nation as a provider of feminized and racialized affective, domestic, and sexual labor within a global capitalist economy.[45] Within the logic of neoliberal capitalism, the global Filipina body—whether a Filipina mail-order bride, OCW, or trafficked woman—is a geobody for the Philippine nation. An analysis of the Filipina/o American *balikbayan* as both a figure and an actor within the

Filipina/o diasporic imagination requires a consideration of his opposite, the global Filipina body.[46] The ubiquity of the global Filipina body within Filipina/o American diasporic imagination demonstrates the pervasive racialized and gendered logic of capitalist globalization, which reduces feminized Filipina/o workers to their corporeal labor, making them "bodies without subjectivity."[47]

The "gender trouble" of Filipina/o American diasporic culture is a legacy of US imperialism; the Filipina/o American *balikbayan* is triangulated between the masculine imperial power of the United States and the feminized Philippine nation. As the child of the heteronormative union between the feminized Philippines and the masculine power of the United States, the figure of the Filipina/o American *balikbayan* evokes anxiety and ambivalence within the Philippine national imaginary. Positioned between Filipina/o American cultural nationalism and Philippine revolutionary nationalisms, the *balikbayan* is also an "imperial remainder or ghost" of the erasure of a US imperialist history.[48] The legacy of epistemic and material violence creates a complex and contradictory relationship of Filipina/o Americans to discourses of the nation: US nationalist exceptionalism, Philippine revolutionary nationalism, Philippine state nationalism, and emergent diasporic nationalisms. The fraught relationship between the dyad of the Filipina/o American *balikbayan* and the global Filipina body embodies the tensions between feminist and queer critiques of the nation and Philippine tropes of national liberation. Never settled comfortably on either side of this discursive divide, the Filipina/o American *balikbayan* both reproduces the heteronormativity and masculinism of revolutionary and cultural nationalism and has the potential to "queer" these normative imaginings of the nation. The figure of the global Filipina body haunts the Filipina/o diasporic imaginary; whether figured as the trafficked woman or the mail-order bride, she persists as a "body without subjectivity."[49]

Within the Eurocentric context of Global North–oriented queer and feminist studies, nationalism has an ambivalent relationship to progressive and radical politics. However, it is crucial to remember that forms of antinationalism in the West draw on older forms of metropolitan antagonism toward anticolonial movements in the Global South.[50] Current scholarly critiques of nationalism within both queer and feminist studies must be situated within an intellectual framework that is inherently inhospitable toward anticolonial and antineocolonial movements in the Global South. While both feminist and queer studies have dismissed the nation as masculinist and heteronormative, this perspective often implicitly assumes a postnationalist, postcolonial framework. Instead, feminist scholars such as Andrea Smith have argued that the nation continues to serve as an essential framework for forms of belonging and political organization, given the ongoing colonial context of Native Americans in the United States.[51]

Historically, Eurocentric feminist theory has either elided the question of the nation or critiqued the nation for its inherent masculinism and heteronormativity. In contrast, some Filipina/o diasporic nationalist feminists argue that national liberation is a prerequisite for gender equality. Arguing against a primarily white, middle-class, US academic feminism that understands issues of nationalism as separate from the notion of gender justice, feminist scholar Delia Aguilar claims, "Freedom from oppression as women can become possible only when the nation is liberated from U.S. domination and when the majority of the people can be released from poverty, illness, malnutrition, and other forms of deprivation rampant in a neocolony."[52] Philippine nationalist feminism foregrounds nationalism as a necessary and central vehicle for social justice, including the achievement of women's liberation from oppressive discourses of gender and sexuality. Unlike mainstream feminist discourses in the United States, many Philippine nationalist feminists foreground anti-imperialist and anticolonial struggles as the necessary foundation for feminist (and other liberation) struggles. As Caroline Hau has noted, "What is noteworthy about the twentieth-century articulation between Philippine nationalism and feminism is the fact that it is made *within* the context of socialist and communist political movements, which positioned themselves in opposition to the (neocolonial) state" (emphasis mine).[53] Unlike most mainstream feminist movements in the United States and other parts of the Global North, nationalist feminisms in the Philippines are explicitly *antistate*, particularly due to the Philippine state's role in facilitating US neocolonial power in the Philippines. The neocolonial relationship of the Philippines to the United States is a primary site of struggle for many Philippine and Filipina/o diasporic feminists.

The ongoing colonial relationship of the Philippines to the United States requires an explicitly *decolonial* approach to understanding popular nationalisms. Nationalist movements in the Philippines and Filipina/o American diasporic nationalisms are key elements of the struggle against the Philippine state, as well as the neocolonial power of the United States. As Bea, PSP faculty member, commented, "Nationalism in the third world is very different to citizens of a first world country. For us, with an experience of colonialism, it [nationalism] means sovereignty, freedom. For citizens of rich countries, the nationalism [of countries in the Global South] might mean losing your power."[54] Antistate popular nationalisms such as the ND movement invoke the nation as a sign of collective struggle and liberation while also working against the Philippine state apparatus. Rico, a PSP language instructor, distinguished between the

nationalism of the Philippine state and the tradition of revolutionary nationalism: "In the Philippine context, it's certainly clear the difference between official
nationalism of the state, the ruling classes. There's a marked difference. There's
a strong and widespread tradition of revolutionary or progressive nationalism
in general and in particular at UP. . . . [In contrast,] the state co-opts or uses
nationalist rhetoric in the service of globalization."[55] Rico's delineation between
the nationalist rhetoric employed by the state to bolster economic globalization (the *bagong bayani* [new heroes] discourse) and the popular nationalism of
the ND movement is a key distinction.[56] Further, Rico stressed the necessity of
emphasizing the historical and geopolitical contexts of ongoing colonialism,
or neocolonialism: "Fil Ams view the ND movement with a certain wariness.
But the main difference is colonialism and neocolonialism. In this context,
nationalism becomes the main form of the struggle for liberation. And of course
it would be different in the States. In the context of the States, nationalism or
patriotism can be oppressive. . . . So that's the difference. I suppose the students
would have to . . . see the different historical contexts . . . in order to make that
leap to some type of action."[57] The contemporary Philippine context of popular
struggle against ongoing forms of US neocolonialism requires an understanding of nationalism in which the hyphen between nation and state is stretched
to its limits.

Pheng Cheah's concept of "cosmopolitics," which untethers the state from the
nation in its understanding of popular nationalisms, is useful for elucidating the
various Philippine nationalisms that intersect within the diasporic context of
heritage language programs such as the PSP. Cheah emphasizes the "loosening
of the hyphen between nation and state" implicit in the idea of cosmopolitics,
which he defines as "popular global political consciousness and community,"
in which the nation and nationalisms are not necessarily yoked to the apparatus of the state or notions of ethnic belonging.[58] Similarly, Filipina/o diasporic
nationalisms organize popular resistance to both the Philippine state and neoliberal globalization in the name of national liberation. Nationalist movements
serve as a vehicle for organizing antistate popular resistance to imperialism and
globalization.

For the decolonizing nation in particular, popular nationalisms are necessary
to organize popular movements *against* the state as the conduit for transnational
capital. Given the Philippine state's role in brokering outward labor migration
as a solution to the crisis of the Philippine economy, nationalist movements
target the state as both the recruiter and the pimp for the devalued racialized
and gendered labor that the Philippines provides within a global economy.
Filipina/o American participation in diasporic social movements occurs within

a framework of popular antistate Philippine nationalisms. Rather than existing as "postnationalist" political formations, Filipina/o American solidarity movements articulate a form of Philippine nationalism that is unique to their position as diasporic subjects—as citizens of the imperial center yet racial minorities within an American racial formation. Bea noted, "Teaching in PSP has confirmed my original impression that Filipinas/os who weren't born in the Philippines are more inclined to be nationalists."[59] Bea's observation resonates with Benedict Anderson's assertion that diasporic subjects, migrants who have left their nation of origin, are more likely to express long-distance nationalism.[60]

Within Filipina/o diasporic culture, I delineate three different modes of Philippine nationalism: (1) *state nationalism*, exemplified by state discourse, particularly in reference to Philippine transnationalism, such as state discourse concerning balikbayans, OCWs, and so on; (2) *popular nationalism*, referring to both a popular understanding of historical movements, such as the revolutionary anti-Spanish movement, the Katipunan, and contemporary antistate nationalist movements, including the National Democratic Front; and (3) *diasporic nationalism*, describing the ways in which the nation is invoked as a mode of solidarity and belonging among Filipina/o Americans, particularly in relation to the Philippines as the "homeland," or site of origin for the Filipina/o diaspora.[61] The discourses of the Philippine nation invoked by Filipina/o American solidarity organizations that support the ND movement in the Philippines, such as BAYAN USA and Anakbayan, are forms of diasporic nationalisms.

Filipina/o American Cultural Nationalism

The masculinism and heteronormativity of the figure of the Filipina/o American *balikbayan* reflect the broader gendered and sexual politics of imagining a Filipina/o American identity. The cultural nationalist project of "Filipina/o America" often relies on an implicit figuration of the national subject as heterosexual and male. David Eng's critique of the heteronormativity and implicit homophobia of Asian American cultural nationalism, particularly in relation to Asian American masculinity, is useful for understanding the politics of gender and sexuality within Filipina/o diasporic nationalisms. Eng argues, "Cultural nationalism's energies focused on not merely defining but prescribing who a recognizable and recognizably legitimate Asian American racial subject should be: male, heterosexual, working class, American born, and English speaking."[62] Similarly, the relationship of the implicitly male heterosexual *balikbayan* to the exploited global Filipina body is shaped by the implicit heteronormativity and masculinism of Filipina/o American cultural nationalism. The spoken word poem performed by Joshua is just one example within a broader gendered and sexual discursive framework in which the Philippine nation is figured as home and homeland. Within the spoken word poem, the (implicitly male) Filipina/o American *balikbayan* not only imagines the Philippine nation as a heterosexual woman to be claimed from white US imperialists but also extends this logic to his daily interactions on the streets of Manila. Several male PSP students expressed their indignation at seeing Filipina women with white US men in public spaces in Manila. Indeed, mixed-race *balikbayans* often trouble the essentialist forms of identity imagined by Filipina/o American *balikbayans*. Jennifer, a biracial PSP student whose mother is Filipina and whose father is a white American, told me about the rude comments she heard about interracial couples on Manila streets. Jennifer remarked on the discomfort and animosity toward interracial relationships between white American men and Filipina women: "There's animosity from both sides—the Filipina/o community in the States and the community in the Philippines. So where do these people go for any kind of community?"[63] Within masculinist narratives of national sovereignty, in which the Philippine nation is represented through the bodies of Filipina women, the children of white American fathers and Filipina mothers serve as a persistent reminder of US militarism and the Philippine sex industry.

In claiming the authentic Filipina body for his own, the male *balikbayan* achieves a level of masculine authenticity impossible in the racial context of the United States, in which Asian American men are feminized and emasculated in relation to white American men. Several feminist-minded students articulated their critiques of such gendered representations of the nation by their fellow Filipino American students. In casual conversation with me, Jennifer expressed her anger and frustration at the conflation of national belonging with sexual conquest/possession that characterized some of her classmates' comments. Students also questioned the heteronormativity of Filipina/o American cultural nationalism, challenging the forms of diasporic identification that assumed a heterosexual relationship as the basis of national belonging.

In the transnational context of the PSP, Filipina/o American cultural nationalism's investment in ethnic/racial identity came into tension with discourses of Philippine revolutionary nationalism, which envisions a revolutionary restructuring of Philippine society from a neocolonial and semifeudal state to a more equitable and just society. When asked about his thoughts on the role of Filipina/o Americans in nationalist movements in the Philippines, Victor, a PSP student from the New York City area, responded, "To me [being a Filipina/o nationalist] is the only step forward. I mean, what are Filipina/o American issues? Identity? World War II veterans? All this stuff that doesn't really matter when everyone here is dying, and they don't have the money to feed their kids or send their kids to school. . . . The only way to get involved [with the people's movements in the Philippines] is to join a group like BAYAN."[64] Victor's statement reveals the tension between the identity-based politics of Filipina/o American cultural nationalism and discourses of revolutionary Philippine nationalism. Instead of working with identity-based Filipina/o American organizations, Victor advocates for Filipina/o American involvement with National Democratic solidarity organizations such as BAYAN USA. Victor critiqued his peers' ignorance of the economic and political crisis in the Philippines: "The majority of the leaders of Fil Am student organizations don't know anything about the situation in the Philippines."[65] Indeed, Dylan Rodriguez argues that Filipina/o American cultural nationalism is a form of "deformed nationalism" that reproduces both the white supremacy of US multiculturalism and the carceral violence of the US state while maintaining class hierarchies within Filipina/o American communities.[66]

In their binational position as diasporic subjects, Filipina/o Americans also negotiate the implicit investment in US exceptionalism characteristic of Filipina/o American cultural nationalism. The cultural nationalist discourse of Filipina/o American ethnic/racial identity contributes to the broader elision of US imperialism in US culture. Cultural nationalist discourses of Filipina/o American identity often elide the violence of US empire as the historical condition of possibility for such claims to American identity.[67] As Dylan Rodriguez argues, the pursuit of Filipina/o American studies as an academic discipline entails a disavowal of the genocide enacted by the US military during the Philippine American War.[68] The very articulation of a Filipina/o American identity within the national context of the United States implies the epistemic violence of the erasure of American imperialism from both the US national and Filipina/o American psyches. Inversely, Allan Isaac argues that the "operation and production of empire is predicated on the legislative and cultural institutionalization of the disavowal of these American subjects [Filipina/os, Puerto Ricans, Guamanians]."[69] This national disavowal allows the US empire to remain invisible to itself.

Queer Nationalisms

The notion of queer nationalisms interrupts the cultural nationalist dyad of the male heterosexual *balikbayan* and the global Filipina body. Situated in relation to Filipina/o American cultural nationalism, Philippine revolutionary nationalism, and the homonationalism of mainstream LGBT politics in the United

States, queer Filipina/o American *balikbayans* occupy an ambivalent relationship to the nation. The relationship between queer sexuality and the nation has a complicated history within US-based queer studies. US queer studies scholars such as Lisa Duggan, Lauren Berlant, and Elizabeth Freeman have discussed the politics of "gay nationalism" within the history of queer politics, focusing largely on the 1990s organization Queer Nation.[70] While many US queer theorists have critiqued the nation, few theorists have addressed the relationship of queer subjects to decolonial, antistate nationalisms.[71] On the other hand, an increasing number of queer theorists have critiqued the incorporation of a (primarily white and male) queer subject into the hegemonic US nation-state through homonationalist projects such as the legalization of gay marriage and the repeal of Don't Ask Don't Tell.[72] Within Filipina/o diasporic political culture, a sustained analysis of the relationship of queer subjects to Philippine nationalist movements is uncommon.[73] Although it is not unusual for members of the ND movement (both in the Philippines and in the United States) to identify as LGBT, *bakla*, or *tomboy*, critiques of the heteronormativity and masculinism of nationalist discourse are rarely articulated within the Filipina/o diasporic culture.[74]

As a queer Filipina American *balikbayan*, I was particularly interested in how PSP students as actors within the transnational social movements engaged with the politics of queer sexuality and nationalism in terms of both the US and Philippine nations. While only a handful of PSP participants openly identified as queer or LGBT, I had particularly fruitful discussions with Joey, a Filipino American PSP student from southern California who identifies as gay. My discussions with Joey illuminated the tensions and contradictions for LGBT subjects within the intersecting discourses of Filipina/o American cultural nationalism and Filipina/o diasporic nationalisms. At the time of our interview, Joey was an undergraduate student attending the University of California who was very active in Filipina/o American politics on his campus and within his community. Joey later became a founding member of a southern California chapter of the Philippine nationalist youth movement Anakbayan (Sons and Daughters of the Nation).

Joey spoke of his early experiences growing up in a Filipina/o American community in California. For Joey, "It was much easier for me to deal with being queer [than being Filipino]. I couldn't deal with all my identities at once. The reason I couldn't deal with the Filipina/o community at first was because I was queer."[75] He went on to say that as a teenager, he felt like an outsider in his local Filipina/o American community because he was openly gay. Joey's sexual orientation set him apart from the upper-middle-class community in which he was raised. Joey described how he participated in activities similar to those of other Filipina/o American boys his age, such as playing tennis, but he did not feel comfortable at community gatherings. As a teenager, Joey was openly gay and involved with queer youth organizations in high school. However, it wasn't until college that Joey felt like he was part of a Filipina/o American community, when he found queer allies at the Filipina/o American student organization at his university.

Many of the Filipina/o American students in PSP were undergraduate students who were politicized within the cultural nationalist context of Filipina/o American student organizations in California. Similarly, Joey only came to identify with his Filipino heritage later, when he became a member of the Filipina/o American organization at the University of California. It is within the context of Pilipino Cultural Nights (PCNs) and other forms of Filipina/o American cultural production that cultural nationalist discourses intersect with Philippine state discourses in the formation of diasporic nationalisms. Because Joey is a queer Filipina/o American *balikbayan*, his relationship to cultural nationalism was a fraught one.[76] Joey described his experience with the PCN at his university, which focused on the Philippine myth about Malakas and Maganda. The story of Malakas and Maganda is a Philippine origin myth in which the Philippine nation is descended from two deities, the male, Malakas (Strong), and the female, Maganda (Beautiful). At a meeting of the Filipina/o American student organization at his university, Joey asked why the PCN, an iconic cultural production that often reproduces the heteronormativity of Filipina/o American cultural nationalism, focused on an origin myth centered on a heterosexual pairing.[77] Another student responded, "Well, it's about a family. You have to have a man and a woman to have a family." Joey responded, "Where do I fit in within the story of Malakas and Maganda?"[78] Although he is an active participant within Filipina/o diasporic nationalist movements, Joey struggled with the heteronormativity of the PCN. Indeed, the dramatic narrative of Filipina/o American PCNs often revolves around a heterosexual romance. Within the discursive logic of the PCN, the queer subject is often unrepresentable as a cultural nationalist subject. Narratives such as the Maganda and Malakas myth reiterate the reproductive logic of the nation within the cultural nationalist framework of Filipina/o American identity.

As a queer Filipina/o American *balikbayan*, Joey both mobilizes nationalist narratives as a mode of resistance to US neocolonialism and capitalist globalization and critiques the nation as an uneasy site of belonging for queer subjects. While he supports the ND vision of Philippine national liberation, Joey recognizes the inherent violence of the nation-state, commenting specifically on groups that have historically been excluded from the Philippine state: "Muslim, NPA, activist—they don't matter to society. . . . The idea of nation suppresses the minority. It calls for a homogeneous society."[79] Perhaps because of his critique of the Philippine state, Joey believes strongly in the ND vision for the Philippine nation, which explicitly contests the authoritarian Philippine state. As a queer Filipino American participant within Filipina/o diasporic social movements, Joey negotiates the tension between conflicting discourses of the nation: the heteronormativity and masculinism of Filipina/o American cultural nationalism, the inherent violence of the Philippine nation-state, and the explicitly antistate discourse of Philippine revolutionary nationalisms. While Joey critiques the tendency of nation-building projects to enforce a homogeneous dominant culture, he also believes in the potential of the nation as a mode of organizing for minority subjects, including queer subjects. For example, Joey commented positively on the use of the rainbow American flag, a symbol that fuses discourses of gay pride with US nationalism: "Some [queer] people want to retake Americanism."[80] The rainbow American flag is an iconic symbol for the homonationalism that characterizes the contemporary US mainstream LGBT movement. The primarily white mainstream LGBT political movement's focus on gay marriage and gay inclusion into the military has alienated queer of color and queer migrant organizations, which have critiqued the lack of an intersectional analysis that centers issues of racial and economic justice within queer organizing.[81] Despite Joey's homonationalist desire for queers to retake Americanism, queer Filipina/o Americans are constituted as the racial Others of the white homonationalist subject. Joey's statement about retaking Americanism suggests the inherent tension between US homonationalism, which bolsters the sexual exceptionalism and violence of the US state, and the antistate popular nationalism of the ND movement. Queer Filipina/o American *balikbayans* must contend with both the homonationalism of the mainstream US LGBT movement and the heteronormativity of Filipina/o diasporic nationalisms. At the same time, queer of color organizations in the United States tend to implicitly focus on the context of the United States, with few discussions of anti-imperialist organizing beyond the borders of the US nation.

The tension between Joey's support of Philippine nationalist movements, his critiques of the heteronormativity of Filipina/o American cultural nationalism, and his own investment in US homonationalism reveals the complexity of queer Filipina/o American engagement with nationalisms. Joey's ambivalent feelings about nationalism mirrored my own. While we both supported Philippine popular nationalist movements, we had reservations about the limits of notions of national unity. Joey's discomfort with the implicit heteronormativity of Filipina/o American cultural nationalist forms of cultural production such as Pilipino Cultural Nights echoed my own mixed feelings. A tension exists between feminist and queer critiques of the heteropatriarchal nation and the trope of national liberation. Indeed, as a feminist, queer, and female-identified *balikbayan* myself, my personal, political, and intellectual commitments coalesce in contradictory and at times divergent ways. Even as I articulate scholarly critiques of nationalism, I am cognizant of my deep political investments in Filipina/o diasporic nationalist struggles against ongoing forms of US imperialism and the violence of capitalist globalization. Simultaneously, I am aware of the need to disentangle the violence of the state from popular movements that organize in the name of national liberation. As a US citizen, I am faced daily with the violence of the US state, which is reproduced within mainstream LGBT culture through insidious forms of homonationalist integration into the apparatus of the state. For example, with the end of Don't Ask Don't Tell, transgender inclusion in the military has become the next political stage for homonationalist political movements.[82] Likewise, I recognize that the antipathy among US feminist and queer critics toward nationalism must be contextualized within a broader intellectual context that is inherently resistant to anticolonial movements.[83] The experiences of queer *balikbayans* must be contextualized within this contact zone of contradictory and divergent discourses of the nation.

The figure of the queer Filipina/o American *balikbayan* disrupts the normative gendered notions of diasporic citizenship upon which diasporic nationalisms relies. As Robert Diaz notes, the figure of the male *balikbayan* indexes heteronormative discourses of "economic stability, appropriate respectability, and familial commitment."[84] Thus, the figure of the *balikbayan* is always already gendered in heteronormative ways, implying a heterosexual subject with appropriate familial and national commitments whose return to the Philippines represents both the values of the traditional nuclear family and the notion of American modernity.[85] As Martin Manalansan notes, "Traditional renderings of diasporic travel naturalize links between heterosexuality, family life, masculinity, and modernity."[86] Indeed, as Manalansan suggests, the presence of the queer *balikbayan* troubles notions of diasporic return and home.[87] The queer *balikbayan* unsettles the gendered and sexual politics of the notion of a home or "homeland." Ultimately, the queer *balikbayan* is a figure whose multiple (trans) national political and affective affiliations disrupt the articulation of diasporic nationalisms. As both a figure within diasporic cultural production and an actor within diasporic political movements, the queer *balikbayan* interrupts gendered and sexual notions of citizenship, national belonging, and home. Imbricated within multiple and at times contradictory forms of nationalism, the figure of the queer Filipina/o American *balikbayan* challenges the dyad of the (implicitly male heterosexual) Filipino American *balikbayan* and the present absence of the global Filipina body. This tension, between the gendered and sexual violence of the nation as a form of collectivity and the nation as a form of liberation from neocolonialism and capitalist globalization, organizes the structure of this book.

While this chapter critiques the gendered and sexual politics of diasporic nationalisms through the figure of the Filipina/o American *balikbayan*, the next chapter focuses primarily on the figure of the Filipina trafficked woman / sex worker. Similarly to diasporic nationalisms, transnational Filipina American feminist movements often draw on notions of diasporic solidarity in the name of liberating the global Filipina body. As such, the political and discursive stakes are particularly significant in the discourse of the "traffic in women." In the context of diasporic nationalisms, the present absence of the global Filipina body is a foil against which the (implicitly male heterosexual) *balikbayan* makes claims of national belonging. In contrast, within the traffic in women discourse, the figure of the Filipina trafficked woman / sex worker embodies not only the failure of the Philippine state to survive without outward labor migration but also the sexual subjection and subordination of the Philippine nation to neoliberal globalization.

Transitioning from an analysis of a heritage language program to Filipina/o American film and performance, the next chapter shifts methodologically from an ethnographic approach to a visual and textual analysis. While the global Filipina body exists at the edges of the analysis in this chapter—as that which is ever present yet absent—in the next chapter I focus squarely on a particular iteration of the global Filipina body, the Filipina trafficked woman / sex worker. In doing so, I move theoretically from a critique of the heteronormativity and masculinism of diasporic nationalisms to a consideration of the politics of Filipina American feminism. Ultimately, both figures remind us of the risk of epistemic and bodily violence in representing the global Filipina body as a sign of the Philippine nation.

CHAPTER 2

Imagining the Filipina Trafficked Woman / Sex Worker

The Politics of Filipina/o American Solidarity

*N*ational Heroes, a dramatic vignette presented at the 2006 Pilipino Cultural Night (PCN) ReCreation, at the University of California at Berkeley, begins with a completely silent, dark stage. Alongside hundreds of Filipina/o American students and their families, I wait in the dark for the scene to unfold onstage. As haunting orchestral music plays in the background, the figures onstage are lit sequentially. One by one, the characters' tear-streaked faces become visible. The main character, a Filipina OCW named Baby, cries out, "This is not my country. This is not my home. This is not my family. This is not my daughter. My daughter is far away, sick, dreaming of me holding her in my arms. Yet I hold someone else's child. It does not matter how much my bones ache, or that I am so tired. I will work as hard as I can to pay for her school, and her medicine, and her clothes."[1] This emotional monologue embodies both the affective and pedagogical roles of the PCN within Filipina/o American culture. Vignettes such as *National Heroes* teach young Filipina/o Americans about the crisis of the Philippine nation's reliance on overseas labor migration.

National Heroes narrates the gendered effects of globalization on the lives of two Filipina domestic helpers working abroad, Flor and Baby. The theme of familial separation and sacrifice structures the narrative of *National Heroes*. Flor must work to support her sick mother and son in the Philippines, and Baby must pay for medicine and healthcare for her sick daughter. While Baby takes care of her employer's child, her interaction with her own daughter is limited to transnational phone calls. In addition to this pedagogical role, *National Heroes* serves the affective purpose of inciting both national and transnational affects— the mourning for the victims of neoliberal globalization and the yearning for a sovereign Philippine nation. The Filipina/o American audience is meant to *feel for* and *with* the Philippine nation.

National Heroes embodies the collective mourning and loss invoked by the figure of the Filipina trafficked woman / sex worker within multiple genres of diasporic Filipina/o cultural production, from Pilipino Cultural Nights to film/ video and the internet. I use the term "trafficked woman" to refer to a constellation of Filipina laboring bodies that provide domestic, affective, and sexual labor for a global economy. Women who migrate—both within and across national borders—to do sexual, affective, and domestic labor are collapsed in the figure of the Filipina trafficked woman / sex worker within the discourse of the "traffic in women." The pervasiveness of the figure of the trafficked woman / sex worker, spanning multiple forms of Filipina/o diasporic cultural production and global popular culture, mirrors the global capitalist logic that reduces Filipina women to the forms of labor they provide for the world economy. Both state and activist uses of the traffic-in-women discourse often conflate diverse forms of gendered labor migration within the figure of the Filipina trafficked woman / sex worker. I am *not* arguing that trafficked labor is equivalent to sex work, nor am I arguing that sex work is equivalent to the various forms of domestic and caretaking feminized labor—whether as domestic workers, eldercare providers, nannies, or nurses—that Filipina migrant workers provide for a global economy. Instead, I contend that the traffic-in-women discourse often conflates sex work with exploited and coerced labor, including the various forms of gendered labor that migrant Filipinas/os provide. The US and Philippine states, as well as Filipina/o American political organizations, use the discourse of trafficking for distinct political purposes. The goals and effects of the circulation of the traffic-in-women discourse by state and popular political actors vary. The Philippine state discourse of "new heroes" (*bagong bayani*) portrays overseas contract workers as heroines of the nation in order to justify the Philippine state's policies of labor exportation.[2] Within the Filipina/o American diasporic imagination, the figure of the Filipina sex worker / trafficked woman often embodies the inability of the Philippine nation to maintain the heteronormative family in the context of transnational labor migration as women are forced to leave their husbands and children to perform both sexual and domestic labor for a global economy. Within the traffic-in-women discourse, the figure of the Filipina migrant laborer often represents the failure of the Philippine nation to maintain its borders in the face of economic globalization, as well as the "pimping out" of migrant labor by the

Philippine state. The ubiquitous figure of the Filipina trafficked woman / sex worker haunts not only Philippine popular culture but also Filipina/o American cultural production.

The narrative of the exploited Filipina trafficked woman / sex worker is central to the affective structure of the Filipina American film *Sin City Diary* (1992), directed by Rachel Rivera. From the 1990s into the 2000s *Sin City Diary* has screened in diverse venues, including the St. John's International Women's Film Festival (1993), a screening organized by the University of California at Irvine chapter of the Filipina American feminist organization GabNet (2008), and a screening organized by the Women and Gender Studies Institute at the University of Toronto (2008).[3] Part personal autobiography and part documentary, *Sin City Diary* documents the lives of Filipina sex workers and their mixed-race Amerasian children in Olongapo, a city that was the site of a major US naval base in the Philippines for almost one hundred years.[4]

Through her personal narrative as a diasporic Filipina American, Rivera tells the story of her childhood departure from Olongapo, Philippines, after her mother married a white American man. *Sin City Diary* articulates a Filipina/o American diasporic subjectivity formed in opposition to two figures, the Filipina sex worker and her biracial Amerasian child. In the film, Filipina/o American diasporic subjectivity is shaped affectively through the narratives of loss and abandonment that frame the representation of the Filipina sex worker. These narratives of loss, against and through which the Filipina American subject defines herself, form the basis for the mode of Filipina/o American diasporic belonging articulated in *Sin City Diary*. In this binational family drama, the Filipina/o American *balikbayan* and the Amerasian child are triangulated between the feminized Philippine nation and the masculine imperial power of the United States. However, while the Filipina/o American *balikbayan* is positioned as the inheritor of US social and material capital, the Amerasian child is figured as the illegitimate offspring of US military masculinity and Philippine sexual labor. Although Rivera's representation of herself as the *balikbayan* who escaped the Philippines departs from the masculinist subjectivity of the Filipino American diasporic nationalism critiqued in the previous chapter, both forms of Filipina/o American subjectivity emerge in opposition to the abject figure of the Filipina trafficked woman / sex worker. As such, the Amerasian child of the Filipina sex worker and a US serviceman is an extension of this abjectness. Within *Sin City Diary*, the Amerasian child is the excess that cannot be enfolded into the binational union of the United States and the Philippines.

This focus on the figure of the trafficked woman / sex worker in *Sin City Diary* marks a methodological and theoretical departure from the previous chapter's analysis of the Filipina/o American *balikbayan* within the social world of the Philippine Studies Program (PSP), a heritage language program. While the previous chapter employed an ethnographic methodology to examine how heteronormative and masculinist discourses of Filipina/o diasporic nationalisms were both articulated and contested in the transnational space of a heritage language program, this chapter shifts its focus to the performance and visual texts in which the figure of the Filipina trafficked woman / sex worker emerges in Filipina/o American cultural production. This methodological transition from ethnographic to visual and textual analyses is required by the breadth of the archive of Filipina/o American diasporic cultural production examined in *The Global Filipina Body*. From the classrooms of a heritage language program to the visual text of the Filipina American film *Sin City Diary*, *The Global Filipina Body* encompasses a range of cultural objects and transnational sites that make up the archive in which the figure of the global Filipina body circulated from the 1990s to the mid-2010s. I shift my optic of analysis from the reproduction and contestation of heteronormative and masculinist notions of diasporic nationalisms in the PSP to a critique of the figure of the trafficked woman / sex worker within *Sin City Diary* and Filipina/o American political discourse more broadly. Both the figure of the Filipina/o American *balikbayan* in chapter 1 and the Filipina trafficked woman / sex worker in chapter 2 index an ongoing concern with the ways in which the crisis of the Philippine nation under global capitalism is often narrated in heteropatriarchal terms in the context of the diaspora. While the Filipina/o American *balikbayan* is both a figure and an actor within transnational discourses of Filipina/o discourses of diasporic nationalisms, the figure of the Filipina trafficked woman / sex worker often signifies the collective mourning for a sovereign nation in the face of neoliberal capitalism.

The Figure of the Filipina Trafficked Woman / Sex Worker

While both the sex worker and the overseas contract worker (OCW) are collapsed within the figure of the Filipina trafficked woman / sex worker, contradictory iterations of this figure are mobilized for distinct political purposes within the Filipina/o diasporic imagination, from Filipina/o American PCNs to Philippine popular film. As the title of the PCN vignette *National Heroes* demonstrates, the Philippine state discourse of OCWs as national heroes has traveled from the Philippines to California university campuses. The representation of overseas domestic helpers has emerged within the genre of PCNs, which have historically focused on the Filipina/o American experience, primarily drawing on the experiences of second-generation Filipina/o American youth.[5] The inclusion of a vignette on Filipina overseas contract workers in a PCN is a departure from the usual story lines, which are often based on excavating one's cultural/ethnic identity within a white dominant culture. Shifting the focus away from belonging to the collective body of the US nation, *National Heroes* instead incites a form of affective affiliation with the exploited global Filipina body of the OCW.

Former Philippine president Cory Aquino introduced the discourse of national heroes in 1988 when she addressed a group of Filipino domestic workers in Hong Kong, saying, "Kayo po ang mga bagong bayani" (You are the new heroes).[6] The "new heroes" discourse has circulated throughout Philippine popular culture from the 1990s onward, especially through films such as *Anak* and *The Flor Contemplacion Story*, which dramatize the lives of Filipina OCWs abroad. While the film *The Flor Contemplacion Story* tells the story of the Filipina domestic helper who was convicted and executed by the Singaporean state for allegedly murdering another Filipina domestic helper (DH), *Anak* describes a Filipina DH who returns to the Philippines to find her family estranged from her. *The Flor Contemplacion Story* was immensely popular throughout the Filipina/o diaspora. Patrick Flores describes the reception of the film in Hong Kong: "An eyewitness recounts that when *The Flor Contemplacion Story* was shown in Hong Kong at the Mandarin Theater inside the second-class mall Pinoy World, the reception of Filipina maids to the event was tremendous. The films played for four weekends, two screenings a day, to standing-room crowds. The theater accommodates 1,500–3,000 people and tickets were priced at HK$50. The film grossed US$3.3 million worldwide."[7] The popularity of the Philippine films *The Flor Contemplacion Story* and *Anak* in diverse sites such as New York, Los Angeles, Hong Kong, Vancouver, and Toronto demonstrates the ubiquity of the national-heroes discourse across the Filipina/o diaspora.[8] The wide dissemination of such films suggests that the Philippine state has been successful in promoting the new-heroes discourse to combat the increasing criticism of the Philippine government's inability to protect its workers from physical and sexual abuse abroad.[9] In particular, the execution of Filipina domestic worker Flor Contemplacion by the Singaporean state in 1995 provoked an outcry among the Philippine public. Contemplacion's death also incited a sense of collective mourning for the Philippine nation's failure to keep itself whole against the onslaught of global capital.[10] This outcry prompted former Philippine president Fidel Ramos to push for the passing of Republic Act (RA) 8042 (The Migrant Workers and Overseas Filipinos Act of 1995), which marked a shift in government policy from exporting labor to "managing" labor migration.[11] Despite the fact that RA 8042 explicitly states that the Philippine government "does not promote overseas employment as a means to sustain economic growth and achieve national development," the act institutionalized policies of overseas employment.[12] Within this larger context of criticism of the Philippine state and its promotion of labor migration, the discourse of national heroes has served to justify the state's reliance on remittances from abroad by valorizing the women and men who choose to work abroad.[13]

Within popular films such as *Anak* and *The Flor Contemplacion Story*, Filipina DHs are represented as "heroines" or "martyrs" who have paid the ultimate sacrifice for their family and, by extension, the Philippine nation. In this nationalist discourse, the Philippine nation is figured through the trope of the nuclear, heteronormative family, which is disrupted by the necessity of overseas labor migration. The national-heroes discourse perpetuates what Sarah Raymundo describes as "a cultural logic that participates in the production and reproduction of capital, rather than a mirror of its logic."[14] The ideological framework of the film *Anak* implicitly legitimizes the Philippine state's policies of labor migration, thereby affirming the Philippine state's collusion with transnational capital. As such, popular films such as *Anak* contribute to the production of what Raymundo terms the "transnational imaginary" of the state, discourses that "normalize and render as natural the exploitative conditions of neoliberal globalization."[15] The PCN vignette *National Heroes* and Philippine popular films such as *Anak* and *The Flor Contemplacion Story* reflect the diasporic circulation of the Philippine state's transnational imaginary of domestic workers as national heroes. The Filipina/o American actors in the *National Heroes* vignette corporealize the figure of the global Filipina body onstage, interpellating the audience into the affective structures that position DHs as signs of national mourning. Here the logic of capital, as mediated by the Philippine state, is reproduced within the diasporic context of Filipina/o American performance.

In contrast to the national-heroes discourse promulgated by the Philippine state, the Filipina trafficked woman / sex worker is figured as the "damaged Other" of the Filipina/o American *balikbayan* in *Sin City Diary*.[16] Jo Doezema describes how British imperial feminists used the figure of the Indian prostitute as the "damaged Other" to bolster white British women's participation in the public sphere.[17] Similarly, the figure of the trafficked woman signifies the exploitative conditions of Philippine outward labor migration within Filipina/o American political discourse. Making no distinction between those who are coerced into sex work and those who choose to do forms of sexual, affective, and domestic labor, the traffic-in-women discourse draws on a heteronormative, anti–sex worker logic to critique the gendered effects of globalization in the Philippines.[18] Within this discourse, the trafficked woman represents the subordination of the feminized Philippine nation, as the Philippines is reduced to the forms of exploited, gendered labor that it provides for a global economy. Roderick Ferguson describes the figure of the sex worker of color as the Other of the heteropatriarchal US nation.[19] Within the logic of *Sin City Diary*, the Filipina trafficked woman / sex worker functions as the Other of the heteropatriarchal Philippine nation. As the embodiment of Philippine sexual, domestic, and affective labor, the Filipina trafficked woman / sex worker is a sign of the failure of the Philippine nation to maintain the heteronormative, patriarchal family in the context of feminized labor migration. This crisis of the Philippine national family is reproduced in the transnational context of the diaspora, particularly through the figure of the Filipina trafficked woman / sex worker. As the vignette *National Heroes* demonstrates, the crisis of the Philippine nation is not limited to Philippine films such as *Anak* and *The Flor Contemplacion Story* but is present in Filipina/o American cultural production as well.

The use of the traffic-in-women discourse by Filipina American feminists is an inherently risky enterprise, as this discourse has the tendency to discursively position the Filipina trafficked woman / sex worker as the "fallen woman" who represents the sexual victimization of the Philippine nation under capitalist globalization. The circulation of the US-based GABRIELA Network's Purple Rose Campaign—a campaign focused on ending the trafficking of Filipina women—exemplifies the circulation of the traffic-in-women discourse within Filipina/o American political culture, beginning in the 1990s and extending into the mid-2010s. Established in 1989 in Chicago, GABRIELA Network (GABNet, now reconvened as the organization AF3IRM) was a multiracial network of primarily Filipina American women who worked in solidarity with the Philippine women's organization GABRIELA.[20] At the time of its inception, GABNet worked with GABRIELA Philippines as part of the movement to oust the US military bases in Clark (air force) and Subic Bay (navy) in the Philippines.[21] According to the GABNet website, "Since our inception we have focused our efforts on organizing, educating, networking, and advocating around the issues of sex trafficking, globalization, militarism, labor export and other structural adjustment programs imposed by international finance agencies like the International Monetary Fund and the World Bank."[22] GABNet's political campaign is explicitly framed through a gendered critique of both neoliberal capitalism and neoimperialism. In the Purple Rose Campaign, various forms of domestic, sexual, and affective transnational labor are conflated in the traffic-in-women discourse. On the former GABNet website, statistics and descriptions of the dire conditions of domestic helpers, sex workers, and mail-order brides were included under the sections titled "Why Campaign Against Trafficking of Filipino Women and Children" and "Trafficking in the United States."[23] Women who marry American men through online dating websites are equated with sex workers in the sex tourism industry in the Philippines. Citing the violence that many mail-order brides face at the hands of their American husbands, GAB-Net conflates being a mail-order bride with both coerced and paid sex work. By including mail-order brides, domestic workers, and sex workers within the discourse of trafficking, multiple kinds of domestic, sexual, and affective labor are included within the figure of the Filipina trafficked woman / sex worker, who is universally portrayed as a victim.

Within the discourse presented on Gabriela Network's website, mail-order brides, domestic workers, and sex workers are often conflated, as all are equally figured as victims without agency. The Purple Rose Campaign has continued throughout Gabriela Network's transformation to AF3IRM. On February 14, 2014, AF3IRM marked the fifteenth anniversary of the Purple Rose Campaign, stating on its website, "For fifteen years, we have engaged in speaking out and advocating for labor and sex trafficked women; we have lobbied for the passage of the International Marriage Broker Regulation Act and pushed for protections for mail-order brides."[24] The statement goes on to note how the Purple Rose Campaign has expanded to include sexual violence more broadly: "The endemic and problematic commodification and fetishization of women's bodies is not just about trafficking—it is about prostitution, it is about pornography, it is about the racist, sexist, and misogynist views that people normalize and spit out as easy as their breath. This is about rejecting sexual violence, sexual exploitation, so-called sexual agency and rape culture."[25] Like much of anti–sex work and antipornography discourse, AF3IRM equates sex work and prostitution with sexual violence against women more broadly. Rejecting what they term "so-called sexual agency," AF3IRM leaves no room for the possibility of choice or agency within the practice of sex work. AF3IRM is not unique in its conflation of sex work with sexual violence. This perspective is common to many white Western feminists' approach to both sex work and trafficking.[26] My intention is not to disparage the important work that GABNet (now AF3IRM) has done to combat the gendered effects of US imperialism and neoliberal capitalism but to point to the epistemic risk in reproducing heteronormative narratives of sex work as violence within Filipina American feminisms.

The conflation of sex work with sexual violence and coerced labor implies a moralistic framework in which the Filipina trafficked woman / sex worker embodies the failure of the Philippine nation to maintain the heteronormative ideal of the family. In the context of the Philippines, Nobue Suzuki argues that the figure of the Filipina "entertainer" in Japan evokes a "self-disciplining middle-class women's anti-prostitution hysteria," in which "women's sexuality must be kept for reproduction and within formal heterosexual marriage, which has been designed according to masculinist capitalist discipline, and sex may be had with 'love' but not for money."[27] In the context of Filipina/o American cultural production, the figure of the Filipina trafficked woman / sex worker functions not only as the sign of the failure of the heteropatriarchal Philippine nation in the face of global capitalism but also as the failure of the heteronormative, masculinist framework of the family, which dictates that sex should happen in the context of the heterosexual marriage, not for financial gain. The ubiquity of the traffic-in-women discourse within Filipina/o American cultural production suggests that "any woman who has sex outside of this scheme is commonly considered 'perverse' and 'fallen' and needs to be reformed."[28]

To be clear, the critique of the traffic-in-women discourse offered in this chapter is an implicitly "loving" critique. That is, it emerges from a deep political commitment to the various political movements through which Filipina/o diasporic feminists, in particular, Filipina/o American feminists, work to end the exploitation of gendered transnational labor migration. Many of the specific cases of labor exploitation taken up by Filipina/o American organizations are clearly cases of coerced and/or forced labor, what can accurately be described as trafficking. Thus, I am *not* arguing against the use of the discourse of trafficking writ large, as many cases of transnational labor are rightly defined as trafficking. Rather, I critique the reductive use of the heteronormative discourse of the traffic in women and its simplistic conflation with sex work as one that often produces discursive and material violence. As an anti-imperialist queer diasporic Filipina feminist, my intention is to analyze how Filipina/o American cultural production can, at times, reify this discourse, *not* to malign the activists or migrant workers doing grassroots political organizing to improve the material conditions of Filipina/o migrant labor. This is crucial political work that is absolutely necessary, given the intensification of neoliberal capitalist globalization and its inherent exploitation and dehumanization of labor. However, it is also necessary to highlight the specific positionality of Filipina/o Americans, located as we are in between US empire and the Philippines. That is, while Filipina/o American are clearly not positioned equally to white Western feminists, given the white supremacist racial formations that structure the United States and other countries of the Global North, we do occupy a position of privilege in relation to those who are represented as "trafficked women" within Filipina/o American cultural production. It is an awareness of this privilege and an attention to the ongoing effects of US imperialism that contextualize my "loving critique" of this discourse. In *Sin City Diary*, the privilege associated with the figure of the Filipina American *balikbayan* in the Philippines is contrasted with the abject conditions of the Filipina sex worker. Such a juxtaposition creates a risky politics of representation, one that Filipina/o Americans must negotiate carefully.

Sin City Diary

The traffic-in-women discourse frames the Filipina American film *Sin City Diary*, which positions the Filipina sex worker as the "damaged Other" against which Filipina American subjectivity is constructed. Within the narrative of the film, the trafficked woman / sex worker stands in for the sexualized exploitation of Philippine labor, while the *balikbayan* signifies the American dream of upward mobility. Directed and narrated by the Filipina American filmmaker Rachel Rivera, *Sin City Diary* describes the journey of Rivera's return to the Philippines after a seventeen-year absence. The film is structured as a narrative of Rivera's familial and personal history as a Filipina American who left the Philippines during childhood to migrate to the United States with her Filipina mother and white American stepfather. *Sin City Diary* also tells the story of three Filipina sex workers in Olongapo City, Philippines, the site of a former US naval base. The frequent presence of Amerasian children in the film is an embodied reminder of the betrayal and abandonment of the Philippines by the United States. The relationship of the white American serviceman to his spurned Filipina lover / sex worker structures the film's portrayal of the relationship between the United States and the Philippines. Within this familial narrative, the exploited bodies of sex workers in Olongapo corporealize the subordinated Philippine nation. Filipina/o American *balikbayan* subjectivity is triangulated between the feminized Philippine nation and the masculine military power of the United States. As the child of two nations, the Filipina/o American *balikbayan* is an interlocutor in the family drama of the United States and the Philippines. In contrast to the Filipina/o American *balikbayan*, the Amerasian children of Filipina sex workers are figured as the illegitimate offspring of the United States / Philippine union, whose mixed-race features serve as physical reminders of the history of US empire in the Philippines.

Sin City Diary is framed through the affective lens of Rivera's *exilic memories* of the Philippines. José Esteban Muñoz describes his exilic memories as an immigrant from Cuba as "the ephemera and personal narratives that signify 'Cuba' for me . . . not only possessing a certain materiality, but also providing a sense of 'place.'"[29] Similarly, Rivera's nostalgic return to her childhood home is the affective framework in which the Filipina sex worker is figured as the "damaged Other" of Filipina American diasporic subjectivity. Rivera's *affective need* to memorialize the Philippines of her childhood frames the representation of the Filipina sex worker within *Sin City Diary*.[30] Rivera's voice-over narration threads together her autobiography of diasporic return with a documentary exposé of the plight of Filipina sex workers in Olongapo. Rivera's voice-over narration connects the disparate visual and aural elements of the film: scenes of sex workers, images of US Navy aircraft, archival photographs, US pop songs, and images of Rivera's childhood. The cross-cutting from long shots of Olongapo streets to Rivera's childhood photographs juxtaposes the lives of Filipina sex workers with Rivera's exilic memories of her childhood in the Philippines. Rivera's voice-over narration guides us through her affective landscape, an emotional terrain of mourning, loss, and abandonment.

 Sin City Diary was filmed in the city of Olongapo in 1989, a few years before the closure of the nearby naval base at Subic Bay, Philippines, in 1992. The film begins with a shot of children playing in a shantytown in Olongapo, a scene of poverty and destitution that is repeated throughout the film. In the next shot, a US military helicopter flies through the sky. The opening introduces the viewer to the sex industry, which is central to Olongapo's local economy, which is dependent on the presence of the US naval base at Subic Bay. The next several shots are images of Filipina sex workers and their American customers walking through the streets of Olongapo, interspersed with shots of Filipina go-go dancers in the dark interiors of the nightclubs. Haunting music plays as the camera pans across a scene of Filipina women waiting in line. The images of women waiting—in lines, in the street for customers—reverberate throughout the film, invoking the theme of abandonment that structures the film. As photographs of Rivera as a child and young adult fill the screen, Rivera narrates, "Summer 1989. After being away for seventeen years, I return to the land of my childhood to see a city known to sailors as Liberty City, Sin City . . . where America meets my homeland in massage parlors and nightclubs. . . . Thousands of women have come here, drawn by the promise of opportunity, the dream of the American rescue." Rivera's exilic memories shape the affective structure of mourning and loss that frames the depiction of the Filipina sex worker in *Sin City Diary*. The narrative juxtaposition of Rivera as the Filipina American heir to US capital and the American Dream with the abject figure of the Filipina sex worker is fundamental to the construction of Filipina/o American diasporic subjectivity in the film. As such, the articulation of Filipina/o American belonging relies on the presence of her damaged Other, the Filipina sex worker. Here the diasporic loss of the *balikbayan* is figured in relation to the mourning of the Filipina sex worker for her former American lover. Rivera reminisces, "Childhood. I grew up never knowing my own language," suggesting that the fulfillment of the American Dream is accompanied by the loss of one's ethnic and cultural identity. Rivera's loss of her native language, the cost of her upward social mobility in the United States, is contrasted with the unfulfilled longing of Filipina sex workers for the American Dream that they will never achieve. The film cuts between photographs of Rivera's Filipina mother and white American stepfather and scenes of Filipina sex workers walking through the streets in Olongapo. In this binational family drama of the United States and the Philippines, the Filipina American *balikbayan* is triangulated between the sexual exploitation of the feminized Philippine nation and the masculine military might of the United States. The Filipina American *balikbayan* is positioned as the legitimate heir to US capital, while the Filipina sex worker is figured as the victim of US military masculinity. This asymmetrical union is visualized in a photograph of Rivera's Filipina mother and white American stepfather, who provided the means for her family's migration to the United States. The sequence shifts from images of Rivera's childhood to a scene of a class for prospective Filipina wives of American servicemen in Olongapo organized by the US Navy. Rivera's voice-over narration frames the shots of young Filipina women listening carefully in class, eager to learn how to become a wife to an American serviceman. In a shot of Filipina women paying rapt attention to their male Filipino instructor, Rivera narrates, "Sitting in this class, I'm reminded how, as a child, I used to think the States as up in heaven, because people had to fly so high in the sky to get there." In Rivera's exilic memories, her childhood departure to the United States is a flight to the heavens, which the hopeful women in the class can only dream about. Several women then describe their desire for an American husband, echoing the dream of rescue through which Rivera narrates her departure from the Philippines as a child. Against the backdrop of Filipina women eager to find an American husband, Rivera positions herself as envied *balikbayan* who embodies the possibility for upward social mobility in the United States.[31] Rivera narrates, "*I was one of the lucky ones.* . . . I see that it is stories like mine that keep the dream alive for *those of us* who were left here" (emphasis mine). This classroom of prospective Filipina brides, a scene of imperial pedagogy, is juxtaposed with photographs of Rivera at various stages of educational achievement: a baby-faced Rivera in an elementary school graduation photograph, a candid photograph of a teenage Rivera smiling. Rivera narrates, "I became an American citizen. I went to American schools, and I graduated from an American college." Rivera's ascent through the US education system, made possible through her mother's marriage to a white American man, contrasts with the pedagogical aims of the prospective Filipina brides, whose purpose is to learn how to be an American wife. Rivera's diasporic subjectivity relies on the juxtaposition of her status as a Filipina American *balikbayan*, as the inheritor of the American Dream, with the abject position of the Filipina sex worker.

Sin City Diary's affective structure is constructed by Rivera's voice-over narration, which positions her as an omniscient figure. Rivera's voice-over narration sutures the disparate images into a cohesive structure of longing and loss. The sex workers' direct address to the camera bolsters Rivera's narrative authority while reifying the objectification of the women interviewed. The structure of the film reinforces a relation of power in which the sex workers are presented as victims to be pitied, in contrast to the empowered position of the Filipina American *balikbayan*. Always focused *on* the women, the camera does not allow the point of view *of* the women to be envisaged on-screen. Here the risky politics of representation become most clear. The depiction of the abandoned Filipina sex worker in *Sin City Diary* risks the reproduction of the imperialist tendencies of Western feminism, which has historically represented women from the Global South as static figures, victims of both traditional patriarchy and histories of colonialism and imperialism.[32] Rivera narrates herself as *belonging to* the collective of Filipina women exploited by US imperialism while simultaneously positioning herself *apart* from them as the Filipina American *balikbayan* who escaped, achieving the dream of American rescue. As such, the film's portrayal of Filipina sex workers is strikingly similar to the problematic semiotics of the images of trafficked women / sex workers that circulate within Western feminist discourse and US popular culture more broadly. Julietta Hua describes the thorny nature of popular representations of the traffic in women, arguing that the visual imagery of sex workers constructs racialized and gendered notions of US national belonging.[33] Similarly to the way in which liberal forms of US national identity are bolstered by images of the abject sex worker / trafficked woman in US popular culture, Rivera's Filipina American feminist subjectivity is constituted in opposition to the Filipina sex worker as damaged Other. Within the logic of the film, the Filipina American *balikbayan* claims a diasporic affiliation with the Philippine nation while simultaneously reproducing the US exceptionalism inherent in the narrative of the American dream. Gendered discourses of US exceptionalism, which present the United States as a site of freedom for women, resonate with the affective logic of *Sin City Diary*.

The rendering of the Philippines as a site of sexual subjection and exploitation is integral to the articulation of Filipina American *balikbayan* subjectivity within the film. *Sin City Diary* weaves together Rivera's personal narrative with the stories of three Filipina sex workers in Olongapo: Glenda, Juliet, and

Josephine. Scenes of each woman going about her daily life are interspersed with scenes in which each documentary subject addresses the camera directly. Juliet, Josephine, and Glenda begin their stories by describing their reasons for migrating from other parts of the Philippines to Olongapo to do sex work. Glenda, who came to Olongapo from a rural province in the Philippines, works as a go-go dancer / sex worker. Juliet, who works as a seamstress and sex worker, has a three-year-old child by an African American serviceman who has returned to the United States. Josephine, whose face is obscured from the camera throughout the film, is an HIV-positive former sex worker who now works in a public health clinic. The stories of Glenda, Juliet, and Josephine are threaded together in a narrative of betrayal and abandonment. Juliet shows the camera photographs of her Amerasian son, A.J., with his father, James, then reads letters from James out loud, invoking a tone of longing and loss. In the next shot, Juliet attends church with her son while saying to the camera, "I pray that the baby's father comes back for him." This theme of abandonment is threaded throughout the film. The scenes of Filipina sex workers narrating their abandonment by their US boyfriends and lovers cut to archival photographs of US soldiers during the Philippine American War. While Rivera narrates, "So many here speak of being betrayed by America, yet the dream lives on," images of Filipino soldiers killed by the US military fill the screen, signifying the ultimate betrayal of the Philippine nation by the United States. In the Philippine American War, the Americans failed to fulfill their promises of benevolent assimilation, meting out death and destruction instead. By connecting the life stories of Juliet, Josephine, and Glenda to the Philippine American War, *Sin City Diary* frames the narrative of betrayal and abandonment through the dyad of the feminized Philippine nation and the masculine military power of the United States.[34] The loss and longing experienced by the abandoned Filipina sex worker and her Amerasian child is an extension of the collective mourning for the sovereign Philippine nation, betrayed by the United States during the Philippine American War.

While Rivera's diasporic subjectivity is made possible through the figuring of Juliet (as the mother of a fatherless child) and Josephine (as an HIV-positive former sex worker) as the "damaged Others" of the Filipina American *balikbayan*, Glenda's self-representation resists this affective framing. Although Glenda relates an earlier experience of "falling in love" with a US serviceman, her self-narration challenges the narrative of abandonment that structures *Sin City Diary*. Glenda tells the camera, "Most of the sailors, they talk a lot of bullshit. I tell myself, don't trust nobody." Glenda resists the lie of the American Dream, unsettling the trope of romance that inspires the faith of many women in Olongapo. In the next shot, Glenda carefully applies makeup to her face, getting dressed for a night of work at the bars. As she looks at herself in the mirror, Glenda defiantly exclaims, "Even if they don't respect me, I respect myself." In contrast to the tone of abandonment and loss that shapes the narratives of Juliet and Josephine, Glenda repudiates the Filipina American gaze. Through her refusal to be figured within the trope of American abandonment, Glenda introduces a sex worker subjectivity that fractures the narrative of sex worker as damaged Other. Glenda deflects the pity and guilt of the Filipina/o American gaze; in doing so, her self-narration resists the dominant affective structure of the film.

Within *Sin City Diary*, the narrative of betrayal and abandonment is most poignantly embodied in the scenes of Amerasian children. The children's mourning for their absent fathers is parallel to the feminized Philippine nation's mourning for the paternal presence of the United States. As the children of the spurned Philippine nation/mother, Amerasian children are the ultimate embodiment of this mourning and loss. Their white American and African American facial features and skin tone echo the legacy of their American fathers. A sequence in the latter half of the film begins with a shot of Amerasian street children who have been abandoned by their Filipina mothers, followed by photographs of more Amerasian children. Meanwhile, Rivera's voice-over narration describes the plight of Amerasian children who have been given up for adoption or abandoned altogether. In the following scene, Amerasian children are shown playing baseball through a church-organized program in Olongapo while Rivera narrates, "I watched them as they played this game inherited from their absent fathers." Medium shots of the children laughing as they play baseball are interspersed with the children addressing the camera directly. One shy young girl, Michelle, states to the camera, "I would like to meet my father." Another girl says, "If my father were here, I would ask him why he left us." While the children laugh and enjoy their game, Rivera's voice-over narration describes the children's "shared longing concealed in laughter." Here the emotional tone of the scene is shaped by Rivera's exilic memories, creating a lens of mourning and loss through which the Amerasian children are represented. During the children's baseball game, the camera pans across the field, focusing on two white American men jogging through the park. Off-screen, a child's voice says, "There are many American guys here we don't even know. They could be our fathers." The camera pans across the field to follow the American men as they jog past the baseball field. As the white American men run off-screen, they embody the children's mourning for their absent fathers. While the Amerasian children are figured as the offspring of the union between Philippine sexual labor and US military masculinity, the *balikbayan* Rivera struggles with a sense of guilt as the Filipina American who is positioned between US masculinist power and Philippine feminized subjection. Off-screen, Rivera's voice-over narration expresses her frustration due to her inability to prevent the Amerasian children from the fate of abandonment by their absent US nation/father: "I wish there was a way for me to go with just a smile and a wave. But in the end there was nothing that I could do . . . just like another visitor from America."

Mourning the Nation

Circulating within multiple sites of Filipina/o diasporic cultural production, the figure of the Filipina trafficked woman / sex worker embodies the anxieties and tensions of the Philippine nation in the contemporary context of capitalist globalization. More specifically, the figure of the Filipina trafficked woman / sex worker signifies the diasporic mourning for a sovereign Philippine nation, as well as a threat to the heteropatriarchal order of the family. While the Filipina/o American *balikbayan* is often represented as the inheritor of US capital within the Philippine national imagination, the figure of the Filipina trafficked woman / sex worker incites the mourning for a sovereign Philippine nation and betrayal by the United States. Within the Filipina/o diasporic imagination, the Filipina trafficked woman / sex worker is the Other of the heteropatriarchal Philippine nation, despite attempts by the Philippine state to depict Filipina OCWs as "national heroes." The diasporic investment in maintaining the sanctity of the heteropatriarchal Philippine nation reproduces the masculinism and heteronormativity of dominant forms of Philippine state and popular nationalism and Filipina/o American cultural nationalism. In *Sin City Diary*, the trope of the heteronormative family of the nation is implicit in the invocation of loss and abandonment that structures the affective landscape of the film. In particular, the Filipina sex worker stands in for the feminized Philippine nation's inability to maintain a heteronormative family structure in the context of contemporary gendered labor migration, as well as the ongoing presence of the US military on the islands.[35] Despite the promises made by her American boyfriends/clients, the Filipina sex worker will rarely, if ever, achieve the status of (heterosexual) wife. As such, her Amerasian child is disavowed within the heteronormative family of the Philippine nation. While her labor is necessary for the economic survival of the nation, both she and her child are positioned as illegitimate members of the national (and diasporic) family.

While the Filipina trafficked woman / sex worker reveals the permeability of Philippine national borders in the face of global capitalism, the Filipina/o

American *balikbayan* signifies the omnipresent power of US capital. The Filipina/o American *balikbayan* is a figure that incites both envy and distrust within the Philippine national imagination. As the embodiment of the American Dream, the narrative of the Filipina/o American *balikbayan* as expatriate success story reinforces the US colonial logic of benevolent assimilation. While the Filipina/o American *balikbayan* is often perceived as the beneficiary of US privilege, the Filipina trafficked woman / sex worker exposes the story of benevolent assimilation to be a lie. Her offspring, the Amerasian child, is the *excess* that embodies the exploitation and subordination inherent to the asymmetrical union between Philippine gendered labor and US military/capital. *Sin City Diary* presents a narrative in which the positioning of the Filipina/o American *balikbayan* as the privileged inheritor of US capital is intrinsically linked to the abjection of the Filipina trafficked woman / sex worker. The Philippine state reproduces this dichotomy as it courts Filipina/o American *balikbayan* capital, encouraging Filipina/o American tourism and investment in the islands while simultaneously brokering gendered labor migration abroad.

Although the "trafficked" Filipina woman / sex worker is positioned as the Other to the heteropatriarchal Philippine nation, she is simultaneously invoked in the service of Filipina/o American political solidarity with the Philippine nation. In Filipina diasporic feminist campaigns such as the Purple Rose Campaign, the plight of the trafficked Filipina woman functions as both a rallying call for transnational Filipina/o American activism and a point of cathection for affective structures of belonging and political solidarity across the Filipina/o diaspora. While political organizing against the exploitation and abuse of Filipina/o migrant workers is absolutely necessary, the politics of representing the global Filipina body within Filipina/o American cultural production are contentious. All too often, Filipina/o American cultural production depicts the trafficked Filipina woman as either a national heroine to be admired for her martyrdom or a victim to be saved from the exploitation of global capitalism. Both iterations of this figure have the tendency to reproduce the heteronormative discourse of the national family. A critical analysis of the politics of gender and sexuality in Filipina/o American cultural production is crucial—particularly the discourse of political solidarity through which many Filipina/o Americans imagine our diasporic connection to the Philippines. Without this critical, self-reflexive analysis, Filipina/o Americans risk complicity with a Western imperialist feminist lens that has historically figured women from the Global South as static victims of tradition or global capitalism.[36] Filipina American feminist film theorist Celine Parreñas Shimizu describes her approach to writing about visual representations of Asian and Asian American sex workers: "Rather than speak for these women, I highlight their unknowability as subjects and the unreliability of representation as a process. I aim to accomplish a form of 'speaking nearby' rather than 'speaking for' these subjects."[37] Similarly, Filipina/o American cultural producers and activists must interrogate the politics of representing the gendered Filipina/o workers who are most exploited by capitalist globalization. Are we "speaking for" or "speaking nearby" Filipina sexual and domestic workers?

CHAPTER 3

Performing the Filipina Mail-Order Bride

Queer Neoliberalism, Affective Labor, and Homonationalism

One of the first appearances of the figure of the Filipina mail-order bride within LGBT popular culture in the Global North occurred in the 1994 Australian film *The Adventures of Priscilla, Queen of the Desert*, directed by Stephan Elliott. In the now infamous ping-pong-ball scene, three Australian drag queens, Bernice, Felicia, and Mitzi, take the stage at a local pub in the Australian outback to the confusion and disgust of the mainly heterosexual male clientele. Interrupting the drag queens' performance, the Filipina bride character, Cynthia, bursts onto the stage, to the delight of the straight male customers. Wearing a leopard-printed bustier, thigh-high boots, and garter belt, Cynthia performs a striptease for the audience. Her performance culminates with the unlikely act of popping ping-pong balls out of her vagina to the enthusiastic audience. *Priscilla* introduced the figure of the Filipina bride, one that is sexually available to the first world, to both mainstream global popular culture and an LGBT subculture.

I was a teenager in the 1990s, and *The Adventures of Priscilla, Queen of the Desert* was my first exposure to the figure of the (implicitly white) drag queen and the figure of the Filipina mail-order bride within Global North popular culture. While the 1990s marked the introduction of the figure of the drag queen into the pop cultural mainstream, the figure of the Filipina mail-order bride also gained widespread notoriety during this time period. Termed "commercial drag" by José Muñoz, films such as *The Adventures of Priscilla, Queen of the Desert*; *To Wong Foo,*

Thanks for Everything! Julie Newmar; and the American remake of *The Bird Cage*, as well as the VH-1 broadcast of drag queen RuPaul's television show, presented a message of "integrationist liberal pluralism" centered on a "sanitized and desexualized queer subject for mass consumption."[1] Simultaneously, the 1990s marked the widespread circulation of the figure of the Filipina mail-order bride within global popular culture.[2] Although the queer Filipina American women's organization Kilawin Kolektibo protested *The Adventures of Priscilla, Queen of the Desert* because of the portrayal of the Filipina bride character, Cynthia, few, if any, mainstream LGBT organizations in the United States critiqued the politics of representation within the film.[3]

The Adventures of Priscilla, Queen of the Desert signified the confluence of the mainstreaming of LGBT culture through "commercial drag" and the emergence of the Filipina mail-order bride as a recognizable trope within global popular culture, highlighting the intersection of gendered and racialized labor under globalization and LGBT cultural politics. The stereotypical representation of the Filipina character, Cynthia, a gold digger who manipulates her white Australian husband and is sexually available to the white male bargoers, reproduces the trope of Filipinas as mail-order brides who exchange sexual labor to obtain a green card. While few LGBT groups—with the exception of Kilawin Kolektibo—protested the portrayal of Cynthia in *Priscilla*, the figure of the Filipina mail-order bride has elicited both outrage and embarrassment within Filipina/o American cultural production more broadly. The ubiquity of the figure of the Filipina mail-order bride within Filipina/o American cultural production reveals broader anxieties about the role of the Philippine nation as a provider of gendered labor within a global economy. Within popular discourse, the Filipina mail-order bride often stands in for the devalued sexual, domestic, and affective labor that Filipinas and other women from the Global South provide for the Global North. Filipina/o American activists, artists, and cultural producers have responded to the popular cultural representations of Filipina mail-order brides in myriad ways—from protests and calls for "positive" images of Filipinas within popular culture, to kitschy appropriations of the term "mail-order bride."

The collaborative art project *Always a Bridesmaid, Never a Bride* (*AABNAB*) (2005–10), by the Filipina American performance and video art group the Mail Order Brides / M.O.B. (M.O.B.), reconfigures the trope of the Filipina mail-order bride. Inspired by a set of performances and art installations at various San Francisco Bay Area art and cultural institutions (Yerba Buena Center for the Arts, Kearny Street Workshop, and the Manilatown Heritage Center), the video I examine is part of the larger performance and visual art project of *AABNAB*. Focusing on the cultural politics of representing the figure of the

Filipina mail-order bride within the testimonial-style video in *AABNAB*, this chapter examines M.O.B.'s performance of feminist camp and ethnic drag to *queer* the figure of the Filipina mail-order bride. The term "feminist camp" refers to M.O.B.'s use of the hyperbolic aesthetic of camp to foreground and critique the forms of gendered and racialized labor performed by Third World women. Similarly, "ethnic drag" describes M.O.B.'s exaggerated embodiment of gendered Filipina/o ethnicity, which makes evident the ethnic/racial performativity inherent to the enactment of domestic and affective labor. In doing so, *AABNAB* implicitly connects critiques of homonationalism to gendered and racialized labor under globalization, linking an analysis of US queer cultural politics to a broader framework of transnational feminisms. M.O.B.'s use of feminist camp and ethnic drag destabilizes the heteropatriarchal notions of Filipina femininity and domesticity that characterize the depiction of the Filipina mail-order bride within Filipina/o American diasporic cultural production, such as the now-defunct website Bagong Pinay / New Filipina.com, which I discuss later in this chapter. *AABNAB* queers the figure of the Filipina mail-order bride within both global popular culture and Filipina/o American cultural production. My two-pronged argument links a critique of the heteropatriarchal politics of Filipina/o American respectability to an analysis of the inability of US homonationalist politics to account for racialized labor. *AABNAB* presents an implicit critique of the homonormative LGBT political discourse of "marriage equality" through their feminist camp representation of gay weddings.[4] Through the figure of the Filipina bridesmaid, these seemingly distinct discourses coalesce in the video, a faux "infomercial" that advertises a rent-a-bridesmaid service for same-sex couples and binational couples marrying for purposes of citizenship. These two forms of marriage are juxtaposed in the figure of the Filipina bridesmaid, whose exploited affective and domestic labor makes her "always a bridesmaid, *never a bride.*" As a bridesmaid, she is essential to the ritual of marriage, whether for immigration or for gay marriage, while she is simultaneously positioned outside the respectability politics of marriage. Through their queering of the figure of the Filipina mail-order bride, who embodies the intersection of marriage for purposes of immigration and gay marriage, *AABNAB* foregrounds the relationship of migration and racialized labor to queer politics.

While chapters 1 and 2 critiqued the heteronormative and masculinist tendencies of dominant representations of the global Filipina body as a sign of the diasporic nation, chapters 3 and 4 explore the ways in which the figure of the global Filipina body is queered within Filipina/o American cultural production. As chapters 1 and 2 argue, dominant representations of the global Filipina body often reproduce the heteropatriarchal politics of the nation within the diaspora and complicate notions of diasporic solidarity within transnational social movements. As I discuss in chapters 1 and 2, the figure of the global Filipina body is a sign of the diasporic nation in which the gendered and sexual politics of state and popular nationalisms are cathected. In contrast to chapters 1 and 2, chapters 3 and 4 shift to an analysis of Filipina/o American video and performance art that reworks or queers the figure of the global Filipina body within both Filipina/o American culture and mainstream LGBT popular culture in the United States. The video and performance art that I examine in the latter half of the book queer the figure of the global Filipina body in multiple senses of the term. In particular, this chapter focuses on the figure of the Filipina mail-order bride in *AABNAB*, integrating a critique of the racial politics of mainstream LGBT culture in the Global North with a discussion of the heteropatriarchy of Filipina/o American respectability politics, both of which inhere in the figure of the Filipina mail-order bride. More broadly, this chapter queers the figure of the Filipina mail-order bride by highlighting the absence of an analysis of gendered and racialized labor and migration within mainstream LGBT politics in the Global North.

As a site in which racialized and gendered labor and migration coalesce, it is fitting that *AABNAB* takes place in San Francisco, a city in which Filipina/o American and LGBT cultural politics intersect. As the home of one of the largest Filipina/o communities outside of the Philippines, as well as a hub of LGBT culture on the US West Coast, San Francisco draws multiple migrants: queers, Filipinas/os, and queer Filipinas/os. In addition to more recent migrants, second- and third-generation Filipina/o American communities reside in the San Francisco Bay Area, from Daly City to the south to the East Bay city of Vallejo in the north. Simultaneously, San Francisco possesses an iconic quality within US LGBT culture as the home of gay civil rights leader Harvey Milk and multiple iterations of LGBT and queer political movements. M.O.B.'s choice of San Francisco City Hall as the location of their fictional bridesmaid service embodies the confluence of discourses of LGBT "marriage quality" and the politics of Filipina/o American nationalism(s). The varied sites of reception of M.O.B.'s work indicate the intertwining of their multiple audiences—queer, Asian American, and Filipina/o American—from their appearance at a Lunar New Year parade in Oakland's Chinatown to a screening at the Manilatown Heritage Center and various queer film festivals.[5] M.O.B. use humor and parody to extend their work beyond the confines of a museum setting. As M.O.B. member Jenifer Wofford states, "Our photos are so ridiculously campy, and they exist on a level where it's meant to be fun for everybody."[6] The multiple genres represented within their work, including karaoke videos, infomercials, and public poster art, allow M.O.B. to reach a broad audience, from everyday San Franciscans waiting for public transit to those who visit art galleries to experience M.O.B.'s installation and video art. The screening of their work in Asian American community spaces in the San Francisco Bay Area such as Kearny Street Workshop and the Manilatown Heritage Center, as well as performing during the Lunar New Year parade in Oakland's Chinatown, reflect M.O.B.'s participation in broader discourses of Asian American and Filipina/o American cultural politics. Their larger oeuvre offers multiple conceptual entry points into their work, from their critique of heteropatriarchal notions of Filipina femininity to their provocations on the politics of Philippine nationalist dress.[7] Through these numerous sites of reception, M.O.B. engage with intersecting communities—Filipina/o Americans, queers, San Francisco public transit passengers—to challenge the discursive construction of the Filipina laboring body within racialized and gendered discourses of neoliberal capitalism.

While M.O.B.'s parody of marriage in their video is an implicit critique of the politics of migration and racialized labor, it simultaneously offers critical commentary on the homonationalism of LGBT movements for "marriage equality." *AABNAB* challenges the invisibility of Third World women workers' labor within a US-based liberal LGBT agenda, particularly the affective labor provided by Filipinos/as performing forms of feminized labor (whether female-assigned or not).[8] This chapter brings together transnational feminist critiques of gendered labor with critiques of homonationalism to examine how affective labor is both a source of value for neoliberal capitalism and a necessity for the constitution of gay marriage as a form of US national belonging. Despite the celebratory public discourse about the end of the Defense of Marriage Act (DOMA), gay marriage is not so much a "right" as it is a means for white middle-class LGBT couples to consolidate the material and discursive privilege that previously only white middle-class married heterosexuals possessed.[9] The neoliberal logics of homo- *and* heterosexual forms of marriage bolster the continued invisibility of the affective and domestic labor that third world women workers provide within a global capitalist system. M.O.B.'s focus on same-sex marriage and marriage for purposes of immigration makes evident how affective labor—such as the labor provided by their fictional bridesmaid service—is necessary for state-sanctioned forms of the hetero- and homonormative family.

Ultimately, I argue against the appeal to depoliticized domesticity as the basis for legitimate belonging to the nation-state, a foundation of the mainstream LGBT movement's political goal of legalizing gay marriage. Moreover, I analyze the racism and sexism of homonationalism by focusing on the subordination of the third world woman worker within a political-economic context of queer neoliberalism. M.O.B. denaturalize the affective and domestic labor performed by Filipina bodies through their appropriation of camp as a performative strategy. In their enactment of feminist camp, M.O.B. shift from the gay white male subject to a feminist queer of color subject.[10] Through their use of feminist camp and ethnic drag as performative strategies, M.O.B. make visible the role of affective labor in constituting the privileged subject of homonationalism.[11] Simultaneously, this chapter critiques the heteropatriarchal politics of respectability and gendered domesticity that undergird diasporic anxiety about the figure of the Filipina mail-order bride within Filipina/o American cultural production. By linking marriage for purposes of immigration with gay marriage in *AABNAB*, my analysis of M.O.B. juxtaposes a critique of the gendered politics of Filipina/o American diasporic and cultural nationalism with a consideration of mainstream LGBT cultural politics in the United States. These two discourses coalesce in *AABNAB*, connecting a critique of homonationalism with the politics of racialized labor and transnational migration. More broadly, I argue that the queering of the Filipina mail-order bride offers an alternative to dominant tropes of the global Filipina body, a figure that embodies heteropatriarchal notions of the nation within the diaspora.

Figure 3.1 Photograph courtesy of the Mail Order Brides / M.O.B.

The Figure of the Filipina Mail-Order Bride

AABNAB is a response to the broader discourse of the Filipina mail-order bride within global popular culture as she is represented in film, television, and websites. As I discuss in the introduction to this book, examples of the Filipina mail-order bride and the global Filipina body more broadly proliferate within popular culture from the 1990s onward, from television and film to the vast expanse of the internet. *AABNAB* intervenes in a broader epistemic landscape in which global Filipina bodies are represented as easily available sources of sexual, domestic, and affective labor.[12] Although this chapter focuses primarily on the figure of the Filipina mail-order bride, my analysis of *AABNAB* is situated within a constellation of representations of the global Filipina body that circulates within global popular culture, from the hyperexploited Filipina overseas domestic laborer (maid, nanny, or eldercare provider) to the Filipina sex worker. Filipina women are especially visible within the ongoing feminist debates on the global sex trade, transnational labor, and the traffic in women as representations of Filipinas as sex workers and "entertainers" in Japan circulate within both popular and scholarly discourse.[13]

The figure of the Filipina mail-order bride is a contested one within Filipina/o American cultural production, evoking both moralistic condemnation and feminist outrage about the politics of Filipina labor, femininity, sexuality, and domesticity. This is especially evident in online Filipina/o American cultural production, such as the (now defunct) website Bagong Pinay, also known as New Filipina.com. Started in 1998 by Perla Daly, a Filipina American woman living in New Jersey, Bagong Pinay / New Filipina.com was designed for the purpose of creating an online community for Filipina women worldwide. Bagong Pinay included editorials, advice columns, message boards, an online art gallery, and news articles. The site allowed for discussions through the multiple message boards on the site, which served as online forums for conversation. Perla Daly describes Bagong Pinay as a public space in which Filipinas could negotiate and articulate a form of transnational identity, one that "connect[s] Filipinas to other Filipinas around the world."[14] Despite Daly's vision of Bagong Pinay as a global Filipina/o community, the website suggested a form of community that was predominantly middle class and heteronormative.[15] In describing her reasons for creating the site, Daly states:

> It was during that time that I was learning web design, that I looked up www.filipina.com and I found out that it was a mail-order bride site. I was deeply offended, dismayed and angered to discover that the representation of Filipinas on the Internet was direly lacking in quality and scope. In 1996, a query done

on the word "filipina" at major Internet search engines resulted in the appalling amounts of 1) Filipina mail-order-bride sites, 2) pen-pal service sites, 3) personal web pages of Filipina women looking for men-friends, and 4) porn sites that overwhelmed the number of very few web pages that mentioned Filipinas in alternative ways.[16]

Daly's motivation for starting the website was to intervene in a dominant visual economy of the internet—in which Filipina women are primarily represented as mail-order brides or sex workers—that reflects the existing racialized and gendered international division of labor under neoliberal globalization. Originally, Daly focused her anger toward women seeking foreign husbands in order to leave the Philippines. Daly has described her previous "biased, angry attitude toward MOBs."[17] Her indignation at being perceived as a mail-order bride is a response to the blurring of boundaries between her position as a middle-class Filipina subject and the abject social location of a mail-order bride. In an online discussion on Bagong Pinay, Daly described her concerns about being perceived as a mail-order bride when meeting her white husband's family:

> I also won't forget the time when I met my future sister in law. . . . I couldn't help but notice her disdainful inspection of my person, looking me up and down haughtily as her brother introduced us. *I pushed down the feeling of embarrassment and hurt at being possibly stereotyped as a maid*, or *gold-digging* Filipina looking for a "rich" husband. I gathered every ounce of my personal dignity and held my chin up and smiled at her nicely. It took a few more encounters over a course of months before she withdrew her initial assumptions of whatever she thought me out to be. (emphasis mine)[18]

Daly's embarrassment and indignation exemplify the moralistic tone that frames middle-class Filipina/o American outrage at mail-order brides' transgression of bourgeois notions of feminine respectability. Middle-class notions of appropriate Filipina femininity and sexuality buttress the contentious nature of the figure of the Filipina mail-order bride within Filipina/o American discourse. Such politics of respectability haunt Filipina/o American cultural nationalism, making evident the heteronormativity and masculinism of representations of Filipina mail-order brides within Filipina/o American cultural production.

Despite her initial embarrassment at being mistaken for a mail-order bride, Daly transformed her message to one of "tolerance" for her Filipina sisters who choose to use online matchmaking sites in order to meet a husband from abroad: "We must keep on hearing the stories of our fellow Filipinas who have gone the path of matchmaking services, AKA mail-order bride services. We must listen, learn, and let love in."[19] Other participants on Bagong Pinay with a less accepting view responded with harsh indictments. According to this post directed toward mail-order brides, "What happened to dignity and honor? What's the matter with you? *GIRLS like you give Filipinos a bad name*. Why don't you just ####ing go to school and make a life for yourself rather than using your body to get what you want? Life is hard, yes, but it doesn't mean you have to give up your dignity just to survive! Get a life!" (emphasis mine).[20] The writer's admonition to Filipina mail-order brides to "go to school and make a life for yourself" signals middle-class Filipina/o American anxiety about the excessive sexuality of the Filipina mail-order bride, a form of sexuality that blurs the boundary between sex work and marriage. The post above indicates that the intended subject of the imagined community of Bagong Pinay was a Filipina American with the social and material capital to conform to bourgeois notions of femininity and domesticity. This diasporic anxiety reflects the inherently heteropatriarchal politics of representation that undergirded Bagong Pinay. Filipina American feminist filmmaker and theorist Celine Parreñas Shimizu critiques the masculinist pressure to present "positive images" of the Filipina/o Americans within her films: "This is a very regressive political move that doesn't serve any of us—to return to a unified notion of community that enabled us once but never truly was."[21] In contrast to the moralistic condemnation of Filipina mail-order brides on Bagong Pinay, Shimizu embraces "bad" womanhood as "a contradictory experience of her body against national narration."[22] Shimizu's claiming of "bad womanhood" contests the implicit masculinism of calls for "positive" representations of Filipinas online, creating other possibilities for Filipina American self-representation beyond the trope of woman as nation.

Always a Bridesmaid, Never a Bride

While Bagong Pinay evoked the heteropatriarchal anxiety that bolsters mainstream Filipina/o American discourses about the Filipina mail-order bride online, M.O.B. queers this figure through their video, performance, and installation art. Filipina American artists Eliza Barrios, Jenifer Wofford, and Reanne Estrada formed the San Francisco Bay Area–based performance and visual art ensemble M.O.B. largely in response to the representation of "fallen" Filipina women that characterizes Filipina/o American cultural production such as Bagong Pinay.[23] In contrast to the moralistic tone of the discourse of mail-order brides on Bagong Pinay, M.O.B. use humor to contest the broader racialized and gendered discourses through which Filipina bodies are constituted and made visible under global capitalism. M.O.B. create work in a variety of media, including installation art, photography, video art, karaoke videos, and performance. In their biography, they describe their collective work:

> For over a decade, Eliza "Neneng" Barrios, Reanne "Immaculata" Estrada and Jenifer "Baby" Wofford have worked collaboratively as Mail Order Brides/M.O.B., a trio of Filipina American artists engaged in an ongoing collaborative investigation of culture, race and gender. While traditionally, "real" mail order brides are thought of as ideal obedient domestics, it has not escaped this trio's attention that, acronymically speaking, "Mail Order Brides" abbreviates down to a more sinister series of initials that inform the darker subtext of their connivings and conspirings.
>
> They have taken matters into their own well-manicured hands, using their innate graciousness, good fashion sense, and interior decorating/decorum skills to gently pry open the eyes of the closed-minded. They have pursued this vision through a cornucopia of creative endeavors, including photographic psycho-dramas, parade performances, public service posters, karaoke music videos, museum makeovers, and educational workshops. Their recent successful business venture, Always A Bridesmaid Never A Bride™, has provided the world with long-needed services of three Professional Bridesmaids™ for weddings, commitment ceremonies and immigration-inspired marital arrangements.[24]

Calling attention to what they term the "women in distress" persona of Filipina women within popular culture, M.O.B. satirize hegemonic notions of Filipina/o American femininity and ethnic identity.[25] While M.O.B. reference the trope of the Filipina bride specifically, their exploration of the politics of gendered domestic and affective labor resonates with scholarly and activist feminist debates on gendered transnational labor more broadly.[26] M.O.B. satirize conventional artists' statements, as well as notions of bourgeois femininity and the institution of marriage. Their brilliantly colored, exquisitely decorated vision of reality materializes in the jewel-toned images of hyperbolized femininity that they present in their photographs and videos. Their emphasis on interior decorating and inner decorum references the affective element of their work as they bring the interior forward into the public space. M.O.B. suggest that "exterior" tropes of femininity ("well-manicured hands, innate graciousness, good fashion sense") are intrinsically linked to "interior" elements of affective labor (nurturing, care giving). In doing so, M.O.B. demonstrate how discourses of racialized and gendered labor under global capitalism rely on the performance of both interior *and* exterior tropes of affective labor.

M.O.B.'s project *AABNAB* includes performances, art installations, video info-mercials, and glossy color brochures and postcards "advertising" their fictional bridesmaid services. This chapter focuses on a video testimonial, one of a series of four videos in *AABNAB*. The video series promotes the services of this rent-a-bridesmaid service. From 2005 to 2010 the video series screened in multiple community and academic venues, mainly in the San Francisco Bay Area, Los Angeles, and Manila, Philippines.[27] *AABNAB* is structured as a faux infomercial, featuring testimonials by satisfied clients of M.O.B.'s fictional bridesmaid service, Always a Bridesmaid, Never a Bride.[28] The video features short vignettes of the group's past successful weddings, highlighting same-sex weddings and weddings for purposes of immigration. The video juxtaposes still images of M.O.B. in their various bridesmaid costumes with video sequences, while voice-over "testimonials" from "satisfied customers" describe the various services that the bridesmaid service offers. M.O.B.'s use of the infomercial genre and the testimonial form in particular highlights the commodification of affective labor within the institution of marriage. M.O.B.'s parody of gay marriage as a business challenges the discursive production of the white gay consumer-citizen as the subject of homonormativity.[29] In particular, M.O.B.'s satire of "customer testimonials" emphasizes the constitution of the white homonationalist subject as a citizen-consumer of third world women workers' labor. At the same time, the video's satire of marriage challenges the moralistic and masculinist notions of

Figure 3.2 Photograph courtesy of the Mail Order Brides / M.O.B.

Filipina femininity that bolster popular representations of Filipina mail-order brides within Filipina/o American cultural production such as Bagong Pinay. M.O.B. contest the politics of heteropatriarchal respectability within Filipina/o American representations of the Filipina mail-order bride while critiquing gay marriage as a form of homonormativity.

In their satire of the marriage industry, M.O.B. play with the representation of Filipina women as innately hospitable and domestic, a discourse that positions Filipina women as naturalized sources of gendered labor. In her description of M.O.B.'s public art series *A Public Service Message about Your Private Life*, which featured images of Filipina/o American family life, Lucy Mae San Pablo Burns argues: "Hospitality becomes understood as one of the categories under which Filipina subjects are evaluated and distributed globally."[30] The "Filipina drag" performed by M.O.B. reveals how notions of Filipina femininity are imbricated within racialized discourses of domesticity and hospitality. M.O.B.'s satirical bridesmaid service is both a reiteration and a critique of discourses of contemporary global capitalism that render ethnically marked Filipina femininity as essentially linked to both affective and domestic labor.[31] In *AABNAB*, M.O.B. satirize marriage for purposes of immigration, as well as LGBT weddings, linking critiques of homonationalism with the broader politics of racialized migration.

M.O.B.'s staging of *AABNAB* occurred in San Francisco immediately after the mayor at the time, Gavin Newsom, declared gay marriage legal.[32] The image that M.O.B. include in their print advertisement for *AABNAB* features a queer couple, a light-skinned, feminine-presenting woman and a darker-skinned, masculine-presenting, female-assigned person. As a hub for queer culture and a destination for queer tourism, as well as the home of well-established Asian American and recent Asian migrant communities, San Francisco is a global city in which neoliberal citizenship, racialized migrant labor, and queer cultural politics coalesce. The video begins with a close-up image of a satisfied customer extolling the virtues of *AABNAB*, describing their "utmost professionalism . . . forsaking themselves and only thinking about the bride." Here the gendered affective labor of emotional sacrifice—putting others' needs before one's own—is highlighted as a service that M.O.B. offer to LGBT couples. A still image of M.O.B. in similar formal gowns, each in a bright primary color, is followed by a still image of San Francisco City Hall. In a voice-over, a satisfied gay male client with a faux southern accent describes how he and his partner made use of *AABNAB*'s services:

> The announcement came while my honey and I were working out at the gym. It was like a bolt out of the blue—they were marrying gays at City Hall! But we

didn't know how long it was gonna last. So we rushed down, and we realized that we didn't have any witnesses, we didn't have any wedding party. Thank goodness for Always a Bridesmaid, Never a Bride! They sure did come through for us. Boy, that teary-eyed hysteria, it was perfect! I tell you, it made our wedding photos. And their confetti cleanup.... Those girls must come from a long line of domestic workers.... They put the "maid" into "bridesmaid!" (emphasis mine)

During this voice-over is a still image of the M.O.B. kneeling on the steps of city hall. They are wearing identical pink dresses, elaborate makeup, and matching gauzy white aprons. In their hands they carry a feather duster, a broom, and a dustpan, with which they are cleaning up fallen rose petals from a wedding ceremony. The still images of M.O.B. in whiteface makeup, jewel-toned *ternos* (the Filipina nationalist dress, identified by its signature butterfly-shaped sleeves), and identical candy-pink pantsuits are interspersed with several still and video images of same-sex couples (both male and female) on the steps of city hall. The dialogue and images articulate the capitalist logic that renders

Figure 3.3 Photograph courtesy of the Mail Order Brides / M.O.B.

Filipina bodies as the naturalized embodiment of domestic labor for a neoliberal global economy; as one of their clients testifies about their services, "They put the 'maid' into 'bridesmaid'!" In particular, this dialogue foregrounds the gay citizen-consumer as the beneficiary of gendered and racialized labor. Through this satire of customer testimonials, M.O.B. undermine the assumed verisimilitude of the testimonial as a mode of performance. M.O.B.'s camp performance of the testimonial form challenges the "reality" of global capitalism—that Filipina/o workers necessarily embody devalued domestic and affective labor.

M.O.B.'s performance of ethnic drag demonstrates how racial/ethnic and gender performativity is an essential aspect of labor within capitalist globalization.[33] The next still image in the video shows M.O.B. lined up in a row wearing whiteface, which contrasts with their drawn-in, heart-shaped dark lips. Their vacant facial expressions and identical pink dresses with elaborate lacy white collars emphasize the doll-like effect of their countenances. The stark contrast of their white makeup with their brown skin makes evident the performance of race essential to the figuring of Filipina bodies as naturalized sources of domestic, affective, and sexual labor. M.O.B. implicitly critique the logic of exchangeability—visualized through their identical pink outfits—that characterizes third world women as replaceable sources of devalued labor. In a voice-over, one M.O.B. explains her decision to serve as a professional bridesmaid: "I remember when we first heard our calling. . . . Every couple is special; every couple needs a different kind of support." M.O.B.'s satirical description of their vocational "calling" as professional bridesmaids highlights the discursive construction of Filipina/o workers as "caring" and "warm," which serves to naturalize the affective and domestic labor that they provide. In the background of the voice-over testimonials, saccharine electronic music plays, much like the musical accompaniment of a karaoke video (another genre that M.O.B. employ in their art). The next set of images implies the availability of the professional bridesmaids for sexual labor as well. In a faux southern accent, a client describes his recent wedding: "My cousin Francis came to town not knowing no one. He's real awkward with the ladies and such . . . and Neneng, she made him feel right at home." This voice-over is accompanied by still images of Neneng seducing the groom's cousin, much to his surprise and delight. This scene invokes the figure of the Filipina sex worker, particularly the role of Filipinas as overseas entertainers in Japan. As such, Neneng suggests both the sexual availability of Filipina entertainers and the affective labor of making Francis feel "right at home." In contrast to the indignation with which Bagong Pinay depicts the sexual labor of Filipina mail-order brides, M.O.B. use the humorous method of feminist camp to emphasize the historical and contemporary discourses that position Filipina mail-order brides as sources of sexual labor. M.O.B.'s invocation of the Filipina sex worker, made up in whiteface, calls to mind the figure of the geisha.[34] Within the Western popular imagination, the figure of the geisha is the penultimate Orientalized embodiment of affective and sexual labor; her role is not solely to satiate the sexual desires of heterosexual men but to make them feel comfortable and sexually attractive. The Orientalist representation of the geisha / sex worker / bridesmaid within *AABNAB* reveals the necessity of ethnic drag, a specifically ethnic/racialized performance of gendered affective and sexual labor intrinsic to the work that Filipina women do for a global economy. M.O.B.'s invocation of the figure of the geisha also references the history and ongoing present of Filipinas as sources of sexual labor for a global economy—from the forced servitude of Filipina comfort women during World War II, to the "rest and recreation" of US servicemen at US military bases in the Philippines, to the global sex trade—suggesting that contemporary forms of Filipina/o labor are always already imbricated in multiple histories of colonialism and neocolonialism.[35]

Through its parody of the commodification of affective labor in the service of same-sex marriage, *AABNAB* presents an implicit critique of queer neoliberalism. Speaking "in character" in my interview with her, Mail-Order Bride Reanne Estrada discussed the LGBT clientele of Always a Bridesmaid, Never a Bride: "Inclusion is our business strategy. . . . As a business you want to make sure you have a lot of customers. It's a way to bring our services to individuals who have been shut out of this ritual."[36] Estrada's emphasis on the ritual of marriage as a means of inclusion into the broader consumer-citizenship of the United States exemplifies the logic of homonormativity.[37] M.O.B.'s parody of the consumer nature of gay inclusion into the national family is also an implicit critique of the racialization of this process. A particularly striking image is one of a white newly married lesbian couple wrapped in a gigantic American flag and embracing on the steps of city hall. The image visualizes the affective connection between the institution of marriage and US nationalism. Here, ideologies of US national belonging are intertwined with the ideology of "marriage equality," reifying the imbrication of whiteness with marriage and belonging to the US nation. The implicit visual narrative of this image connects notions of US liberal democracy and freedom to the rights-based claim of "marriage equality," suggesting that the United States (and San Francisco in particular) is a site of freedom for queers.[38] Despite the celebratory discourse surrounding the United States Supreme Court's 2015 ruling of the Defense of Marriage Act as unconstitutional, the benefits granted to same-sex married couples are largely limited to documented, white, middle-class, property-owning, monogamous couples. M.O.B. link their critique of gay marriage as a form of inclusion into the nation-state with the broader politics of racialized migration through their depiction of marriage for purposes of citizenship. Interspersed with images and video sequences of gay weddings are scenes of "INS interventions," in which M.O.B. prevent Immigration and Naturalization Service (INS) agents from disrupting the weddings of binational couples.[39] In one image, M.O.B. pose triumphantly over the figures of fallen INS agents, clad in dark suits and wearing earpieces, who failed in their attempt to disrupt the wedding ceremony of a heterosexual binational couple. As a result of M.O.B.'s successful intervention, the happy couple is able to go through with their marriage, assuring citizenship for the Filipina bride. Through the juxtaposition of binational weddings with gay marriage, *AABNAB* introduces a critique of racialized migration and labor into the affective politics of gay marriage.

M.O.B.'s enactment of feminist camp within a context of racialized and gendered transnational Filipina/o labor migration highlights the invisibility of third world women workers' labor. As a genre that has historically been associated with white gay male culture, camp has been critiqued for its "blatantly misogynistic images of female excess."[40] In contrast, M.O.B. enact a form of feminist camp to critique the discursive embodiment of Filipina workers as sources of affective labor. Building on theorists Pamela Robertson's and José Muñoz's discussions of feminist and queer of color interventions in camp as a performance strategy, I argue that M.O.B.'s use of feminist camp calls attention to the performance of ethnicized gender and gendered ethnicity required of Filipinas as providers of affective labor. M.O.B.'s enactment of feminist camp critiques both the racialized homonationalism of mainstream US LGBT politics and the position of third world women workers within a broader international division of labor. M.O.B. suggest that racialized and gendered labor itself is a form of ethnic drag. Their performance of gendered Filipina/o ethnicity is visually signified by their wearing of *terno* gowns and their use of whiteface.[41] M.O.B.'s performance of corporeal and sartorial markers of ethnic and racial difference exposes the nature of affective labor within capitalist globalization, which requires ethnic/racialized subjects to perform banal forms of ethnic/racial difference. M.O.B.'s performative embodiment as "eternal bridesmaids" visualizes forms of corporeal and affective labor—cleaning up after the wedding party, kneeling to roll out the carpet for their "trademarked Aisle Service," shedding tears during the ceremony—that position the global Filipina body as essentially outside of both hetero- and homonationalist subjectivity. While the domestic and affective labor of the global Filipina body is necessary for the constitution of the white middle-class hetero- and homonationalist subject (*AABNAB*'s ideal "customer"), M.O.B. are never able to access this form of national respectability themselves. As their title suggests, the global Filipina body is "always a bridesmaid, never a bride." As figures whose racialized corporeal labor (domestic, affective, sexual) is rendered outside of the norm of bourgeois respectability and marriage, their bodies are instead circumscribed by global capitalist discourses that figure transnational Filipina bodies as sex workers, trafficked women, gold diggers, or maids.[42] In Pamela Robertson's words, the Mail-Order Bride "plays at what she is already perceived to be."[43]

M.O.B.'s use of feminist camp and ethnic drag to denaturalize the labor of Filipina bodies illuminates the crucial absence within scholarly and popular critiques of homonationalism of analyses of racialized and gendered labor and migration within LGBT cultural politics. By juxtaposing binational marriages for purposes of immigration ("INS interventions") with LGBT weddings, *AABNAB* introduces a crucial connection between critiques of homonationalism and analyses of racialized migration. While some theorists have addressed the intersections of queer identities and global capitalism, few critics of homonationalism have explicitly addressed its relationship to racialized transnational labor. The scarcity of political economic discussions of labor within critiques of homonationalism leaves undertheorized the vital connection between queer cultural politics and social movements focused on migration and racial and economic justice. *AABNAB* addresses this gap in scholarly and popular critiques of queer neoliberalism and racialized homonationalism by explicitly foregrounding the ways in which transnational labor is both gendered and racialized in relation to queer politics. Through their parody of gay marriage, M.O.B. problematize the invisible role of third world affective and domestic labor in the constitution of gay marriage as a site of freedom and national belonging. M.O.B.'s use of a feminist camp aesthetic, evident in their ostentatious, brightly colored costumes and exaggerated makeup, reveals the artifice of their hyperbolized performances of commodified racialized and gendered labor. *AABNAB*'s intertextual advertising of "trademarked" services reveals the consumer nature of the video as a "marketing" tool, pointing to both the homonormativity of mainstream US LGBT cultural politics (in which citizenship is consolidated through consumerism) and the commodification of Filipina bodily labor more broadly. Interspersed with still images of M.O.B. are the intertextual phrases "We always go the extra mile, down the aisle™" and "Our Signature W.M.D.s™" (Wedding Maid Duties). M.O.B.'s "trademarked" services include Sycophancy™, Sentimental Toasts™, Flattery™, Fawning™, Tears of Emotion™, Best Friends Forever™, Deluxe Applause™, Confetti Cleanup™, Bouquet Skirmish™, and Aisle Service™, and there are short video sequences of M.O.B. performing each of these forms of affective labor. *AABNAB* also includes images of M.O.B. per-forming physical labor, from their Confetti Cleanup™ to their Aisle Service™, in which they roll out the carpet for the wedding participants. In these images, M.O.B. are literally on their knees, embodying the physical and affective labor necessary to uphold marriage as a neoliberal social institution. The ability of the nuclear family to serve as an independent, self-sufficient economic unit that is financially independent of the state relies on the subordinated labor of US women of color and women from the Global South. As such, women of color in the United States and Global South women globally bear the burden of the gendered effects of neoliberal globalization, as structural adjustment policies and anti-immigrant policies in the United States severely limit access to social services, education, and healthcare.[44] M.O.B.'s identical pink suits and dresses suggest a logic of exchangeability within which the laboring bodies of third world women are reduced to indistinguishable, replaceable sources of labor.

Through their performance of the figure of the third world woman worker, M.O.B. present a crucial intervention in the critique of racialized homonation-alism, highlighting the relationship of queer cultural politics to labor. Simul-taneously, the juxtaposition of LGBT weddings with binational marriages for purposes of citizenship in *AABNAB* connects a critique of gay marriage with the

Figure 3.4 The Mail Order Brides / M.O.B.'s trademarked Aisle Service.™ Photo courtesy of the Mail Order Brides / M.O.B.

broader politics of racialized migration and citizenship under capitalist globalization. M.O.B.'s campy depiction of Filipina mail-order brides challenges
the masculinism of Filipina/o American cultural nationalist calls for "positive" representations of Filipina women. In contrast to the bourgeois discourse
of respectability that characterizes the representation of Filipina mail-order
brides on Bagong Pinay, *AABNAB* challenges the logic of capitalist globalization that aligns heteronormative discourses of femininity and domesticity with
the Filipina laboring body. M.O.B.'s parody of the ethnic drag that is required
of Filipina workers within a global economy also contests the discourse of heteropatriarchal respectability that haunts the figure of the Filipina mail-order
bride within Filipina/o American discourse. The diasporic anxiety incited by
the figure of the Filipina mail-order bride—and other global Filipina bodies
who provide affective and domestic labor for a global economy—exemplifies
the masculinism and bourgeois heteronormativity that undergird many forms
of Filipina/o American cultural production.

Affective Labor, Surplus Value, and the Gendering
of Filipina/o Bodies

AABNAB emphasizes the role of commodified Filipina affective labor in uphold-
ing the social institution of the family under global capitalism, as well as the
specific role of affective labor in constituting neoliberal homonationalist subjectivity through gay marriage. Affective labor is a form of "immaterial labor,"
which, according to Michael Hardt, is labor that produces immaterial goods,
such as service, knowledge, and communication.[45] Hardt argues that within a
contemporary global capitalist economy that is geared toward the circulation
and exchange of information and services rather than durable goods, affective
labor is the most value-producing form of labor for global capital.[46] The affective and domestic labor of transnational Filipinas, who clean the houses, care
for the children, and satisfy the husbands of middle- and upper-class families
in the Global North, reflects the neoliberal logic that places the responsibility of economic survival on the nuclear family, relieving the state of its duty
to ameliorate the disastrous effects of budget cuts and structural adjustment
policies. Filipinas, like other poor women of color from the Global South, are
most impacted by capitalist globalization. The performance of labor by M.O.B.
suggests the biopolitical function of affective labor in producing and differentiating racialized and gendered subjectivities within global capitalism.[47] The
affective labor of Filipina bodies serves a biopolitical function both through the
production of value (in Hardt's theorization of the term) for nuclear families

in the Global North and by differentiating which bodies have access to racialized homonationalist subjectivity. That is, their performance of affective labor in the service of the heteronormative family is precisely that which forecloses Filipina women from participating in homonationalist structures of feeling. This foreclosure from racialized homonormativity is made evident in M.O.B.'s motto, "Always a bridesmaid, never a bride." As racialized and gendered providers of affective labor, Filipinas and other women of the Global South are rendered outside of the racialized frameworks of national belonging inherent within the institution of gay marriage. Simultaneously, Filipina mail-order brides are positioned outside the heteropatriarchal notions of bourgeois respectability and normative femininity that undergird Filipina/o American cultural nationalism. In a global capitalist system that relies on affective labor to produce forms of sociality and collectivity, Filipina wives, nannies, and maids are a crucial source of value. The forms of affective labor required to produce feelings of community, as well as social institutions such as the family, can be understood as a form of biopower.[48] These feelings of community and family, achieved through affective labor, are the forms of surplus value / biopower that Filipinos/as provide for a global economy. Through their parody of the inherent commercial value of the affective labor necessary to create the hetero- and homonormative family through marriage—signified by their "trademarking" of their various services—M.O.B. make evident the forms of biopower provided by Filipina bodies for the functioning of global capital.

M.O.B. emphasize the surplus value created by Filipina labor through their "marketing" of forms of affective labor in the service of gay marriage—Sycophancy™, Sentimental Toasts™, Flattery™, Fawning™, and Tears of Emotion.™ The devaluing of affective labor, such as caregiving and nurturing, within a wage labor economy positions Filipina wives, maids, and nannies as a cheap source of surplus value for the Global North. This surplus value is accrued precisely because of the devaluation of Filipinas' racialized and gendered bodies, seen solely as a source of unskilled and flexible labor. While Filipinas are discursively constructed as subjects/workers under contemporary global capitalism, they are simultaneously constituted as endless sources of surplus value, as "bodies without subjectivity."[49] It is precisely through the performance of affective labor that surplus value is extracted from Filipina laboring bodies. Indeed, the performance of nurturing and caregiving by Filipinas, whether as wives, eldercare providers, or nannies, is the surplus value or biopower upon which the social institutions such as the nuclear family or the community rely. The "coercive mimeticism" required of Filipina/o workers within a global capitalist logic—performances of racialized gender and gendered race—makes their labor invisible while facilitating the extraction of surplus value from their affective labor.[50]

M.O.B. make this labor visible through their enactment of feminist camp, a hyperbolized performance of Filipina labor that creates a critical distance from the normalized gendered labor of the private sphere—the site in which Filipina women provide affective, domestic, and sexual labor within an economic context of transnational labor migration. M.O.B.'s excessive, humorous style of camp highlights their feminist analysis of gendered labor. The critical distance created by M.O.B.'s enactment of feminist camp illuminates the extraction of surplus value through Filipina/o affective labor. Through the faux infomercial/testimonial style of the video's marketing of their "trademarked" services, M.O.B. name and visualize the labor that Filipina bodies provide, bringing this labor from the private realm to the public domain.

AABNAB destabilizes the conflation of domestic and caregiving work with female-bodied workers. Martin Manalansan challenges the association of affective labor with the bodies of cisgender women in his discussion of the heteronormativity of scholarship on gender and migration.[51] Manalansan critiques feminist scholarship on migration that collapses gendered transnational labor within the essentialized category of women. Like Manalansan, *AABNAB* unsettles notions of affective labor that assume a gendering based on normative conceptions of care, love, and other emotions, a "[gender] essentialism [that] revolves around the crucial assertion that women are domestic, that they are essentially caring and loving."[52] Echoing Manalansan's concerns, M.O.B. suggest an analysis of gendered labor migration and affective labor that is not centered on the biological bodies of cisgendered women or the dominant framework of heterosexuality.[53] The gendering of Filipina/o labor is not limited to the "feminine" qualities of affective labor. As Kale Bantigue Fajardo has shown, Filipino men are also discursively gendered according to masculinist narratives of being good providers and "breadwinners," particularly by the Philippine state.[54] By hyperbolizing the attachment of essentialized Filipina femininity to affective and domestic labor, M.O.B. queer the figure of the mail-order bride. Reanne Estrada describes M.O.B.'s art as "queer" in that it involves an "abnegation of the idea of a fixed identity."[55] Estrada's use of the term "queer" refers less to sexual orientation and more to the unfixing of essentialized relationships between ethnically marked femininity, racialized labor, and female-assigned bodies.

The *AABNAB* video "infomercials" and print brochures present an implicit critique of a broader neoliberal capitalist logic in which racialized and gendered "cultural traits" are essentialized as a sign of national difference, naturalizing the performance of affective labor by Filipina bodies. M.O.B.'s "trademarking" of their affective labor is also a parody of the Philippine state's marketing of Filipina/o laborers to a global market. Robyn Rodriguez and Anna Guevarra discuss the role of the neoliberal Philippine state, as well as private agencies, in creating a "cultural logic of labor migration."[56] Both Rodriguez and Guevarra analyze Philippine state discourse, which lauds the affective qualities that distinguish Filipinos/as as exemplary workers in a context of global labor migration. Rodriguez cites an anecdote from an official at the Philippine Overseas Employment Administration (the state agency that both manages and promotes overseas Filipina/o labor) in regard to Filipina/o medical workers: "The Philippines is still top. Filipinas have a warmth and care that people like."[57] Guevarra points to the racializing and essentializing of "cultural traits" attributed to Filipina/o workers by the Philippine state in her analysis of a brochure circulated at a predeparture seminar for Filipina/o migrant workers titled *Filipino Workers: Moving the World Today*. The brochure describes the "added bonus qualities" of Filipina/o workers, including "hospitality," "charm and cheerful efficiency," "an innovative spirit," and "a strong desire to heal."[58] These essentialized qualities, or at least the performance of these qualities, is integral to the "racialized (and gendered) work hierarchies upon which the global division of labor, and hence capitalism's profits, depends."[59] M.O.B.'s parody of the commodification of affective labor is a simultaneous critique of the wedding industry—and gay marriage in particular—as well as the role of the Philippine state in discursively constructing gendered migrant labor as "products for export."

Queering the Filipina Mail-Order Bride

As a departure from the first half of the book, which critiqued hegemonic figurations of the global Filipina body as a sex worker and *balikbayan*, this chapter introduces a queering or reworking of this figure as a sign of the nation. The queering of the Filipina mail-order bride in *AABNAB* links two critiques that are often seen as separate: critiques of the queer neoliberalism of US homonationalism, and critiques of the heteropatriarchal gendered politics of respectability within Filipina/o American cultural nationalism. Yet both of these discourses coalesce in M.O.B.'s *AABNAB*, which juxtaposes US homonationalist discourses of gay marriage as a site of citizenship and the Filipina bride as a sign of the racialized migration and gendered labor that the Philippines provides for global capitalism. The figure of the Filipina mail-order bride often incites a heteropatriarchal discourse of respectability that haunts Filipina/o American cultural production, evident in the website Bagong Pinay. This fraught figure embodies the diasporic anxiety surrounding the failure of the feminized Philippine nation to maintain its borders in the face of capitalist globalization. The queering of the Filipina mail-order bride presented in *AABNAB* is a dual-pronged reworking of the global Filipina body as a sign of the multiple forms of nationalism—from Filipina/o American cultural nationalism to Filipina/o diasporic nationalisms. On the one hand, *AABNAB* challenges the politics of respectability that undergird cultural nationalist calls for "positive" representations of Filipinas in the face of the "bad womanhood" of Filipina mail-order brides.[60] The diasporic anxiety incited by the blurry boundaries between Filipina sex workers and mail-order brides coincides with heteropatriarchal exhortations for more "positive" representations of Filipina women. Inversely, the figure of the Filipina mail-order bride in *AABNAB* also signifies the exclusion of racialized, gendered labor within the dominant homonationalism of mainstream US LGBT movements for gay marriage. The juxtaposition of gay weddings with marriages for the purposes of immigration puts these seemingly disparate frameworks in conversation with each other. Ultimately, *AABNAB* challenges notions of a hegemonic homonationalist US nation, united by the push for gay marriage, by calling attention to the failure of mainstream US LGBT politics to account for racialized and gendered labor and migration.

This is a difficult task for the mainstream US LGBT movement, given that discussions of race are largely elided, perpetuating the fallacy that race and sexuality are inherently distinct axes of difference.[61] In this queer neoliberal discourse, racial and sexual civil rights are positioned as parallel but separate discourses.[62] *AABNAB* challenges the "colorblindness" of a queer neoliberal discourse that implicitly excludes queers of color and queer immigrants while centering the normative white, gay, middle-class subject. *AABNAB*'s foregrounding of marriage for purposes of immigration highlights the invisible position of undocumented, racialized queer immigrants within a mainstream discourse of "marriage equality," revealing that gay marriage is not so equal after all.[63] The name of the piece, *Always a Bridesmaid, Never a Bride*, suggests how marriage as a form of inclusion into the nation-state—a form of national respectability / middle-class heteronormativity—is possible only for the white citizen-subject.

While many queer theorists have discussed the homonormativity of the marriage equality movement, few critics have addressed the relationship of homonationalism to racialized and gendered labor.[64] Keeping in mind Lisa Duggan's original theorization of the queer consumer-citizen, a key component of a neoliberal queer culture, my analysis of M.O.B. extends Duggan's analytical framework to encompass not only the consumer nature of homonormative politics but also the relationship of homonationalism to racialized and gendered labor.[65] Echoing mainstream anti-immigration discourses that seek to withhold rights to citizenship from undocumented migrants while simultaneously relying on their labor, the mainstream LGBT movement's failure to address issues of immigration is indicative of its broader rhetoric of "colorblindness."

AABNAB elucidates how homonationalism, exemplified by gay marriage, is integral to an implicitly racialized national affect.[66] *AABNAB*'s juxtaposition of an image of white lesbians wrapped in a gigantic American flag with voice-over testimonials of gay men extolling M.O.B.'s exquisite attention to detail and "customer service" suggests the forms of immaterial labor required for this performance of national affect. Echoing Lauren Berlant and Michael Warner's argument that "national heterosexuality is the mechanism by which a core national culture can be imagined as a sanitized space of sentimental feeling and immaculate behavior, a space of pure citizenship," *AABNAB* demonstrates how the performance of citizenship is necessarily affective.[67] As such, M.O.B. critique the conflation of citizenship with whiteness within performances of homonationalist belonging.[68] In particular, the creation of a (white) homonationalist structure of feeling is similar to the "public comfort" of heteronormativity, in which only particular (white, middle-class) queer bodies are allowed to occupy the "space of pure citizenship."[69] By denaturalizing the "public comfort" of gay marriage, M.O.B. make clear how a homonationalist structure of feeling centered on the white homonuclear family both relies on and fails to recognize the labor of people of color (queer and otherwise).

Introducing a crucial intervention into the homonationalist project of marriage equality, *AABNAB* underscores issues of migration and racialized, gendered labor within queer politics.[70] As such, M.O.B.'s work resonates with a queer vernacular counterdiscourse that contests two key tenets of neoliberal logic: the conflation of consumerism with citizenship, and the prioritization of rights claims over a more equitable societal structure.[71] As artists, M.O.B.'s work contributes to queer of color political movements that integrate an analysis of queer politics with issues of racism, migration, neoliberalism, imperialism, and incarceration and policing. M.O.B.'s commentary on gay marriage echoes the many existing critiques within this antihomonationalist and radical queer political culture that conceptualizes "economic issues" such as labor and welfare rights for people of color and migrants as inherent to social justice struggles to improve the lives of queer people.[72] *AABNAB* critiques the forms of affective labor that Filipinas perform in the service of maintaining heteronormative families in the Global North, an analysis that links feminist critiques of the exploitation of third world women's labor with queer of color critiques of racialized homonationalism. While many queer of color scholars argue that a queer political agenda must focus on social transformation and a critique of the status quo, not an attempt to assimilate into the dominant structures of nationalism, incarceration, neoliberalism, and imperialism, the politics of racialized and gendered labor in relation to queer politics are often overlooked.[73]

AABNAB's circulation within many Asian American and Filipina/o American community venues also points to its contribution to debates over the representation of Filipina femininity, domesticity, and sexuality within the context of Filipina/o American cultural nationalism. Formed in response to the pop cultural representations of "bad" Filipina womanhood, M.O.B. present a queer reconfiguration of the figure of the Filipina bride beyond the narration of the Filipina body as nation.[74] In contrast to the heteropatriarchal politics that underlie depictions of Filipina mail-order brides on websites such as Bagong Pinay, *AABNAB* reminds its viewers of the broader global political economy that renders Filipina bodies as natural sources of affective, sexual, and domestic labor. Using feminist camp and ethnic drag, M.O.B. use humor to make evident the necessity of racialized and gendered performance to global capitalism's extraction of surplus value from women's bodies in the Global South. Ultimately, *AABNAB* questions not only the heteronormative and masculinist politics of Filipina/o American cultural nationalism or the neoliberalism of the movement for marriage equality but also the discursive production of the Filipina body under capitalism writ large. Through the use of feminist camp and ethnic drag, *AABNAB* shifts the discursive terrain beyond the Filipina body as a sign of the heteropatriarchal nation or an accessory to the production of homonationalist affect to other forms of Filipina being in the world.

CHAPTER 4

The Queer Cyborg in Gigi Otálvaro-Hormillosa's *Cosmic Blood*

> The search is for art forms which express the experience of the body
> (*and* the "soul"), not as vehicles of labor power and resignation, but
> as vehicles of liberation. This is the search for a *sensuous culture*,
> "sensuous" inasmuch as it involves the radical transformation of
> man's sense experience and receptivity: their emancipation from a
> self-propelling, profitable, and mutilating productivity.
>
> —Herbert Marcuse, *Counter-Revolution and Revolt*

Although the representation of the global Filipina body is often overdetermined by the "mutilating productivity" of global capitalism, it is through "art forms which express the experience of the body" that the Filipina body can be reimagined, "not as vehicles of labor power and resignation, but as vehicles of liberation."[1] While previous chapters explored the ubiquitous figure of the global Filipina body that pervades both Filipina/o American cultural production and global popular culture—the mail-order bride, the *balikbayan*, the sex worker / trafficked woman—this chapter enters the science fictional space of the future through the figure of the queer Filipina cyborg. Within the performance and video art piece *Cosmic Blood*, by the queer Colombian and Filipina American artist Gigi Otálvaro-Hormillosa, the figure of the cyborg embodies the utopian promise of queer futurity. From 2002 to 2004 *Cosmic Blood* was performed at both national and international venues, from Asian American arts festivals and queer/trans arts festivals in the San Francisco Bay Area, to university campuses in Hawai'i and Colorado, to international art exhibitions in Spain, Canada, Peru, and Latvia. This performance of *Cosmic Blood* took place on March 1, 2003, at Bindlestiff Studio, a small theater in the South of Market district of San Francisco, a neighborhood that has historically been home to a large Filipina/o American community. Described as the "epicenter of Filipino American arts," Bindlestiff Studio serves as a center for Filipina/o American theater, live music, spoken word, dance, and other performing arts.[2] Otálvaro-Hormillosa's piece, which combined video art with performance art and live electronic music, was accompanied by Melissa Dougherty, a DJ and electronic music composer.

Building on José Esteban Muñoz's foundational text, *Cruising Utopia*, I analyze the cyborg as a utopian figure for imagining other forms of corporeality for the global Filipina body, beyond the biologism of kinship as the heteronormative model for both nation and diaspora. Here, the potential of a queer diaspora rests not in the corporeal organic body but rather in the cyborg body. As both a utopian gesture and a surrealist form of imagination, *Cosmic Blood* is a science fictional homage to African American author Octavia Butler's novel *Parable of the Sower*. *Cosmic Blood* posits a utopian future through its reimagining of the past, focusing on an alternative moment of contact between the colonizer and the colonized, one that is shaped by queer desire. In particular, Otálvaro-Hormillosa draws on Gloria Anzaldúa's notion of "mestiza consciousness" to theorize a queer, post/neocolonial subject.[3] Similar to Afrofuturist longings for an alternative future, *Cosmic Blood* uses a science fictional mode to critique and exceed the material conditions of the global capitalist present, in which Filipina bodies are constrained by the racialized and gendered discursive construction of their labor. In doing so, *Cosmic Blood* presents a vision for collectivity beyond the biological materiality of blood and family that undergirds cultural nationalist models of nation and diaspora. It is through the figure of the cyborg that we can imagine a queer Filipina/o diaspora.

The cyborg promises the potentiality of queer utopias. In his discussion of utopia, Muñoz describes queerness as a "longing that propels us forward, beyond romances of the negative and toiling in the present. Queerness is that thing that lets us feel that this world is not enough, that indeed, something is missing."[4] The potentiality of queer utopias in *Cosmic Blood* exceeds the limits of "gay pragmatism," exemplified by mainstream LGBT issues such as gay marriage.[5] As I argued in chapter 3, gay marriage is a homonationalist form of neoliberal queer citizenship. Drawing on Muñoz, this chapter imagines the "not-quite conscious"—other forms of queer politics beyond the limited scope of gay pragmatism of the present.[6] A queer utopian practice imagines a future that exceeds the material conditions of the present, beyond the global capitalist logic that produces Filipinas/os as "bodies without subjectivity," discursive constructions that are rooted in older colonial taxonomies of racial difference.[7] The queer futurity of the cyborg "is essentially about the rejection of a here and now and an insistence on potentiality or *concrete possibility for another world*" (emphasis mine).[8] In a queer utopian practice, hope is both an affect and a methodology for exceeding the limits of the current moment.[9] Queer utopias are not naive flights from reality; instead, they offer a notion of futurity that functions as a historical materialist critique of the present.[10]

Before we can step into a queer future, we must first gaze backward. The queer utopian impulse of *Cosmic Blood* begins with a return to the colonial past, emphasizing visual metaphors of gestation and birth. A disembodied voice is amplified throughout the theater, describing a "girl with a tail in her ass" who emerges from "a gourd in the shape of a womb." The text, "Change is God," is projected onto a video screen at the back of the stage. The text then rearranges itself to form the statement "God is change." Onstage, an eight-foot-high hollow white gourd-shaped object is visible lit from within. The outline of a pulsing figure can be seen through the gourd's semitranslucent white walls. The disembodied voice continues: "The girl with the tail in her ass, a transformative being she was. . . . Their civilizations were in different stages of evolutionary process. . . . The earth people were quite young in the cosmic scheme of existence." Meanwhile, Otálvaro-Hormillosa cavorts onstage with an imaginary "tail," chanting, "Girl with the tail in her ass!" while holding a jaw harp behind her to represent the "tail" of the foreign, half animal, half human, native Other. This scene of gestation is followed by the second scene, which begins with the text "The Approach" projected onto the video screen at the back of the stage. Otálvaro-Hormillosa writhes on the ground, covered by what appears to be a fur skin, in a birthing scene of pain and transformation. While the performer writhes underneath the fur, mechanical sounds accompany her robotic, jerky movements. Still underneath the fur skin, Otálvaro-Hormillosa begins to crawl across the floor, rolling on the ground and partially crawling up the walls. This period of movement stretches temporally, lasting for at least fifteen minutes without dialogue. The tempo is slow and consistent, drawing out the movement onstage. Otálvaro-Hormillosa's character suggests the birth of a new figure, a mestiza of mixed "cosmic blood," as well as the animalistic corporeality of the native Other within colonial paradigms of racial and gender difference.

Cosmic Blood is simultaneously a reimagining of the past, a restaging of the colonizer/colonized dichotomy, and an envisioning of the utopian future. Otálvaro-Hormillosa's "girl with the tail in her ass," described as "young in the cosmic scheme of existence," invokes a colonial past through a reimagining of first contact. Referring to evolutionist paradigms of visualizing the native, primitive Other, Otálvaro-Hormillosa reimagines the moment of colonization through a speculative science fictional mode. Analogizing evolutionist paradigms of the native Other to scenes of gestation and birth, Otálvaro-Hormillosa performs the birthing scene of the "girl with a tail in her ass." The gestation and birth represented onstage are corporeal manifestations of Otálvaro-Hormillosa's vision of a "new mestiza," a figure whose subjectivity emerges as the painful result of histories of colonization, genocide, and sexual violence. *Cosmic Blood*'s reimagining of the relationship of colonization to the queer racialized body is visualized primarily through images of queer eroticism. This eroticism is more ambiguous than liberatory, implicitly referencing the sexual violence of conquest while centering queer desire. Video images are projected onto a screen at the back of the stage throughout the duration of the performance. Otálvaro-Hormillosa's dialogue, movement, and percussion are juxtaposed with the images on the video screen behind her. The videos are a series of short scenes, each a few seconds long, with fast cutting from one disparate image to another. The first scene shows a barely clad young Filipina woman with long flowing hair standing on a beach, invoking the image of virgin, unspoiled land. The next scene visualizes both a symbolic and a literal conquest/rape. In this scene, Otálvaro-Hormillosa, wearing a helmet and cape, plays the character of an androgynous conquistador who straddles the now-naked young woman from the previous scene. Otálvaro-Hormillosa's conquistador figure struggles with the naked woman as she mounts her. The scene alludes to bondage and sadomasochism as the sensual, violent interactions between the two women vacillate between eroticism and domination. In the next moment, the naked woman strikes the conquistador figure with her helmet. The naked woman then straddles the conquistador figure while she ties her up with a silky scarf. Interspersed between these scenes of violence and eroticism is a scene of the Filipina woman walking hand in hand with a light-skinned Latinx man on a beach. Breaking up the sequence is a close-up image of a miniature *nipa* hut, a sign of Filipino rural/indigenous culture that is made ironic by its representation as a piece of tourist art. Meanwhile, Otálvaro-Hormillosa is onstage, performing what appear to be sexual gestures onstage while wearing a conquistador helmet. The video projected onscreen behind her shows Otálvaro-Hormillosa's conquistador character pantomiming anal penetration of the naked Latino man. These graphic images of eroticism and domination reference the sexual trauma of colonization through the lens of queer desire. The next video scene shifts to an image of Otálvaro-Hormillosa's conquistador figure passionately kissing the naked young Filipina woman. Onstage, Otálvaro-Hormillosa ends this

Figure 4.1 Gigi Otálvaro-Hormillosa's conquistador character in the *Cosmic Blood* performance at Espacios Mestizos, Gran Canaria, Spain, 2003. Photograph courtesy of Nacho Gonzalez.

portion of the performance lying on her back. Is she defeated or merely sated with corporeal pleasure?

The next scene begins with the following text projected on the video screen: "El Otro Encuentro / A neo-queer / precolonial imagining." In the next video image, Otálvaro-Hormillosa, dressed in a sarong, is sitting on a blanket in an open field, playing the jaw harp, followed by the text, "When did you see me first?" The subsequent depiction shows an African American woman who is dressed in a white gauzy material and who cautiously approaches Otálvaro-Hormillosa. The following text appears: "How would we see each other now . . ." In the accompanying video image, Otálvaro-Hormillosa and an African American woman carefully consider each other as they draw closer, followed by the text ". . . if we had never been taught to see each other?" In between the lines of text on the screen, brief video images fill the screen: two women embracing, two men (Latinx and Filipino) struggling and having sex, a close-up of two women's bodies moving against each other, two men engaging in oral sex, hands gripping a back and caressing it from behind, and finally, a return to the original scene in the open field, in which Otálvaro-Hormillosa is lying on top of the African American woman. Throughout this scene, the electronic music shifts from a slow and ethereal mood to a quicker, more frenetic beat, increasing the intensity and tempo of the cross-cutting between images.

In these video images, Otálvaro-Hormillosa presents an alternative imagination of the "contact zone," what she terms a "neo-queer precolonial imagining."[11] *Cosmic Blood* is a reimagining of the past in which queer desire is a locus of relations of power between the colonizer and the colonized. Through the temporal disjuncture implied by the juxtaposition of "neo-queer" with "precolonial" ("across time and space"), Otálvaro-Hormillosa suggests both a different moment of contact and an alternative mode of recognition between colonized peoples, one that is visualized through queer eroticism. This is not a liberatory vision of queer desire but a more ambiguous eroticism that at times resembles the sexual violence of conquest. Within the "contact zone," queer desire functions as a mode of recognition beyond colonial taxonomies of racial difference. Otálvaro-Hormillosa asks, "How would we see each other now, if we had never been taught to see each other?" Interspersed between scenes of the nude feminine Filipina woman walking hand in hand with a light-skinned Latino man are scenes of physical conflict and eroticized violence between the nude Filipina woman and Otálvaro-Hormillosa's androgynous conquistador figure, as well as explicit gay male sex. Through the sequence titled "El Otro Encuentro: A Neo-queer Precolonial Imagining," *Cosmic Blood* presents images of queer bodies struggling to both dominate and comprehend each other, an intimate act that is ultimately a dance of recognition. The animated sequence that follows depicts two figures, one emerging from the Americas, the other from the African continent, superimposed upon a map of the world, suggesting an imagining of the past in which colonized subjects learn to see each other's racialized bodies across national and hemispheric borders. Here the sensual exploration of bodies functions as a different way of *knowing each other*, a form of resistance to the epistemic violence of colonial taxonomies of racial difference.

Cosmic Blood presents a *resignification* of the signs of Native and Empire framed within a lens of queer desire.[12] These visual images—the naked Filipina woman standing on a beach, the macho, yet androgynous, conquistador figure, the "girl with a tail in her ass"—reenact and resignify colonial relations of power through queer eroticism. Their struggles to both recognize and dominate each other are represented through the visual images projected onscreen and through the dialogue and movement onstage. In "El Otro Encuentro: A Neo-queer Precolonial Imagining," Gigi Otálvaro-Hormillosa presents a reimagining of the first meeting of "African" and "Native" peoples. This imagining of an alternative moment of first contact contests overdetermined discourses of colonial visuality by imagining queer bodies of color that resist the taxonomizing imperative of colonial visual regimes.

Aeromestizaje

Drawing on Gloria Anzaldúa's concept of "mestiza consciousness," Otálvaro-Hormillosa describes her concept of *aeromestizaje*: "My concept of (a)eromestizaje challenges stereotypical representations of identity, community and sexuality that I explore through the aerodynamic filter of a new 'mestizaje' (the term that describes the Spanish/indigenous race mixture of Latin America and the Philippines) in which there is a constant, yet shifting interplay between racial and sexual identities."[13]

Otálvaro-Hormillosa draws on her experience as a gender-nonconforming person of Filipina and Colombian descent in her concept of *aeromestizaje*. Her appellation of *aeromestizaje* connotes a sense of travel and movement, displacing static notions of *mestizaje* while implying a connection to the science fictional trope of interstellar travel. In the fourth scene, Otálvaro-Hormillosa plays conga drums as she states, "Cumbia! A product of *mestizaje*," invoking the Afro-Latin dance the cumbia as a metaphor for postcolonial hybridity. Otálvaro-Hormillosa exhorts the audience to begin a "mixed-race movement." She begins a litany of praises for ethnic and racial mixes in the San Francisco Bay Area: "Thank Creator for the Bay Area! Thank Creator for Mexipinos! Thank Creator for Chicanoriquenos! Thank Creator for Afro-Korean military children! Thank creator for JaimaicArgentinians!" She then goes on to discuss her own body as a sign of *mestizaje* by humorously referencing the racial and ethnic stereotypes that her queer Filipina Colombian body negotiates in the multiracial context of the United States. Shifting from her self-description as "petite Oriental girl" to "macho/a oversexualized Hispanic—whoops, I mean Latino!" Otálvaro-Hormillosa demonstrates the shifting codes through which her queer mixed-race body is read within discourses of US multiculturalism. Although located in a humorous monologue, Otálvaro-Hormillosa's call for a mixed-race movement is earnest in its yearning for forms of belonging that exceed the existing modes of reading the racialized queer body.

The title of the performance, *Cosmic Blood*, is a play on José Vasconcelos's idea that the mix of European, indigenous, Asian, and African peoples in the Americas creates a "cosmic race."[14] Within the piece, Vasconcelos's notion of the cosmic race is emblematic of a reimagined past and a hopeful future, both of which rely on a notion of *mestizaje* as a mode of survival and resistance, implicitly referencing Anzaldúa's notion of mestiza consciousness. In *Borderlands / La*

Frontera: The New Mestiza, Anzaldúa quotes Jack Forbes in her discussion of José Vasconcelos's notion of the cosmic race:

"José Vasconcelos, Mexican philosopher, envisaged una raza mestiza, una mezcla de razas afines, una raza de color—la primera raza síntesis del globo. He called it a cosmic race, la raza cósmica, a fifth race embracing the four major races of the world." Opposite to the theory of the pure Aryan, and to the policy of racial purity that white America practices, his theory is one of inclusivity. At the confluence of two or more genetic streams, races, rather than resulting in an inferior being, provides hybrid progeny, a mutable, more malleable species with a rich gene pool. From this racial, ideological, cultural and biological cross-pollinization, an "alien" consciousness is presently in the making—*a new mestiza consciousness, una conciencia de mujer. It is a consciousness of the Borderlands.* (emphasis mine)[15]

Anzaldúa utilizes the metaphor of racial/blood mixing in her positing of a feminist, queer understanding of belonging in relation to race and ethnicity. While invoking corporeal metaphors of blood and genes, Anzaldúa's notion of mixing occurs not at the level of the corporeal but rather at the level of consciousness. *Cosmic Blood*'s performance of mestiza consciousness relates less to corporeal notions of blood and more to an understanding of subjectivity and of belonging beyond the reproductive logic of the nation. Resisting masculinist and heteronormative cultural nationalist formations, Anzaldúa's mestiza consciousness proposes a model of belonging that exceeds the trope of woman as a maternal figure for the nation. Anzaldúa argues, "*As mestiza I have no country*, my homeland cast me out; yet all countries are mine because I am every woman's sister or potential lover. (*As a lesbian I have no race*, my own people disclaim me; but I am all races because there is the queer of me in all races.) . . . I am participating in the creation of yet another culture; *a new story to explain the world and our participation in it*, a new value system with images and symbols that connect us to each other and to the planet" (emphasis mine).[16] In contrast to teleological narratives of belonging, Anzaldúa calls for other origin stories beyond the heteronormative framework of kinship that position women as the (re)producers of a stable national culture.

Cosmic Blood is another kind of origin story, one that imagines forms of belonging beyond the corporeality of the national family. The mestiza body in *Cosmic Blood* challenges the epistemic violence of the colonizer/colonized dichotomy, a distinction that reduces women's bodies to the territory of the nation.[17] Through the framework of queer desire, Otálvaro-Hormillosa presents images of the colonized queer body that exceed the trope of woman as the narration of the nation. The ambiguous eroticism in *Cosmic Blood* includes a queer subject who simultaneously desires and resists the violence of the colonizer. As a desiring queer subject, the nude Filipina woman is neither a figure for the nation nor a passive victim of colonial violence. The mestiza body contests the epistemic violence of colonial taxonomies of racial difference. The ambiguity suggested by the sadomasochistic interaction between the feminine figure of the nude Filipina and Otálvaro-Hormillosa's masculine conquistador figure suggests a multivalent relationship that troubles the colonizer/colonized dichotomy. Here, the figure of the feminine Filipina woman exceeds the trope of the colonized nation; instead, she is a desiring subject whose pleasures are not easily positioned within the frameworks of nationalism and coloniality.

Otálvaro-Hormillosa's concept of *aeromestizaje* draws on historical understandings of *mestizaje* within both Latin American and Philippine contexts. Within both contexts, *mestizaje* is intertwined with notions of national identity and nation building. Despite the utopian dimension in which *Cosmic Blood* imagines *aeromestizaje*, particularly the invocation of Anzaldúa's notion of "mestiza consciousness," the concept of *mestizaje* has a complicated history throughout both Latin American and the Philippines. While a full consideration of the history of *mestizaje* is not possible here, it is worth noting that within the Latin American context, *mestizaje* has been critiqued for its connection to masculinist forms of ethnonationalism.[18] Similarly, the use of *mestizaje*, or what Vicente Rafael terms "mestizoness," in the Philippines has an ambivalent relationship to the history of nation building. Within the mythology of Philippine nation-state building, mestizos such as national hero José Rizal played a privileged role in consolidating critiques of Spanish colonialism. However, as I noted in chapter 1, the narrative of José Rizal as leader for the nation was critiqued during the 1960s by nationalists who claimed that Andres Bonifacio was the true national hero.[19] Despite this challenge to the enduring historical legacy of Rizal, Rafael notes that "in the Filipino historical imagination, the mestizo/a has enjoyed a privileged position associated with economic wealth, political influence, and cultural hegemony."[20] As Rafael has noted, the figure of the mestizo is central to narratives of Philippine revolutionary nationalism:

> For this reason, mestizos/as (and those who come to identify with them) have historically had an ambivalent relationship with sources of power, whether the masses below or colonial rulers above. They have collaborated with one against the other at different moments, or with both at the same time. They can thus claim the privilege to solicit as well as contain the workings of power, whatever its source. And because of their dual association with the history of revolutionary nationalism and counterrevolutionary colonial regimes since the late nineteenth century, mestizos/as—whether as Chinese, Spanish, or North American—have been regarded as the chief architects of the nation-state.[21]

Indeed, it is impossible to separate the concept of mestizoness from discourses of national revolution in the Philippine context. Simultaneously, mestizoness has an enduring association with the workings of power, whether Spanish colonial power or the contemporary power of US neocolonialism. While the term "mestizo" has come to mean mixed-race Filipinos of Chinese and white American descent, as well as Spanish mestizos, the term continues to be associated with forms of privilege in the Philippines.

In contrast to the discourse of mestizoness in the Philippines, *mestizaje* has had a different valence within Chicana feminist theory, a legacy of the work of Anzaldúa. In *Queering Mestizaje*, Alicia Arrizón details the varying contours of the use of *mestizaje* within both the Philippine and Latin American contexts.[22] Drawing on Mary Louise Pratt's notion of "transculturation" and Anzaldúa's notion of mestiza consciousness, Arrizón presents *mestizaje* as a mode of articulating alternative subject positions beyond the dichotomy of colonizer/colonized.[23] Arrizón draws on Pratt's discussion of the contact zone as "the imaginary space of colonial encounters, where [for Pratt] the 'relations among colonizers and colonized . . . [are expressed] not in terms of separateness and apartheid, but in terms of copresence, interactions, interlocking understandings and practices, often within radically asymmetrical relations of power.'"[24] This contact zone is the space of *Cosmic Blood*'s "neo-queer precolonial imagining," where Otálvaro-Hormillosa imagines a different scene of first contact that is shaped by queer desire and a mutual recognition of colonized peoples—her mixed-race Filipina and Colombian character and the African American woman with whom she performs a sensual dance. Otálvaro-Hormillosa's concept of *aeromestizaje* departs from the conflation of mestizos with nation-building projects. Instead, *aeromestizaje* draws less on the mixed-race heritage of mestizos—steeped as they are in colonial taxonomies of difference that are rooted in the corporeality of blood—and more on notions of belonging that exceed the nation. Here, blood is "cosmic" in the sense that it is actually not rooted in the organic body at all. Instead, "cosmic blood" is found in the cyborg body.

The Cyborg Body

Cosmic Blood ends with the figure of the cyborg, a hybrid form exceeding the corporeality of the organic body. Transitioning from a "neo-queer precolonial imagining," *Cosmic Blood* shifts to the science fictional site of the future. The cyborg embodies the utopian possibility of queer diasporas as an alternative to the biological kinship structure of the nation. The last scene of *Cosmic Blood* begins with the following text on a video screen at the back of the stage, "Beginnings of Endings," accompanied by Otálvaro-Hormillosa stating,

"Blood. Dispersion. Thought. Time. And. Space. Hybridization as survival." In this scene, the body of Otálvaro-Hormillosa shifts from the excessive corporeality of the Native body to the hybrid body—part machine, part organic—of the queer cyborg. The next video scene is an animated image of a spaceship arriving on the surface of a planet, followed by the text, "Mestiza from Another Planet." Here, Otálvaro-Hormillosa links her notion of *aeromestizaje* to the trope of interstellar travel. The following video scene is a close-up of Otálvaro-Hormillosa's shaved head, her entire face and scalp painted blue. Her face undergoes multiple contortions, eyes shifting back and forth in robotic, jerky movements, while mechanical noises can be heard in the background. Onstage, Otálvaro-Hormillosa has transformed into an alien creature inside the huge gourd, which has been stripped of its walls and now only exists as a skeleton. Otálvaro-Hormillosa's cyborg form is constituted by the performer's shaved blue head atop a compact body draped in white cloth, a white fur tail, and a mechanical motorized bottom half that propels her across the stage. With jerky, robotic movements, the blue cyborg travels across the stage, transported by the wheels of its mechanical bottom half. At first, the cyborg appears limbless, but later it raises its "arms," made of shiny, metal rods. The slow, shaking movements with which the cyborg raises its "arms" seems to be a process of growth, an expansion accompanied by the facial contortions of Otálvaro-Hormillosa's cyborg figure. The last scene of *Cosmic Blood* is a dark stage with a spotlight on a hole in the floor of the stage, through which the blue alien creature's head protrudes. The head slowly rises and descends through the hole in the stage as Otálvaro-Hormillosa's face contorts. Is this pain? Growth? Transformation? The final scene then ends with words from *Parable of the Sower*: "The destiny of Earthseed is to take root among the stars."[25]

Beginning with the words "Mestiza from Another Planet," this scene analogizes European colonization to interstellar travel, a move that situates Otálvaro-Hormillosa's retroping of the past in a science fictional mode. Beginning her performance with the words "Change is God . . . God is change," Gigi Otálvaro-Hormillosa frames *Cosmic Blood* as a response to Octavia Butler's science fiction novel *Parable of the Sower*.[26] Throughout the performance, Otálvaro-Hormillosa references the words of the character Lauren Olamina, the African American prophet and leader of the multiracial collective called Earthseed, described in *Parable of the Sower*. In the context of a postapocalyptic United States, the members of Earthseed gather around their shared belief that "God is change"; that is, the only higher power to which one can pledge one's faith is the inevitability of change and the necessity of adapting to one's surroundings. The novel is set in the year 2025 in a town close to Los Angeles. The context is one of urban violence

Figure 4.2 Gigi Otálvaro-Hormillosa's cyborg character in the *Cosmic Blood* performance at Espacios Mestizos, Gran Canaria, Spain, 2003. Photograph courtesy of Nacho Gonzalez.

and decay, in which few people have access to food, water, or shelter, and the material infrastructure is deteriorating or nonexistent. Few people drive cars, as there is no more fuel; water is expensive; and the few people who can afford homes live in walled-off communities. Diseases such as cholera and measles have become epidemics, as few people have access to clean water or health care. Arson, murder, mutilation, and robbery are the everyday risks of survival.

Within this postapocalyptic setting, Lauren Olamina's collective, Earthseed, views change and adaptation as the only means of survival. As part of their beliefs, Earthseed idealizes space travel as the only path of redemption for the human race. Implicit in Octavia Butler's description of Earthseed is both an affirmation of the need for a multiracial coalitional politics and an insistence on the pervasiveness of race in all social contexts. Otálvaro-Hormillosa's reference to Butler's *Parable of the Sower* suggests the centrality of a mestiza consciousness to a vision of the future that can exceed the boundaries of colonial taxonomies of difference. A multiracial coalitional politics, not a transcendence of race, must develop in order for the human race to survive the apocalypse.

Repeating Earthseed's belief in the necessity of adaptation, Otálvaro-Hormillosa's blue cyborg is the physical manifestation of the *mestizaje* as a necessity for survival in the science fictional future. Otálvaro-Hormillosa's transformation to the blue alien cyborg forces a shift in the audience's perception of the performer's body. This is both a shift in embodiment and a foregrounding of the body of the colonized as the ground upon which struggles between colonizer/colonized take place. The overt bodily presence of the previous scenes, of Otálvaro-Hormillosa's writhing form, draped in fur, and the naked forms of Filipina/o, African American, and Latinx women and men struggling/engaging in sexual acts in the video scenes, shifts to the forced disembodiment of the blue alien's cyborg form, whose only movement is propelled by its mechanical lower half. The science fictional site of the future, embodied in the cyborg, is the utopian site of possibility. The mestiza embodiment of the cyborg is the result of bodily pain through the metaphor of birth and sexual violence, as well as the *disembodiment* of the transformation from human to machine. *Cosmic Blood* retropes the historical narrative of colonization through the imagining of a *disembodied* future—a future in which Filipina bodies can exist as more than "bodies without subjectivity."[27]

Cosmic Blood echoes the ideals of surrealism, which emphasized practices of imagination in the service of radical social change. In *Freedom Dreams* Robin Kelley describes Afrofuturism as the surrealist practice of envisioning a different future through a reimagining of the past. As a utopian artistic movement, surrealism sought to create a different world through the imagination of an alternative future. According to the Chicago Surrealist Group,

> Surrealism is the exaltation of freedom, revolt, imagination, and love. . . . Its basic aim is to lessen and eventually to completely *resolve the contradiction between everyday life and our wildest dreams.* By definition, subversive, surrealist thought and action are intended not only to discredit and destroy the forces of repression, but also to *emancipate desire* and supply it with new poetic weapons. . . .

Beginning with the abolition of imaginative slavery, it advances to the creation of a free society in which everyone will be a poet—a society in which everyone will be able to develop his or her potentialities fully and freely. (emphasis mine)[28]

Kelley links the futurist mode of popular musicians such as Sun-Ra to surrealist art, describing both as utopian practices that produce counterimaginations, alternative visions of the future that exceed the material conditions of the present. Afrofuturism accomplished this through a reimagining of the past in a futuristic mode. Linking the music of Sun-Ra to the "Back to Africa" movement, Kelley describes Sun Ra and his band, the Arkestra, modeled after Sun Ra's idea of an intergalactic Ark that could return to Egypt through the metaphor of outer space. Sun Ra and other proponents of Afrofuturism "looked backward in order to look forward, finding the cosmos by way of ancient Egypt."[29] Similarly, *Cosmic Blood*'s science fictional/futurist approach is a surrealist intervention in the present that exceeds the discursive construction of the global Filipina body, whose corporeality is circumscribed by both contemporary discourses of gendered labor under global capitalism and colonial taxonomies of racial difference. In discussing the Afrofuturism of Sun-Ra, Kelley states, "At the heart of Sun-Ra's vision was the notion of alter/destiny—the idea that through the creation of new myths we have the power to redirect the future."[30]

Otálvaro-Hormillosa's *Cosmic Blood* accomplishes a similar goal of creating new origin stories, reimagining the colonial past in order to envision a different future. As a practice of imagining that retropes the past in order to posit a more hopeful and perhaps revolutionary future, *Cosmic Blood* employs the metaphors of intergalactic travel and cyborg transformation to reimagine a different relationship of the body of the colonized—specifically of Otálvaro-Hormillosa's mixed-race, queer, Filipina-Colombian body—to a history of colonization and forced assimilation. It is through a reimagining of the past that a utopian future can be imagined. A mix of the corporeal and the machine, Otálvaro-Hormillosa's cyborg body is a science fictional embodiment of *mestizaje*. Much like Sun Ra's notion of the Ark as a means of returning both to the past and to an alternative future, *Cosmic Blood* functions as a surrealist intervention into the reality of everyday life, in which post- or neocolonial subjects are shaped by multiple histories of colonization and forced assimilation. According to Kelley, "Surrealism recognizes that any revolution must begin with thought, with how we imagine a New World, with how we reconstruct our social and individual relationships, with unleashing our desire and building a new future on the basis of love and creativity rather than rationality."[31] In this sense, *Cosmic Blood* can be understood as a type of surrealist, futurist longing that retropes the past in order to imagine an alternative future—a future in which the queer, racialized body of the Filipina possesses subjectivity outside of the logic of global capitalism. Within the logic of global capitalism, which is both an effect and an extension of colonial taxonomies of difference, the Filipina body is commodified for the sexual and domestic labor that her brown body provides.

As a surrealist intervention into both the legacy of colonial difference and the everyday logic of contemporary capitalism, Cosmic Blood imagines other modes of subjectivity for Filipina bodies. Otálvaro-Hormillosa's shift to the blue cyborg in the last scene of Cosmic Blood is a forced shift in the perception/recognition of embodiment. This shift in recognition destabilizes the codes of racial, sexual, and gender difference that are inscribed onto Otálvaro-Hormillosa's body. Rather than existing as the "petite Oriental girl" or "macho/a oversexualized Latino," Otálvaro-Hormillosa forces the audience to perceive her transformed body, one that is no longer anchored by the organic materiality of a human body but rather exists as a cyborg body. Here the codes of race, gender, and sexuality blur. In the realm of the surreal, the cyborg body allows for a recoding of racial and gender difference. Cosmic Blood is an act of disidentification, in Muñoz's sense of the term, a performative and imaginative act through which subjects resist the interpellating call of race and ethnicity issued by both US multiculturalism and broader discourses of global capitalism.[32]

BEYOND BLOOD

I am sick to death of bonding through kinship and "the family," and I long for models of solidarity and human unity and difference rooted in friendship, work, partially shared purposes, intractable collective pain, inescapable mortality, and persistent hope. It is time to theorize an "unfamiliar" unconscious, a different primal scene, where everything does not stem from the drama of identity and reproduction. Ties through blood—including blood recast in the coin of genes and information—have been bloody enough already. I believe that there will be no racial or sexual peace, no livable nature, until we learn to produce humanity through something more and less than kinship.

—Donna Haraway, Modest_Witness@Second_Millenium.
FemaleMan©_Meets_OncoMouse™

In Otálvaro-Hormillosa's theorization of belonging, blood serves as both solvent and coagulant. Throughout the performance, blood is a metaphor for belonging, kinship, mixing. It is through the biological metaphor of blood mixing that Otálvaro-Hormillosa imagines a different past and future. Invoking Vasconcelos's notion of the cosmic race through the title of the piece Cosmic Blood, Otálvaro-Hormillosa imagines forms of belonging that escape the over-determined corporeality of blood. Historically, blood has served as a biological referent for racial difference. A result of biological discourses that have solidified racial difference in the materiality of the body, blood is pervasive as a sign of kinship and belonging. In her juxtaposition of "cosmic" with "blood," Otálvaro-Hormillosa uses a science fictional mode to retrope the meanings of "blood." This juxtaposition shifts the meaning of "blood" from the level of the flesh to the ethereal nature of the "cosmic," that which is not rooted in the material reality of the earth but rather exists in the stars. In doing so, this juxtaposition unfixes the biologism of blood. Otálvaro-Hormillosa physically manifests the multivalent meanings of blood through her shift in embodiment, from her ambiguously gendered, racially mixed, Filipina-Colombian body to that of the blue cyborg—a shift from the purely organic to the hybrid realm of the cyborg. The shift from the biological fleshiness of the human body to a partially inorganic, alien hybrid destabilizes the corporeal materiality of blood, particularly its relation to race and nation. Otálvaro-Hormillosa's cosmic blood exceeds the organic, biological meanings of the term "blood," rooted as they are in discourses of miscegenation and eugenics. Instead, the cosmic blood of the figure of the cyborg offers possibilities for theorizing notions of belonging beyond the corporeality of blood, kinship, and nation.

The figure of the cyborg introduces a future for the global Filipina body that exceeds the limits of the corporeal, suggesting a queer temporal framework beyond the reproductive logic of the nation. The queer cyborg also looks backward, telling another origin story, one in which kinship is understood beyond the fleshiness of blood. The queer temporality offered in *Cosmic Blood*, like the Afrofuturism of musical artists such as Sun-Ra, is one that gazes backward as it simultaneously envisions a future that is not yet there. *Cosmic Blood* answers Gloria Anzaldúa's call for a "*a new story to explain the world and our participation in it*, a new value system with images and symbols that connect us to each other and to the planet."[33] *Cosmic Blood*'s origin story reimagines the very terms of belonging, beyond the limits of the corporeal. As Haraway notes, "Ties through blood—including blood recast in the coin of genes and information—have been bloody enough already. I believe that there will be no racial or sexual peace, no livable nature, *until we learn to produce humanity through something more and less than kinship*."[34] Echoing Haraway's call for another mode of belonging, *Cosmic Blood* presents a story of origins that exceeds the biological family. In its reimagination of the past, *Cosmic Blood* simultaneously envisions a queer future in which the diaspora is not circumscribed by the reproductive logic of the nation.

Jack Halberstam describes how "queer uses of time and space develop, at least in part, in opposition to the institutions of family, heterosexuality, and reproduction."[35] The queer time of *Cosmic Blood*'s science fictional future allows the Filipina body to exist beyond the reproductive temporal frameworks of the nation. The "reproductive time" of the nation "connects the family to the historical past of the nation, and glances ahead to connect the family to the future of both familial and national stability."[36] In contrast to the reproductive time of the nation, *Cosmic Blood*'s queer time unsettles the heteropatriarchal logic that reduces the global Filipina body to a sign of the nation. In this queer temporal framework, *Cosmic Blood* introduces the possibility of queer diasporas—modes of collectivity that exceed the reproductive time of the nation. If "queerness is that thing that lets us feel that this world is not enough, that indeed, something is missing," then the diaspora imagined by *Cosmic Blood* is one that exists in the queer time of the future.[37]

As a vision of Muñoz's queer potentiality, *Cosmic Blood* presents the possibility of a queer diaspora that challenges the trope of the global Filipina body as the narration of the nation. While I posit a notion of a queer diaspora that resists the trope of the Filipina body as sign of the nation, I recognize the necessity of Filipina/o popular nationalist movements as the primary means of challenging the lasting effects of colonialism and imperialism. As the closing figure of this book, the cyborg is a figure whose mestiza consciousness can encompass the essential tension that animates this project. The mestiza nature of the cyborg—part human and part machine—embodies this duality, between the real political need for nationalist movements to combat the exploitation of neocolonialism and neoliberal globalization and the violence of the Philippine state, and the hope for models of collectivity that can exceed the reproductive logic of the nation. In this sense, the cyborg embodies the culmination of the trajectory that this book explores. The arc of figures explored in *The Global Filipina Body*, from the Filipina/o American *balikbayan* to the Filipina mail-order bride, culminates in the figure of the cyborg in *Cosmic Blood*. The cyborg's mestiza nature offers the possibility for a queer diaspora that resists the violence of the discursive construction of the global Filipina body under capitalist globalization while not relinquishing the political necessity of diasporic nationalist movements that are committed to anti-imperialist and anticapitalist struggle. This ability to hold both sides of the coin, a utopian possibility that the cyborg embodies, makes it an apt figure to conclude the larger project of this book. The cyborg's mestiza consciousness allows it to encompass both the limits and the political promise of nationalisms, which envision a different future and alternative forms of collectivity that exceed the corporeality of blood and kinship. In doing so, the cyborg signifies the promise of queer potentiality, the not-yet-there of other origin stories, other modes of collectivity that exist, if not in our present, in the imagination of a different future.

Conclusion

Queer Necropolitics and the Afterlife
of US Imperialism

In the colony, the "world" is often thought of as the U.S.
After all, that is where you go if you want to be a citizen for
real. But, in reality, the world in the colony is so tiny and
beautiful and heartbreaking, it fits in a dance club.
—Guillermo Rebollo-Gil, "As It Regards the Ones We've Lost"

But for a moment, I want to talk about the sacredness of Latin
Night at the queer club. Amid all the noise, I want to close
my eyes and see you all there, dancing, inviolable, free.
—Justin Torres, "In Praise of Latin Night at the Queer Club"

I was wrapping up the first draft of this manuscript when forty-nine people were killed at Pulse, a queer nightclub in Orlando, Florida, on June 12, 2016. It was Latin night, and most of the patrons were young men of color, many of whom were Puerto Rican. Influenced by the erratic hormones of my first trimester of pregnancy, I started many of those summer days reading social media and weeping. The stories and recollections that my friends on social media told of their formative experiences in queer clubs—iconic places within queer culture—moved me to tears. In the midst of gestating a new life, I was overwhelmed by the collective outpouring of queer grief that filled my computer screen each day. The murderous violation of a gathering of queer people of color at Pulse felt both intimate and terrifying. Although never a "safe space," the dance floors of queer clubs, particularly on queer of color nights, have an almost sacred quality in the collective memories of queer people of color of my generation, the 1970s and 1980s babies who grew up remembering Matthew Shepard and James Byrd Jr.[1] On social media, friends recited names of the queer of color nightclubs of their youth in cities such as Oakland, San Francisco, and New York: Mango, Backstreet, Butta, Lovergirl, Latin night at the Café.

In these dark clubs, among sweaty bodies and pounding beats, many of us felt the most alive and whole, experiencing a life beyond mere survival. As I grieved for those who did not survive the Pulse massacre, I was reminded of the words of Audre Lorde in her poem "A Litany for Survival":

> when the sun sets we are afraid
> it might not rise in the morning
> . . . .
> remembering
> we were never meant to survive[2]

Like the Pulse massacre, Lorde's poem amplifies the precarity of queer of color life, reminding us that our survival is not assured. Even as I was positioned on the edge of creating a new life, I was reminded of the pervasive forms of queer and trans death that surrounded me and my unborn fetus. The necropolitical quality of queer of color life in the current political moment—intertwined with the ongoing War on Terror, US state–sanctioned Islamophobia, white nationalism, and anti-immigrant US state policies—added a layer of apprehension to my feelings about bringing a new human into this world. The resulting homonationalism of the public response to the Pulse shooting facilitated the mobilization of queer grief for Islamophobic purposes, dovetailing with then presidential hopeful Donald Trump's calls for a so-called Muslim ban. The fact that the shooter, Omar Mateen, was a Muslim US citizen of Afghani descent (suspected of being closeted) added fuel to the fire of Trump's Islamophobic rhetoric. A few months after seeing the profile pictures of mostly straight friends on Facebook overlaid with the colors of the rainbow flag, I wept upon hearing the news of Donald Trump's election to the presidency, terrified about what this would mean for my baby, a child of Filipina/o and Arab descent with an Arabic name and queer parents. Unlike most of the recent mass shootings in the United States, the Pulse shooting targeted a community that resembled my own—queer people of color who were either migrants or from a migrant familial background. The shooting happened at a Latinx night at Pulse; most of those victims were black and brown Latinxs.[3] Almost half of the victims were Puerto Rican, reflecting Orlando's status as a migration hub for Puerto Ricans both on and off the island.[4] Many of the rest of the Pulse victims were transnational migrants; some were undocumented, originally from Mexico and the Dominican Republic.[5]

The disposability of queer brown life, of migrant life, haunts the pages of this text. As I theorize the disposability of racialized and gendered migrant labor in the Filipina/o diaspora, I cannot disentangle it from the massive queer and trans death of the Pulse massacre, which, like the Philippines, is overshadowed by the long reach of US imperialism. Similarly to the Philippines, another location in what Allan Isaac has termed the "American tropics," Puerto Rico's status as a (neo)colony is intertwined with the history of outward labor migration from the island.[6] The forms of death experienced by workers in the 2015 Kentex factory fire in the Philippines, discussed in the introduction to this book, resonate with the queer and trans death of the Pulse massacre a year later.[7] The social media accounts of Kentex workers trapped in a fiery sweatshop reverberated with descriptions of friends and lovers struck by machine gun fire in the darkness of the Pulse nightclub.

The juxtaposition of these two massacres highlights the necropolitical afterlife of US imperialism. Since the fall of 2017, Puerto Rico has experienced even worse conditions as the island struggles to recover from Hurricane Maria. The ongoing effects of Hurricane Maria are a result of Puerto Rico's long-standing status as a US neocolony and key military base. As Puerto Rican scholar Javier Arbona notes, "It is precisely Puerto Ricans—historically, fighting grunts in U.S. wars starting with World War I—who are once again being hailed to participate, including through affective mobilizations, in a global war, now without limits or borders, and in *particular, specific ways.* This is a war apparatus that, in fact, also has been deployed—from 1898's invasion—against Puerto Ricans themselves, and has been / is being actively used to pacify insurgency against imperialism and colonialism" (emphasis in the original).[8] In the wake of the Pulse shooting, the use of homonationalist grief to bolster US Islamophobia reminds us of the interconnectedness of the "American Tropics" with current critiques of queer necropolitics. As some queer and trans subjects are folded into life, other queer subjects are consigned to the death worlds of disposability. As Jin Haritaworn, Adi Kuntsman, and Sylvia Posocco argue in *Queer Necropolitics*, the mobilization of homonationalism for queer necropolitical ends is rooted in older histories of colonialism and imperialism.[9] In the days and weeks following the massacre, queer Latinx writers and scholars articulated this connection between US colonialism in Puerto Rico, labor migration, and the Pulse shooting.[10] While queer Latinx scholars such as Lawrence La Fontaine-Stokes wrote about the connections between US colonialism in Puerto Rico, outward labor migration from the island, and homophobia, the LGBT and mainstream US press largely ignored ongoing forms of US colonialism and imperialism as the key political economic context for racialized, homophobic violence.[11] Instead, the deaths of Puerto Rican and Latinx queer migrants at Pulse were largely subsumed within homonationalist calls for unity that implicitly bolstered the growing Islamophobia of the United States, embodied in Trump's slogan, "Make America Great Again."[12] Less than a year after the Pulse shooting, the Trump administration instituted a "Muslim ban" against travelers from Chad, Iran, Libya, Somalia, Syria, and Yemen as President Trump made good on his Islamophobic campaign promises. The same black and brown bodies whose living presence—as queer and trans Latinx migrants—underwrote the perceived threat to Trump's promise to "make America great again" became ammunition for an anti-LGBT, anti-immigrant, and Islamophobic administration in death.

The failure of the mainstream media to recognize the longer history of US empire as the key historical context for the Pulse massacre is far from accidental. In contrast, as American studies scholars such as Allan Isaac and Amy Kaplan have argued, the very notion of a US national identity requires a historical amnesia of the nation's past and current forms of imperialism.[13] US national identity is implicitly constructed by its post- (or perhaps neo-) colonies, what Isaac terms the "American tropics." In particular, the Philippines is strikingly similar to Puerto Rico in this regard. In his media analysis of Andrew Cunanan, the mixed-race gay Filipino American serial killer who murdered fashion designer Gianni Versace in 1997, Isaac points to the "unrecognizability of the Filipino and the Philippines in larger U.S. narratives." The disparate media accounts of Cunanan—the mainstream press focused on his sexual orientation, while the Filipina/o American press emphasized his partial Filipino heritage—reflect the incommensurability of discourses of immigration, colonialism, and sexuality, revealing the "blind limits of the U.S. racial imaginary and its misreading and incomprehension of its imperial history."[14]

The centrality of US empire to US national identity has largely been invisible to itself. As the mainstream media coverage of the Pulse shooting suggests, much of US-based queer politics has failed to address US empire in both its current forms and its afterlife. This inability to contend with the afterlife of US empire is reflected within much of queer studies scholarship in the Global North, reflecting the legacy of antagonism toward anticolonialism in the Global South.[15] As a key formation through which anti-imperialist thought and action manifest, particularly in the Global South, popular nationalisms are a crucial vehicle for anti-imperialist social movements in the age of capitalist globalization. The dismissal of nationalism by much of queer studies scholarship in the Global North is contextualized within a longer history of disregard, if not outright hostility, to anticolonial movements.

In the current political climate of Trump's administration, the Pulse shooting is a reminder of the need to take anti-imperialism and its accompanying formation, popular nationalism, seriously within Global North–oriented queer studies and queer politics more broadly. Indeed, this book's analysis of how the figure of the global Filipina body has both reified and challenged the gendered and sexual politics of Filipina/o diasporic nationalisms in the Filipina/o American context demonstrates how formations of nationalisms can be destabilized, even as they are reworked in queer and feminist ways. In this political context, *The Global Filipina Body* introduces two significant interventions. On the one hand, the reworking of the global Filipina body presents queer and feminist interventions in the politics of Filipina/o diasporic nationalism while holding on to its liberatory potential in the face of both ongoing US imperialism and neoliberal globalization, manifested in the material context of outward labor migration. On the other hand, the queering of the global Filipina body inserts an anti-imperialist framework that foregrounds the promise and necessity of popular nationalisms—while acknowledging queer and feminist critiques of the nation—to queer politics in the United States and beyond. In doing so, *The Global Filipina Body* holds the politics of diasporic nationalisms accountable to broader debates within both transnational feminisms and queer globalization studies.

Queering the Global Filipina Body

"But half of the ND [National Democratic] members are gay!" This was the response from an audience member to a conference presentation that I gave in which I critiqued the heteronormativity and masculinism of expressions of Filipina/o diasporic nationalism within heritage language programs. This response echoes through my mind years later as I am reminded of the pervasiveness of liberal narratives of inclusion. The speaker's assumption is that the inclusion or presence of LGBT members within the National Democratic movement makes a critique of the gendered and sexual politics of nationalism(s) unnecessary. While this project is not focused exclusively on the National Democratic movement but on Filipina/o diasporic nationalisms more broadly, critiques of the gendered tropes of the nation that are mobilized in the name of anti-imperialist and anticapitalist resistance are incredibly contentious within Filipina/o diasporic culture. To challenge the invocation of the nation as the primary framework through which political struggles are imagined within the Filipina/o diaspora could be considered misguided at best, perhaps even detrimental to anti-imperialist struggles at worst. The long-standing tension between nationalisms—whether cultural nationalism or revolutionary nationalism—and feminist and queer critiques of the heteropatriarchal nation has troubled many radical social change movements, from racial justice struggles in the United States to anticolonial and anti-imperialist social movements in the Global South.

Despite the political risk of such a project, the broader goal of *The Global Filipina Body* has been to interrogate the gendered and sexual politics of nationalism—in its state, popular, and cultural forms—that are embodied in the figure of the global Filipina body not only as a mode of critique but to think seriously about what a queer and feminist engagement with Filipina/o diasporic nationalism might look like. Simultaneously, I explore the ways in which *queer* articulations of the global Filipina body have unsettled the gendered and sexual politics of distinct forms of nationalism. Thus, my goal has been *not* to dismiss the nation but to insist that nationalism is still a key theoretical and political framework for anti-imperialist struggle, despite the valid critiques of the heteropatriarchy of the nation within feminist and queer theory. A nuanced consideration of the politics of popular nationalisms is crucial to analyze the relationship between queer politics and US empire both in the United States and in the Filipina/o diaspora. To put it more simply, *The Global Filipina Body* queers our analyses of US empire and Filipina/o diasporic nationalisms. In doing so, my goal is both to claim the necessity of popular nationalisms for anti-imperialist social movements and to argue for a queer and feminist critique of the heteropatriarchy of the nation even as we write, think, and organize in its name.

While nationalism is a slippery formation, one that must be teased out, delineated, and made to work in specific ways—from the Filipina/o American cultural nationalism embodied in Pilipino Cultural Nights, to the state nationalism of Philippine state discourses of "national heroes," to the respectability politics that impugn the figure of the mail-order bride—this project maps the gendered and sexual articulations of Philippine, Filipina/o American, and Filipina/o diasporic nationalism that intersect in the figure of the global Filipina body. The figure of the exploited global Filipina body is positioned as the opposite of the privileged Filipina/o American *balikbayan* within both Philippine popular discourse and the Filipina/o American context.[16] The tension between the figure of the exploited global Filipina body and the privileged Filipina/o American *balikbayan* embodies the larger conundrum at the heart of this project: the relationship between primarily US and Global North–based articulations of feminism and queer politics that critique the heteropatriarchy of the nation as vehicle for social movements and the centrality of nationalism to anti-imperialist and anticolonial movements in the Global South.

The figure of the Filipina trafficked woman / sex worker as a sign of the failure of the heteropatriarchal Philippine nation has galvanized both transnational feminist and Filipina/o diasporic nationalist discourse. Often conflated with each other within the dominant discourse of the "traffic in women," the Filipina trafficked woman and sex worker are figures that suggest the risky politics of representation within Filipina/o American cultural production. Within this discourse, the Filipina trafficked woman / sex worker embodies the inability of the heteropatriarchal nation to maintain its borders given its reliance on transnational labor migration. The dichotomous figures of the Filipina/o American *balikbayan* and the Filipina trafficked woman / sex worker index a broader discursive struggle over the meaning of the global Filipina body, who embodies the contemporary crisis of the Philippine nation under capitalist globalization as well as the subjugation of the Philippine nation as an American tropic.

While hegemonic representations of the global Filipina body often reproduce the heteropatriarchy of the nation, queer reworkings of this figure can unsettle the gendered and sexual politics of Filipina/o state and popular nationalisms. In response to the notion of the "fallen woman" representation of mail-order brides, M.O.B.'s campy performance of the Filipina mail-order bride not only critiques the cultural nationalist discourses in which Filipina women stand in for the broader community but also puts this figure in conversation with the politics of gay marriage. The Filipina mail-order bride is reconfigured outside of the heteropatriarchal politics of respectability, which position her as a fallen figure for the nation. Simultaneously, Mail Order Brides / M.O.B. *queer* the figure of the mail-order bride by juxtaposing the "marriage equality" discourse with issues of racialized migration and gendered labor. The queered figure of the Filipina mail-order bride presents an implicit critique of the homonationalism of mainstream LGBT efforts to centralize gay marriage as a key political issue. *Always a Bridesmaid, Never a Bride*'s queer mail-order bride is equally a critique of the conservative, heteropatriarchal nature of Filipina/o American cultural nationalism, as she is a figure that points to the excess of implicitly white forms of homonationalism, those who cannot be folded into the national body—queer people of color, queer migrants, and working-class queers.

The queer global Filipina body, embodied in the cyborg, offers an alternative figure for imagining a queer Filipina/o diaspora. Much of queer of color studies and queer globalization studies has critiqued the ways in which the nation and nationalism(s) reproduce conservative notions of gender and sexuality, often linking heteronormative notions of the family to the future of the nation.[17] In contrast, the queering of the global Filipina body suggests an engagement with nationalism that holds on to the political potential of nationalism(s) as a liberatory, anti-imperialist form of struggle while acknowledging that the nation must be reimagined beyond its heteropatriarchal origins. Thus, the final figure of this book, the cyborg, exists not in the colonial past nor under the crushing weight of neoliberal globalization that overdetermines the material conditions of the present but in a future whose contours are shaped by desire and imagination.[18] To return to the surrealists, we must harness the power of the imagination to envision a future that seems impossible in the present.[19] *The Global Filipina Body* offers glimpses into this future through alternative figures of the Filipina/o diaspora: Joey, the queer *balikbayan* who critiques the heteronormativity of Filipina/o American cultural nationalism, even as he sees himself as part of a diasporic Filipina/o nationalist youth movement; and the queer Filipina mail-order bride, who exists not as a sign of the sexual subjection of Filipina women but instead as a figure that challenges a mainstream LGBT movement to address its failure to incorporate issues of racialized migration and labor. The reconfiguration of the global Filipina body involves a queering of multiple narratives: the queering of the nation in the context of the diaspora, as well as the reconfiguration of mainstream LGBT politics to imagine a future rooted in anti-imperialist and anticapitalist struggle. These glimpses of alternative configurations of transnational belonging offer a hope for a queer diaspora, one in which the global Filipina body can exceed the narrative of woman-as-nation. The cyborg challenges the discursive construction of the global Filipina body as the embodiment of Philippine sexual and domestic labor.

If the cyborg represents the queer utopian hope for the future, then the Pulse massacre is a chilling reminder of the forms of queer and trans death that haunt the political landscape of the present. The Pulse massacre reminds us that the queer necropolitics of the present have been enabled by the afterlife of US empire, whether manifest in the disastrous impacts of Hurricane Maria on Puerto Rico or the ongoing US military presence in the Philippines in the name of the War on Terror. The Pulse massacre highlights the necessity of critiques of US empire within queer politics, linking homophobic and transphobic violence to the legacies of economic violence in the American tropics. Inversely, the murder of Filipina trans woman Jennifer Laude highlights the intersection of queer and trans organizing with Filipina/o diasporic anti-imperialist politics, making clear the need for an explicitly queer and trans approach to resisting ongoing forms of US empire in the Philippines.

I return to the figure of Jennifer Laude, whom I first discussed in the intro-duction, to reiterate the broader political stakes and contexts in which a queer Filipina/o diaspora is imagined. The 2014 death of Jennifer Laude, a transgender Filipina woman, at the hands of US Marine Joseph Scott Pemberton is a chilling example of the effects of the ongoing presence of US military in the Philippines, a legacy of both US colonization and the ongoing forms of neoimperialism that persist during the seemingly endless War on Terror.[20] Jennifer Laude's death reflects the gendered violence that accompanies the US military presence in the Philippines, which has increased since the beginning of the War on Terror in 2001.

Yet the murder of Jennifer Laude also signals the emergence of an explicitly *queer and trans* mode of Filipina/o American political organizing that links US imperialist violence to homophobia and transphobia. The protests that emerged in New York City in response to the death of Laude suggest the adoption of an anti-imperialist lens within the work of US-based LGBT organizations, the Audre Lorde Project and the New York City Anti-Violence Project.[21] If Laude's murder is a reminder of the forms of queer and trans death that accompany US militarism—despite a post–Don't Ask Don't Tell era that has attempted to fold transgender subjects into US homonationalism—then the organizing in response to her death points to the need for a different political and intellectual trajectory.[22] The protests organized jointly between Filipina/o American anti-imperialist organizations such as BAYAN and broad-based LGBT organizations such as the Anti-Violence Project embody the "coalitional moment" that a queer Filipina/o diasporic framework makes possible.[23] Karma Chávez describes a "coalitional moment" as a moment in which "political issues coincide or merge in the public sphere in ways that create space to reenvision or potentially recon-struct rhetorical imaginaries." She notes that the concept of coalition "connotes tension and precariousness, but is not necessarily temporary. . . . [I]t requires constant work if it is to endure." Thus, the queer anti-imperialist coalitional moment that emerged in response to Jennifer Laude's death marks a moment of possibility, a queer temporality, in which the future hope of a queer diaspora begins to take material shape in the present.[24]

This coalitional moment points to the intersection of transnational feminist critiques of the gendered violence inherent to US militarism and imperialism with a specifically queer and trans analysis of the forms of social and literal death enacted by the state on queer, trans, and gender-nonconforming subjects. Filipina American feminist scholars Robyn Rodriguez and Vernadette Gonza-lez discuss the continuity between contemporary representations of Filipina bodies and the long histories of gendered and sexual violence against Filipina women in the context of US imperialism and militarism.[25] Within queer and trans studies, Eric Stanley and Nat Smith describe the ways in which the state, in particular, the prison-industrial complex, both regulates gender and enacts violence on queer and trans bodies: "Among the most volatile points of contact between state violence and one's body is the domain of gender."[26] In the coalitional moment inaugurated by the protests in response to Jennifer Laude's death, critiques of queer and trans death in the face of state violence intersect with anti-imperialist feminist critiques of gendered violence. In this queer union, queers engage with anti-imperialist nationalism, and anti-imperialists ground their work in critiques of anti-queer and anti-trans violence. It is this convergence that gives me hope for a different future. I end with this example to foreground the dire need for an anti-imperialist framework within US-based queer organizing (including queer-of-color organizations), given the violence of neoliberal capitalism and the endless War on Terror. Inversely, a specifically queer and trans analysis is crucial to articulations of anti-imperialist diasporic nationalism in the Filipina/o diaspora. The coalitional political moment of the present points to a future trajectory for both Filipina/o American politics and Filipina/o American studies more broadly. If the cyborg embodies a potentiality for a queer utopia that is not-yet-there, then the Pulse shooting and the murder of Jennifer Laude point to the queer necropolitics of the present, corporealized through queer and trans death in the afterlife of US empire. The coalitional response to Laude's death from both LGBT and Filipina/o American communities exemplifies the intersectional queer and feminist anti-imperialism—one that links transnational feminist critiques of gendered and sexual labor with an analysis of queer and trans necropolitics—that we need today. The time for the future is now.

Notes

Introduction

1. Baron, "List." I use the popular term "mail-order bride" to refer to women from the Global South who use online matchmaking websites to meet potential husbands. However, in doing so, I recognize the implicitly derogatory nature of such a term. I call attention to the problematic nature of global discourses about Filipina brides.

2. See Philippine Overseas Employment Administration, http://www.poea.gov.ph /ofwstat/stockest/2009.pdf. As of 2009, the population of the Philippines was approximately ninety-one million. For an excellent discussion of the role of the Philippine state in the brokering of Filipino migrant laborers, see Rodriguez, *Migrants for Export*. See also Guevarra's study of the cultural logic of labor brokering in the Philippines in *Marketing Dreams*.

3. Ackerman, *Frasier*.

4. Elliott, *The Adventures of Priscilla, Queen of the Desert*; Nobile, *Closer to Home*. For a discussion of the representation of Filipina bodies on the internet, see Gonzalez and Rodriguez, "Filipina.com." For a discussion of the representation of transnational Filipina bodies, see Tolentino, "Bodies, Letters, Catalogs."

5. Tolentino, "Bodies, Letters, Catalogs."

6. The term "overseas contract worker" (OCW) is popularly used in the Philippines and throughout its diaspora to refer to Filipina/o migrant workers who work abroad on temporary contracts. OCW is often used interchangeably with the term "overseas Filipino worker" (OFW).

7. The term *balikbayan* combines the word *balik* (to return) with the word *bayan* (nation) to describe Filipina/os from the Global North (often the United States, Canada, and Australia) who return to the Philippines. In chapter 4 of this book, I draw on Haraway's foundational essay, "A Cyborg Manifesto," in my analysis of the science fictional video and performance art piece *Cosmic Blood*, by the Filipina and Colombian American artist Gigi Otálvaro-Hormillosa. I argue that the cyborg is a utopian figure for queer forms of diaspora beyond the heteronormativity and masculinism of the nation.

8. Shahani, "Human Trafficking."

9. Morel, *Taken*. The plot of the film *Taken*, starring Liam Neeson, revolves around the abduction of Neeson's character's daughter by a sex trafficking group. For more information on Soroptomists International's anti–sex trafficking campaign, see http://www.soroptimist.org/stoptrafficking.html.

10. Morel, *Taken*.

11. Focusing on the figure of the global Filipina body as it emerges in Filipina/o American cultural production during the first two decades of the twenty-first century, this project builds on scholarship investigating how the Filipina has been constructed as a transnational sign of the nation during earlier historical periods, such as Denise Cruz's analysis of the figure of the transpacific Filipina within Philippine and US literature and popular culture from the early to the mid-twentieth century. See Cruz, *Transpacific Femininities*.

12. Rodriguez, *Migrants for Export*; Guevarra, *Marketing Dreams*.

13. Hau, *On the Subject*; Tadiar, *Fantasy-Production*; Tolentino, "Bodies, Letters, Catalogs."

14. Tadiar discusses the relationship between the "selling of women" and the selling of national sovereignty in Philippine nationalism. See Tadiar, *Things Fall Away*, 72.

15. Ibid., 26.

16. I use the term "heteropatriarchy of the nation" to refer to the ways in which the nation as both a mode of belonging and an organizing principle for the state tends to reproduce and enforce heteronormative and patriarchal norms of gender, sexuality, and family.

17. Although Ferguson uses the term "drag queen" in his discussion of a feminine sex worker character in Marlon Riggs's film *Tongues Untied*, I put this term in quotes to make clear the indeterminacy of such a gender description. I do so in order to hold open the possibility that the gender identification of this character in the film is actually unclear. This character could identify as a transgender woman or another gender. Ferguson, *Aberrations in Black*, 9; Riggs, *Tongues Untied*.

18. Tadlar, *Things Fall Away*, 25.

19. See Quintos, *Anak*; Parreñas, *Children of Global Migration*.

20. At various moments throughout this text, I use the term "queer" as a verb to indicate the methodology of "queering" as a form of disrupting heteropatriarchal norms; at other time, I use "queer" as a noun. I also use "queer" as an adjective to

indicate a form of subjectivity based on a departure from this same heteropatriarchy. I often distinguish between "queer" as a critique of fixed categories of identity and "LGBT," which cements these various categories. However, within popular discourse, these terms are often used interchangeably. The slippage between these two terms is at times reproduced within this text, largely because, given the existing state of the nonprofit-industrial complex that dominates queer politics and the way in which the mainstream LGBT movement has co-opted the term "queer," the distinction between the terms has become, at times, indistinguishable.

21. Gayatri Gopinath argues that the diaspora has the potential to queer (or destabilize) the nation, as well as the possibility of reifying conservative forms of nationalism. See Gopinath, *Impossible Desires.*

22. In 1898 the United States took possession of the Philippines, despite fierce opposition from Filipinos. The ensuing Philippine American War (1899–1902) resulted in the death of over a million Filipinos, the destruction of the nationalist forces, and the US territorial annexation of the Philippines, ostensibly to prepare the Philippines for eventual independence. Waves of Filipino migration to the United States in the 1920s and 1970s established large Filipino American communities in the United States. From the 1920s through the present, Filipino migration to the United States has increased exponentially. The US Navy has been one of the main mechanisms through which Filipinos migrated to the United States due to the former recruitment of Filipinos into the US Navy, as well as the stipulation that allowed Filipinos into the navy. The 1965 Immigration Act ended national-origins quotas and permitted entry into the United States based on family reunification and occupational characteristics, which increased the number of Filipino migrants to the United States. See Espiritu, *Home Bound*, 25.

23. For critiques of the heteronormativity of the nation within queer studies, see Alexander, "Not Just (Any) Body"; Eng, *Racial Castration*; Ferguson, *Aberrations in Black.*

24. Clifford, *Routes*, 251.

25. Alexander, "Not Just (Any) Body"; Eng, *Racial Castration*; Ferguson, *Aberrations in Black.*

26. Gopinath, *Impossible Desires*, 11.

27. Ibid., 11.

28. For a discussion of the differences between anticolonial and anti-imperialist nationalisms in the Philippines and imperialist forms of nationalism in the Global North, see chapter 1 of this book.

29. The Philippine government admits to killing at least 4,854 people as of August 31, 2018. Gabriel Pabico Lalu, "Over 400 Killed in a Month in Drug War," *Philippine Daily Inquirer*, September 26, 2018, https://newsinfo.inquirer.net /1036460/drug-war-death-toll-now-at-4854-govt?utm_expid=.XqNwTug2W6nw DVUSgFJXed.1. According to independent sources such as the International People's Tribunal, this number is closer to 23,000. Azadeh Shahshahani, "The Philippine President Is Waging a Ruthless War on Drugs—and the U.S. Is Complicit,"

In These Times, October 2, 2018, http://inthesetimes.com/article/21500/peoples -tribunal-philippines-rodrigo-duterte-drug-war-executions-repression.

30. Shahshahani, "The Philippine President."

31. Within the territorial confines of the Philippines, the National Democratic movement is one prominent example of popular nationalism. The National Democratic Front (NDF) is connected to local, national, and international organizations. Since the early 1970s, the National Democratic movement has been one of the most consistent and vocal critics of US imperialism and capitalist globalization. As a mass movement, the NDF functions through a multitude of organizations geared toward improving the welfare of various populations, including peasants, workers, women, and youth. The NDF calls for a societal revolution as the solution for the poverty and dispossession that are the result of what the NDF critiques as a semifeudal and neocolonial system. See National Democratic Front of the Philippines, http://www.ndfp.net/web2014/.

32. While I focus primarily on the work of queer Filipina/o American studies, including the work of Martin Manalansan, Allan Punzalan Isaac, Kale Bantigue Fajardo, Robert Diaz, Victor Mendoza, and Joseph Ponce, I also recognize the substantial work within gay and lesbian studies in the Philippines, including the work of J. Neil Garcia and Danton Remoto. See Diaz, "The Limits"; Fajardo, *Filipino Crosscurrents*; Garcia, *Philippine Gay Culture* and *Slip/Pages*; Garcia and Remoto, *Ladlad*; Isaac, *American Tropics*; Manalansan, *Global Divas*; Mendoza, *Metroimperial Intimacies*; Ponce, *Beyond the Nation*.

33. See Chang, *Disposable Domestics*; Guevarra, *Marketing Dreams*; Lowe, *Immigrant Acts*; Mohanty, "Women Workers"; Parreñas, *Servants of Globalization*; Rodriguez, *Migrants for Export*; Tadiar, *Fantasy Production*.

34. Mohanty, "Women Workers."

35. Feminist scholars Doezema, Kempadoo, and Chapkis argue that sex work is a legitimate form of labor. Doezema and Kempadoo argue that migrant sex work, which is often collapsed within the "traffic in women" discourse, is a legitimate form of labor that should come with rights and protections. Anti–sex work feminists, such as Kathleen Barry, argue that all forms of sex work constitute violence against women. See Barry, *The Prostitution*; Chapkis, *Live Sex Acts*; Doezma, "Forced to Choose"; Kempadoo, "Women of Color."

36. As Soto has noted, transnational feminisms also builds on the intellectual legacy of women of color feminisms, particularly foundational scholars such as Moraga and Anzaldúa. See Anzaldúa and Moraga, *This Bridge*; Soto, "Where in the Transnational World?"

37. The scholarship on gender, sexuality, and nationalism is far too expansive to cite. However, several theorists have influenced my thinking, from Visweswaran's work on feminist ethnography and Indian nationalism, to Enloe's work on feminist participation in nationalism. Several key texts have shaped this project, including *Nationalisms and Sexualities*, edited by Parker, Russo, Sommer, and Yaeger, and *Between Woman and Nation*, edited by Kaplan, Alarcon, and Moallen. See Aguilar, *Toward a Nationalist*

Feminism; Enloe, *Bananas, Beaches, and Bases*; Kaplan, Alarcon, and Moallen, *Between Woman and Nation*; Parker et al., *Nationalisms and Sexualities*; Visweswaran, *Fictions*.

38. Aguilar argues that nationalism is a prerequisite for achieving feminist political goals, as the nation must first be liberated from ongoing forms of US imperialism before feminist equality can be achieved. See Aguilar, *Toward a Nationalist Feminism*.

39. Campomanes, "The New Nation's"; Fajardo, *Filipino Crosscurrents*; Isaac, *American Tropics*; Balce, "The Filipina's Breast"; Rafael, *White Love*; Rodriguez, *Suspended Apocalypse*; Rodriguez, *Migrants for Export*; See, *The Decolonized Eye*; Tadiar, *Fantasy-Production*.

40. Chuh, *Imagine Otherwise*, 34.

41. San Juan, *After Postcolonialism*, 13.

42. Campomanes, "The New Nation's," 8.

43. Rodriguez, "A Million Deaths?," 148.

44. Much of Filipina/o American studies scholarship foregrounds US imperialism (including the institution of the US military) as a key analytical framework. The following list offers just a few examples of such scholarship: Balce, *Body Parts*; Gonzalez, *Securing Paradise*; See, *The Decolonized Eye*; Villegas, "Currents of Militarization."

45. Mariano, "Doing Good"; Viola, "Toward a Filipino"; Tungohan, "The Transformative"; Hanna, "A Call for Healing."

46. One could argue that the sites of cultural production that I examine—performance, film/video, websites, and heritage language programs—make up a repertoire, and not only an archive, of US empire's lasting effects on Filipina/o American culture. Thus, US empire constitutes Filipina/o America not only through the archive but also through the momentary and bodily nature of the performative. Theodore Gonzalves draws on the work of performance theorist Diana Taylor to argue for not only an archive but also a repertoire of Filipina/o American performance. On the relationship between US empire and Filipina/o American performance, see Burns, *Puro Arte*; Gonzalves, *The Day*; See, *The Decolonized Eye*.

47. I discuss the film *Sin City Diary* and GABRIELA Network (now AF3IRM) at length in chapter 2. Members of GABRIELA Network, a US-based Filipina American feminist organization, describe it as a "transnational feminist organization." AF3IRM, www.af3irm.org.

48. "Domestic helper" is a term used to refer to Filipinas/os who provide a variety of domestic labor, from childcare and eldercare to cleaning and cooking.

49. The discourse of overseas migrant workers as "heroes for the nation" has been used by the Philippine state since the 1980s to legitimize the Philippine economy's reliance on remittances. Maglipon, "DH in HK," as cited in Rafael, *White Love*, 211.

50. See my analysis of the figure of the Filipina mail-order bride in chapter 3.

51. I build on other ethnographic studies of diasporic Filipina/o subjectivity such as Manalansan, *Global Divas*, and Vergara, *Pinoy Capital*.

52. Hall, *New Ethnicities*, as cited in Louie, *Chineseness across Borders*, 9.

53. Kaplan and Grewal, "Transnational," 358.

54. Ibid., 352.

55. See the discussion of a "loving" critique in Velasco, "Negotiating Legacies." A "loving" critique is articulated from the position of solidarity, sharing similar political investments with the object of critique.

56. Naber, *Arab America.*

57. Pante, "Kentex Factory."

58. "Action and Rally in Response to the Killing of Jennifer Laude," Facebook, https://www.facebook.com/events/349241425253980/.

Chapter 1. Mapping Diasporic Nationalisms

1. Intramuros, the original walled city of Manila, was built during the time of Spanish colonialism. Intramuros was heavily damaged during World War II and was rebuilt in 1951 after it was declared a national monument.

2. Tagalog on Site was affiliated with the University of California's Education Abroad Program during the summer of 2003.

3. Heritage language programs, or Balik-Aral (back to study) programs, offer courses in Filipina/o language, history, and culture, as well as "immersion" or "exposure trips," to Filipina/o American youth. S. Lily Mendoza coined the term "Balik-Aral" to describe heritage language programs for Filipina/o Americans. See Mendoza, "A Different Breed." The term "exposure trip" has its origin in the ongoing practice of "exposing" nationalist youth and students to the conditions of poverty and dispossession in the Philippine countryside.

4. For a discussion of nationalism among Filipina/o Americans, see Vergara, *Pinoy Capital*. Also, see Louie's ethnographic study of heritage travel programs for Chinese Americans in mainland China in *Chineseness across Borders*.

5. While official Philippine state discourse defines a *balikbayan* as someone who was born in the Philippines, immigrated to another country (usually in the Global North, possibly obtaining a different national citizenship), then returned "home," popular use of the term may or may not include Filipina/o Americans. More often, this term refers to Filipina/os within two categories: (1) those who have permanently settled outside of the Philippines, often in the United States, Canada, or western Europe; and (2) overseas contract workers, migrant workers who have left the Philippines temporarily to earn money abroad. There are significant differences in socioeconomic class, cultural capital, and transnational mobility between the two groups. However, for the purposes of this study, I use the term *balikbayan* to refer to Filipina/o American youth, whether born in the United States or in the Philippines.

6. Mendoza, "A Different Breed," 200.

7. Rafael, *White Love*, 208.

8. Leah, interview, August 1, 2006.

9. According to Rafael, "The Thomasites were the first group of U.S. schoolteachers who arrived in the Philippines at the beginning of this century and who figure in

nationalist narrative not as benevolent instructors but as purveyors of the miseducation of the Filipina/o" (*White Love*, 208).

10. Pido, "Balikbayan Paranoia."

11. Ibid.

12. Ibid.

13. Diaz, "Failed Returns," 338.

14. Ibid., 5.

15. Hau, *On the Subject*, 193.

16. Ibid.

17. Jeremy, interview, August 14, 2006.

18. There are multiple examples of the trope of returning/finding home within contemporary Filipina/o American and Filipina/o Canadian cultural production. The theater/movement piece *Pagbabalik* (Return), by Aimee Suzara, a performer, poet, and cultural activist based in the San Francisco Bay Area, explores the theme of return. The play follows the spiritual journey of the main character, Diwata, to the Philippines after growing up in the United States. The Filipina/o Canadian horror film *Ang pamana* (The inheritance, Romeo Candido, 2006) tells the story of two Filipina/o Canadians who visit a haunted house in a rural Philippine province that they have inherited from their Filipina grandmother. During their visit to the Philippines, they come to terms with both their cultural heritage and the spirits of the past. The short experimental documentary *Balikbayan Confessions* (2006), directed by Tina Bartolome, documents the journey of a group of queer Filipina Americans to an international lesbian and gay conference in the Philippines. The film weaves together reflections on sexuality, gender, and race with the experiences of Filipina Americans visiting the Philippines for the first time. The trope of visiting/returning to the Philippines is also a common theme of Pilipino Cultural Nights / Pilipino Cultural Celebrations at universities across the United States.

19. Exposure trips include visits with social movement organizations meant to educate and politicize Filipino Americans. For more on Philippine exposure trips, see Viola, "Toward a Filipino Critical Pedagogy."

20. Philippine Forum, http://www.philippineforum.org/.

21. "Philippine Studies Program," http://www.philippinestudies.org.

22. National Democratic Front of the Philippines, http://www.ndfp.net/web2014/.

23. For example, in past years, students were matched with a political organization such as Anakbayan or GABRIELA in order to facilitate their interest in working with Philippine political movements. Faculty also mentioned that in past years, the speakers came from political organizing backgrounds rather than academic institutions.

24. The University of California's Education Abroad Program in the Philippines was suspended in 2006 due to the US State Department's March 23, 2006, travel advisory against Americans traveling in the Philippines. See the article posted on the website of the UCLA International Institute, http://www.international.ucla.edu/article.asp?parentid=32406, and the current US State Department's advisory against

travel to the Philippines (posted on April 27, 2007) at http://travel.state.gov/travel/cis_pa_tw/tw/tw_2190.html.

25. Bea, interview, August 15, 2006.

26. Ibid.

27. Ibid.

28. Trina, interview, August 15, 2006.

29. Rico, interview, August 16, 2006.

30. See "World Report 2013: Philippines," Human Rights Watch, http://www.hrw.org/world-report/2013/country-chapters/philippines.

31. Ibid.

32. Retired Maj. Gen. Jovito Palparan was found guilty of the kidnapping and illegal detention of Sherlyn Cadapan and Karen Empeño. In 2018, he was sentenced to forty years in prison. Lian Buan, "Jovito Palparan Found Guilty," Rappler, September 17, 2018, https://www.rappler.com/nation/212145-bulacan-court-judgment-kidnapping-illegal-detention-cases-vs-jovito-palparan-september-17-2018.

33. Toribio, "We Are Revolution," 157.

34. Ibid., 158.

35. Ibid., 170.

36. Choy, "Towards Trans-Pacific Social Justice."

37. BAYAN USA is the first and largest international chapter of the Philippine mass organization BAYAN, which coordinates the National Democratic movement in the Philippines. BAYAN USA is an alliance of twenty-six Filipina/o American organizations. See BAYAN USA (Bagong Alyansang Makabayan / New Patriotic Alliance), http://www.bayanusa.org/index.php. Anakbayan is a nationalist youth organization that works to support the National Democratic movement in the Philippines. Anakbayan has chapters in various cities in the Philippines, as well as in the United States (San Francisco, East Bay, Seattle, Los Angeles, Honolulu). "Anakbayan," http://www.anakbayan.org/.

38. See Ileto, *Filipina/os and Their Revolution*. He discusses the two main Marxist critiques of "statist" approaches to Philippine history: (1) Constantino and Constantino, through their text *The Philippines: A Past Revisited*; and (2) the NDF, through Guerrero, *Philippine Society and Revolution*. Both texts argue against the "great hero" narrative of national history, emphasizing the social and economic conditions that have led to the development of a national consciousness.

39. I focus on Joshua not to demonize this individual student but because Joshua's sentiments represent the masculinism and heteronormativity that are common within diasporic nationalist discourse.

40. See Ileto, *Filipinos and Their Revolution*, 185. In his discussion of the anti-Marcos movements of the 1960s, Ileto discusses the "rediscovery" of Andres Bonifacio by Filipina/o nationalist historians such as Teodoro Agoncillo and Renato Constantino. In a context in which student movements and radical nationalist movements were gaining more popular support, a break in popular historical consciousness occurred. For Ileto, "this 'break' consisted of the displacement of the 'reformist Rizal' (a construct

of the church/state establishment) by the 'revolutionary Bonifacio' (a construct of labor / peasant labor movements and the radical left)" (ibid., 189). Within this discourse, Bonifacio serves as a symbol of the revolutionary struggle of the common people, while Rizal represents the reformism of the elite class.

41. Anakbayan Seattle, www.anakbayan.org.

42. Tolentino, "Bodies, Letters, Catalogs," describes the figure of the global Filipina body, particularly the Filipina mail-order bride, as a *geobody* for the Philippine nation. As such, the global Filipina body stands in for the Philippine nation itself.

43. Lisa, interview, August 25, 2006.

44. The New People's Army is the armed wing of the Communist Party of the Philippines.

45. Tadiar discusses the "gender trouble" of the Philippine nation as a feminized provider of devalued sexual and domestic labor within a global capitalist economy. Tadiar, *Fantasy-Production*, 23.

46. I use the pronouns "he" and "him" in reference to the Filipina/o *balikbayan* not to suggest that all *balikbayans* are male-identified but rather to emphasize how the dominant discursive framework of *balikbayans* within forms of diasporic nationalisms can assume a masculinist perspective.

47. Tadiar discusses the racializing discourses through which corporeal difference is made legible on Filipina bodies within a context of global capitalism. Here racial and gender difference becomes the basis for determining which bodies are considered human. Tadiar describes Filipina domestic helpers as "bodies without subjectivity; that is, corporeal objects at the mercy and for the pleasure of those who buy them from the recruitment agency" (*Fantasy-Production*, 104).

48. Isaac describes "imperial remainder or ghosts" as the "persistent but constitutive elements [of an imperial history] that are incorporated, however uncomfortably, into Filipino *and* Filipino American narratives. This uneasy incorporation shapes the lives and imagination of American postcolonial subjects" (*American Tropics*, 12).

49. Tadiar, *Fantasy-Production*, 104.

50. Lloyd, "Nationalisms," 174.

51. Smith, "Queer Theory."

52. Aguilar, *Toward a Nationalist Feminism*, 67.

53. Hau, *On the Subject*, 168.

54. Bea, interview, August 15, 2006.

55. Rico, interview, August 16, 2006.

56. Rafael describes the discourse about OCWs as "national heroes" by both the Aquino and Ramos administrations in *White Love*. President Cory Aquino introduced the term when addressing a group of domestic helpers in Hong Kong in 1998 by telling them, "Kayo po ang mga bagong bayani" (You are the new heroes). Maglipon, "DH in HK," as cited in Rafael, *White Love*, 211. After the execution of Filipina domestic helper Flor Contemplacion by the Singaporean state in 1995, President Ramos described Contemplacion's death as the beginning "of our own soul searching. . . . We have been reborn as a *national family*, mindful of our obligations to take care for

one another, especially for those without the means to sustain or protect themselves" (Rafael, *White Love*, 215, emphasis mine).

57. Rico, interview, August 16, 2006.

58. Cheah, "Introduction Part II," 36.

59. Bea, interview, August 15, 2006.

60. Anderson, "Exodus," 315.

61. I emphasize the invocation of historical movements such as the Katipunan within a state-dominated discourse of nationalism. I do not intend to imply that the Katipuneros themselves were engaged in a project of nation-building but rather that individual figures of the Katipunan and the movement itself are invoked within popular discourses of nationalism in the contemporary Philippines. For example, the existence of Katipunan Avenue near the UP Diliman campus is evidence of such a discourse.

62. Eng, *Racial Castration*, 209.

63. Jennifer, interview, August 25, 2006.

64. Victor, interview, August 8, 2006.

65. Ibid.

66. Rodriguez, *Suspended Apocalypse*, 35, 79.

67. As several Filipina/o American studies and Philippine studies scholars have noted, the very notion of a Filipina/o American ethnic identity relies on the erasure of US imperialism as its constitutive historical condition of possibility. Arguing against the dominant narrative of immigration and assimilation within Asian American studies, scholars such as Campomanes, Rodriguez, and Isaac emphasize instead the violent quasi incorporation of Filipina/os into the US national body through the invasion and occupation of the Philippine nation.

68. Rodriguez, *Suspended Apocalypse*, 146.

69. Isaac, *American Tropics*, 7.

70. Berlant and Freeman, "Queer Nationality"; Duggan, "Making It Perfectly Queer."

71. Queer of color theorists Roderick Ferguson, Jacqui Alexander, and David Eng have critiqued the heteronormativity and masculinism of state and cultural nationalisms. In contrast, queer Native studies scholars have argued that critiques of the nation do not address the ongoing colonial status of Native peoples, particularly in the United States. See Alexander, "Not Just"; Eng, *Racial Castration*; Ferguson, *Aberrations in Black*; Smith, "Queer Theory," 59–61.

72. Puar, *Terrorist Assemblages*; Haritaworn, "Loyal Repetitions."

73. One notable exception is Karen Buenavista Hanna's analysis of homophobia and transphobia in relation to Filipina/o nationalism in a Filipina/o American activist organization. See Hanna, "A Call for Healing."

74. In the Filipina/o American context, few examples of cultural production present critiques of Philippine nationalist movements. One exception was a vignette I watched as part of *The Bakla Show*, a performance at the Filipina/o American theater space Bindlestiff Studio in San Francisco. Written by Lolan Sevilla and Aimee Espiritu, the

skit described the love found between two women involved with a Filipina/o American nationalist youth organization. The skit presents a critique of the heteronormativity and implicit homophobia of the culture of Filipina/o American nationalist youth organizations. *Bakla* is a Tagalog word that, although not analogous to "gay," is often used to describe trans women and gay men in the Philippines. *Tomboy* is a term used to describe masculine-presenting, female-assigned people in the Philippines. Kale Fajardo in "Transportation" argues that *tomboy* is not a synonym for "lesbian"; instead, *tomboy* refers to a specifically working-class masculine identity that is more similar to a transgender male identity.

75. Joey, interview, July 25, 2006.

76. Joey's self-description vacillated between the terms "gay" and "queer" throughout the course of our discussion.

77. Many PCNs revolve around two major narrative themes: (1) the process through which the Filipino American "finds" his or her cultural/ethnic identity; and (2) the framework of heterosexual romantic love. Theodore Gonzalves in "'The Show Must Go On'" describes how the narrative structure of the Pilipino Cultural Night / Pilipino Cultural Celebration is often focused on a Filipino American student's search for her or his identity.

78. Joey, interview, July 25, 2006.

79. Ibid.

80. Ibid.

81. Queer of color and multiracial political organizations such as FIERCE, (the former) Queers for Economic Justice, the Audre Lorde Project, the Sylvia Rivera Law Project, and SUSPECT integrate economic and racial justice issues into their political campaigns. For example, Queers for Economic Justice's welfare rights campaign, Welfare Warriors, "organizes low-income LGBT people on public assistance to fight for a more humane, just and inclusive welfare system" (Queers for Economic Justice, http://q4ej.org/). Welfare rights campaigns inherently address the politics of racialized and gendered labor, particularly domestic and affective labor, in relation to the neoliberal state. See also SUSPECT, http://nohomonationalism.blogspot.com/; Audre Lorde Project, http://alp.org/; FIERCE, http://www.fiercenyc.org/; Sylvia Rivera Law Project, http://srlp.org/.

82. In 2015, Sgt. Shane Ortega, a trans man of color, was featured in several news articles calling attention to the ban on transgender soldiers in the US military. Eilperin, "Transgender in the Military."

83. Lloyd, "Nationalisms."

84. Robert Diaz notes how the male *balikbayan* in particular embodies heteronormative notions of familial responsibility, economic security, and respectability. Diaz, "Failed Returns," 339.

85. Ibid., 7.

86. Manalansan, "Wayward Erotics," 34.

87. Ibid., 46.

Chapter 2. Imagining the Filipina Trafficked Woman / Sex Worker

1. Velasco, "Negotiating Legacies." See my expanded analysis of the traffic in women debate within Filipina/o American feminisms in this essay.

2. For a discussion of how the Philippine state brokers outward labor migration, see Rodriguez, *Migrants for Export*.

3. St. John's International Women's Film Festival, https://www.womensfilmfestival.com/filmarchive/14/1993-films; BakitWhy, http://bakitwhy.com/articles/sin-city-diary-film-screening-tonight; Bonnie McElhinny, CKA Event: Transnational Domesticity Film Series, Women and Gender Studies Institute, University of Toronto *Matters* newsletter, Spring 2008, https://wgsi.utoronto.ca/wp-content/uploads/2010/09/Volume-6-Issue-1-Spring-2008.pdf.

4. The term "Amerasian" refers to the mixed-race children of Filipina women and US servicemen.

5. Gonzalves, "The Show Must Go On."

6. Maglipon, "DH in HK," as cited in Rafael, *White Love*, 211.

7. Flores, "The Dissemination," 92.

8. Ibid., 82.

9. Hau, *On the Subject*, 231.

10. Rafael, *White Love*, 213.

11. Soriano, *Kung Saan Ako Pupunta*, 1, cited in Hau, *On the Subject*, 231.

12. Hau, *On the Subject*, 231.

13. Guevarra (*Marketing Dreams, Manufacturing Heroes*) and Rodriguez (*Migrants for Export*) discuss the role of the Philippine state in brokering overseas labor migration. In particular, they analyze the role of the state in producing a "cultural logic of migration" that emphasizes the gendered, affective qualities of Filipina/o workers such as "care" or "warmth."

14. Raymundo, "In the Womb," 6.

15. Ibid., 3.

16. Doezema, "Ouch!"

17. Ibid.

18. Kempadoo argues that the global sex trade cannot be reduced to a discourse of the traffic in women, which elides the complex histories of colonialism and imperialism in the Global South, as well as the "local cultural histories and traditions which shape the sexual agency of women" ("Women of Color," 28).

19. Ferguson, *Aberrations in Black*, 9. See my discussion of Ferguson's analysis of the sex worker of color as the Other of the heteronormative nation under capitalism in the introduction to this book. In particular, Ferguson's analysis is useful for theorizing the position of the Filipina sex worker in relation to the Philippine nation, given the transnational labor migration made necessary by neoliberal capitalism.

20. AF3IRM, http://www.af3irm.org/af3irm/about/; GABRIELA Network, www.gabnet.org. Although GABRIELA Network focused on Filipina women's issues, the

membership of the organization was not limited to Filipina American women. Women of multiple ethnic backgrounds, including white American women, were involved with the organization. GABNet chapters were spread across the United States—in the San Francisco Bay Area, Los Angeles, New York, New Jersey, Chicago, Seattle, and Washington, DC. In 2010 Gabriela Network reconvened as the organization AF3IRM. My discussion of Gabriela Network is based on analysis of their website in 2007, before the shift to AF3IRM. AF3IRM's political objectives seem to be largely the same as their previous incarnation as AF3IRM, a transnational and anti-imperialist feminist organization, but they are no longer affiliated with Gabriela Philippines. For a brief history of AF3IRM, see their website.

21. GABRIELA Network.

22. Ibid.

23. Ibid.

24. AF3IRM, http://www.af3irm.org/af3irm/2014/02/af3irm-marks-milestone-15-years-of-the-purple-rose-campaign-renews-resolve-for-justice-with-launch-of-transnational-work-here-and-abroad/.

25. Ibid.

26. For an example of this discourse, see the work of antipornography writer Gail Dines, whose appeal transcends the divide between scholarly and popular audiences, as evidenced by her TEDx Talk, her documentary film and book, *Pornland: How the Porn Business Has Hijacked Our Sexuality*, and her role as founder and president of Culture Reframed, "a health promotion non-profit organization that recognizes and addresses pornography as the public health crisis of the digital age" (*Pornland*, http://www.kanopystreaming.com/node/127015; http://gaildines.com/).

27. For a description of the figure of the Filipina Japayuki, the Filipina woman who works as an "entertainer" and (at times) sex worker, within Philippine popular culture, see Suzuki, "'Japayuki.'"

28. Ibid., 448.

29. Muñoz, "The Autoethnographic Performance," 76.

30. Cvetkovich cites Spivak's notion of the "nostalgia for lost origins" as "the way that return depends on and posits as authentic nation based on *affective need*" in her analysis of the film *Brincando el Charco: Portrait of a Puerto Rican*, directed by diasporic Puerto Rican filmmaker Frances Negrón-Muntaner (emphasis mine). *An Archive of Feelings*, 130.

31. Rivera's narration of herself as a Filipina American *balikbayan* reveals the key differences between how Filipina/o American *balikbayans* represent themselves in relation to the Philippine nation and the popular representation of Filipina/o American *balikbayans* in the Philippine national imagination. While Rivera presents herself as the Filipina American who journeys home to discover an inextricable connection to the place she left, popular conceptions of *balikbayans* in the Philippines are often more critical.

32. The representation of "Third World women" has long been a concern within transnational feminisms. See Mohanty's classic analysis of the representation of the Third World woman in "Under Western Eyes." While I am *not* arguing that Filipina/o American *balikbayans* have an equivalent subject position to white Western feminists, I am pointing to the discursive and epistemic risks of representing Filipina sex workers primarily as victims in relation to Filipina/o Americans, particularly in relation to notions of diasporic belonging. For a related discussion of the politics of transnational belonging among Filipina/o American volunteerism in the Philippines, see Faith Kares's discussion of the narrative of Filipina/o American volunteers within the NGO Gawad Kalinga as "heroes of the nation" ("Practicing 'Enlightened Capitalism'").

33. Hua, *Trafficking Women's Human Rights*, 71.

34. This narrative of the betrayal and abandonment of the feminized Philippine nation by the US military also structures the film *Memories of a Forgotten War*. The filmmaker, Camilla Griggers, narrates her mixed-race familial history in relation to the Philippine American War. Griggers and Dalena, *Memories of a Forgotten War*. See Faye Caronan's insightful analysis of this film in Caronan, *Legitimizing Empire*.

35. The 2014 agreement between the Philippine and US governments to allow a US military presence in the Philippines reflects that ongoing reality of US neo-colonialism. See "Philippines Agrees to 10-Year Pact Allowing US Military Presence," April 27, 2014, https://www.theguardian.com/world/2014/apr/27/philippines-us-military-presence-china-dispute.

36. Mohanty, "Under Western Eyes."

37. Shimizu, *The Hypersexuality of Race*, 187.

Chapter 3. Performing the Filipina Mail-Order Bride

1. Muñoz, *Disidentifications*, 99.

2. See my discussion of the circulation of the figure of the Filipina mail-order bride in the introduction, including the film *Closer to Home* (Joseph Nobile, 1994) and actor Alec Baldwin's controversial quip in 2009 (on the television show *Late Night with David Letterman*) that he would expand his family by "looking for a Filipino mail-order bride."

3. Christine Lipat, personal communication, April 4, 2008.

4. I draw on both Hochschild's theory of emotional labor and Hardt's theory of affective labor as immaterial labor. Hardt highlights the centrality of what he terms "immaterial labor" and affective labor in particular to a contemporary global capitalist system. See Hardt, "Affective Labor"; Hochschild, *The Managed Heart*. For an excellent review of both strands of literature, see Weeks, "Life within and against Work." Hardt's theorization fails to address the role of gendered affective labor in consolidating racialized national identities in the postcolonial context. For a now-classic feminist analysis of the coconstitutive relationship of ethnicity, gender, and nationalism, see Anthias and Yuval-Davis, *Racialized Boundaries*; Yuval-Davis and Anthias, "The Citizenship Debate." See also Alexander's germinal essay on the relationship between

black female sexual labor and the postcolonial nationalist state, "Not Just (Any) Body Can Be a Citizen."

5. Kearny Street Workshop is a historically Asian American community arts space in San Francisco, California. The Manilatown Heritage Center is a Filipina/o American community center, also in San Francisco. Oakland's Chinatown is a commercial and residential district that is the hub of Chinese American and Asian American communities in Oakland. M.O.B.'s engagement with Filipina/o American cultural politics reflects their location within the San Francisco Bay Area, which is, according to Espiritu in *Home Bound*, one of the largest, most well-established Filipina/o American communities outside of the Philippines.

6. Brenneman, "Mail Order Brides."

7. Burns presents an insightful analysis of M.O.B.'s invocation of the *terno*. Burns analyzes M.O.B. in relation to the emergence of the *terno* as a nationalist symbol for upper-class Filipina femininity. See Burns, "Your Terno's Draggin'."

8. I use the term "Third World woman worker," coined by Mohanty, to describe the racialization and gendering of devalued labor within a global capitalist political economy. My use of this term allows for a critique of queer neoliberalism that emphasizes the possibilities for transnational solidarity and coalitional politics among those who have been the most exploited by a racialized and gendered international division of labor. In addition, I draw on the rich body of scholarship about third world women's racialized and gendered labor produced by transnational and women of color feminists. See Lowe, *Immigrant Acts*; Mohanty, "Women Workers"; Parreñas, *Servants of Globalization*; Tadiar, *Fantasy-Production*. I use the terms "male-assigned" and "female-assigned" to reference the distinction between the gender one is assigned at birth and one's self-determined gender identity and expression.

9. Although the United States Supreme Court ruled that the Defense of Marriage Act (DOMA) was unconstitutional in 2015, this issue animated mainstream LGBT politics for over a decade prior to the decision. In the current Trump administration, fears of anti-LGBT legislation have continued to make gay marriage an issue of concern for LGBT communities in the United States.

10. Muñoz describes the discourse of camp as one dominated by "middle- to upper-class white gay male sensibilities" (*Disidentifications*, 120).

11. I build on Puar's introduction of the term "homonationalism" to describe the ways in which normative queer subjects, primarily white middle-class gay men, conform to social norms in order to become legitimate members of the national body. See *Terrorist Assemblages*.

12. For a discussion of the representation of Filipina bodies on the internet, see Gonzalez and Rodriguez, "Filipina.com." For a discussion of the figure of the global Filipina body, see Tolentino, "Bodies, Letters, Catalogs."

13. See Parreñas's ethnographic scholarship on Filipina entertainers in Japan in "Homeward Bound" and "Benevolent Paternalism."

14. Bagong Pinay, www.bagongpinay.com.

15. Although Bagong Pinay did include a section titled "Our Lesbian Sisters," this title presumed a straight female audience, reinforcing the site's heteronormativity.

16. Bagong Pinay, www.bagongpinay.com.

17. Ibid.

18. Ibid.

19. Ibid.

20. Ibid.

21. Gonzalves, "Unashamed to Be So Beautiful," 273.

22. Ibid., 264.

23. Brenneman, "Mail Order Brides."

24. "Mail Order Brides / M.O.B.," Wofflehouse, 2008, http://www.wofflehouse .com/mob/.

25. Brenneman, "Mail Order Brides."

26. See my discussion of the politics of gendered transnational labor and sex work in chapter 2.

27. *Always a Bridesmaid, Never a Bride* screened in the following venues: Yerba Buena Center for the Arts, San Francisco, CA (2005), Barbershop Chinatown, Los Angeles, CA (2005), Stanford University, Palo Alto, CA (2006), California State University Monterey Bay, CA (2006), The Living Room art space, Manila, Philippines (2006), Future Prospects art space, Manila, Philippines (2006), University of California at Los Angeles (2006), University of California at Berkeley (2006, 2007, 2008), University of San Francisco (2007, 2008, 2009), Kearny Street Workshop, San Francisco, CA (2007), San Pancho Arts Festival, San Pancho, Mexico (2007), Chela Project, Buenos Aires, Argentina (2007), Manilatown Heritage Center, San Francisco, CA (2008), California College of the Arts, Oakland, CA (2008), Zeum Museum, San Francisco, CA (2008), Queer Conference, University of California at Santa Cruz (2010).

28. Although the project *AABNAB* encompasses work within multiple media (video, performance, photography, installation art), my analysis is primarily focused on the "testimonial" video, one of a series of four videos that M.O.B. created in this artistic collaboration.

29. Duggan's introduction of the term "homonormativity" to describe the consumer nature of an assimilationist LGBT cultural politics introduced a critique of queer neoliberal politics. Duggan describes how a homonormative political agenda does "not contest dominant heteronormative assumptions and institutions but upholds and sustains them while promising the possibility of a demobilized gay constituency and a privatized, depoliticized gay culture anchored in domesticity and consumption." See Duggan, "The New Homonormativity." The creation of the white gay male consumer as the ideal queer subject within the US popular imagination has been critiqued by queer studies scholars Rosemary Henessey and Jacqui Alexander. See Hennessy, *Profit and Pleasure*, and Alexander, "Imperial Desire."

30. Burns, "Your Terno's Draggin'," 213.

31. Ibid., 209.

32. In 2004 San Francisco mayor Gavin Newsom directed the San Francisco city clerk to issue marriage licenses to same-sex couples. See Allday, "Newsom Was Central."

33. Chow uses the term "coercive mimeticism" to describe the ways in which ethnic subjects are discursively constructed in relation to labor. Ethnic subjects (and I would argue racialized subjects as well) are required to perform the stereotypes attributed to them within a dominant racial formation. See Chow, *The Protestant Ethnic*.

34. M.O.B.'s use of whiteface must be contextualized within the racial formation of the United States. As several scholars have noted, the long-standing relationship of the Philippines to US imperialism and the centuries-long colonization by Spain have resulted in a persistent colorism within the Philippines in which whiteness is valued as a sign of beauty and social and economic upward mobility. See Rondilla and Spickard, *Is Lighter Better?*; Pierce, "Not Just My Closet"; Hunter, "The Persistent Problem."

35. For a discussion of the history of Filipina sexual labor, particularly the relationship of military prostitution to the contemporary global sex trade, see Rodriguez and Gonzalez, "Filipina.com."

36. Reanne Estrada, interview by the author, digital recording, July 24, 2009. Philadelphia, PA.

37. Duggan, "The New Homonormativity."

38. For a discussion of gay assimilation and the discursive production of the West as a site of freedom for queers, see Haritaworn, "Loyal Repetitions."

39. In 2003 the former US agency Immigration and Naturalization Service (INS) was replaced by the Department of Homeland Security, which included the US Citizenship and Immigration Services (USCIS), Immigration and Customs Enforcement (ICE), and Customs and Border Protection (CBP).

40. Robertson, "The Kinda Comedy," 57.

41. Although a comprehensive discussion of the practice of whiteface is beyond the scope of this chapter, it is worth noting that M.O.B.'s use of whiteface directly references their emphasis on racial/ethnic performativity. Drawing on multiple cultural references, from the figure of the geisha, to Japanese Kabuki theater, to American blackface and minstrelsy, M.O.B. invoke cross-racial and cross-gender performance traditions. Indeed, their wearing of the traditional Filipino male formal attire, the transparent Barong shirt, reveals the play of both gender and racial performativity in their work. Further, their use of whiteface inverts the dominant paradigm of performing the racial Other, signified by practices such as the wearing of blackface by white performers.

42. The characterization of Filipina brides ranges from the devious, sexually excessive figure of Cynthia in Elliott's Australian film *The Adventures of Priscilla, Queen of the Desert* to the multiple media images of abused and murdered Filipina mail-order brides; see Tolentino, "Bodies, Letters, Catalogs."

43. Robertson, "What Makes the Feminist Camp?," 274.

44. For an excellent discussion of the relationship between anti-immigrant rhetoric in the United States and neoliberal policies of structural adjustment, see Chang, *Disposable Domestics*.

45. Hardt, "Affective Labor."

46. Ibid., 90.

47. For an analysis of the affective labor of the transgender medical tourism industry (in which many Americans and Europeans travel to Thailand to undergo sexual reassignment surgery), where affective labor serves to differentiate racialized and gendered bodies within a framework of global capitalism, see Aizura, "The Romance."

48. For Hardt, "affective labor is itself . . . the constitution of communities and collective subjectivities" ("Affective Labor," 89). This affective labor in the service of producing the social is what Hardt, drawing on Foucault, terms "biopower." Unlike Foucault, however, Hardt argues that biopower is not solely exercised by the state. Hardt describes a "biopower from below," defining biopower as "the creation of life; it is the production of collective subjectivities, sociality, and society itself" (ibid., 98).

49. Tadiar discusses the racializing discourses through which corporeal difference is made legible on Filipina bodies within a context of global capitalism. Here racial and gender difference are the basis for determining which bodies are considered human. Tadiar describes Filipina domestic helpers as "bodies without subjectivity; that is, corporeal objects at the mercy and for the pleasure of those who buy them from the recruitment agency" (*Fantasy-Production*, 104). For Tadiar, the corporeality of the Filipina body is objectified as a commodity, while the subjectivity of these women is foreclosed. In the case of Filipina domestic helpers, it is their very corporeality that is sold. Tadiar argues, "Domestic helpers are paid not for a specific skill but rather for their gendered bodies—for their embodiment of a variety of functions and services which they are expected to provide at the beck and call of their employers" (ibid., 104).

50. Chow, *The Protestant Ethnic*.

51. Manalansan, "Queering," 4.

52. Ibid.

53. Both Manalansan and Isaac analyze how the performance of affective labor by Filipina trans women and Filipino gay men in Israel disrupt the heteronormative paradigm of gendered labor migration. See Manalansan, "Queering the Chain"; Isaac, "In a Precarious Time."

54. Fajardo, *Filipino Crosscurrents*.

55. Reanne Estrada, Skype interview with the author, August 1, 2009.

56. Guevarra, *Marketing Dreams*, 4; Rodriguez, *Migrants for Export*.

57. Rodriguez, *Migrants for Export*, 61.

58. Guevarra, *Marketing Dreams*, 66.

59. Rodriguez, *Migrants for Export*, 63.

60. Gonzalves, "Unashamed to Be So Beautiful," 273.

61. On April 2, 2012, Kevin Naff, the editor of the Washington, DC, LGBT weekly newspaper, the *Washington Blade*, critiqued a statement issued by the National Gay and

Lesbian Taskforce on the National Gay and Lesbian Taskforce Blog, signed by twenty-nine national LGBT organizations, condemning the killing of African American teenager Trayvon Martin by George Zimmerman. Nash argued that these LGBT organizations "jumped onto the bandwagon" of race. http://thetaskforceblog.org/2012/04/02 /national-lgbt-rights-groups-issue-joint-open-letter-on-the-killing-of-trayvon -martin-it-is-a-national-call-to-action. In contrast, on April 10, 2012, Jeff Krehely, vice president of LGBT Progress, and Aisha Moodie-Mills, advisor of LGBT Progress's FIRE Initiative for racial equality, argued against Nash's statement that "the spotlight on Trayvon somehow casts a shadow on LGBT victims of hate crimes." Krehely and Moodie-Mills went on to critique the assumption that victims of LGBT hate crimes are white, citing research that most victims of LGBT hate crimes are people of color. Think Progress, http://thinkprogress.org/lgbt/2012/04/10/461681/gay-newspaper-editorial -on-trayvon-martins-death-ignores-reality-of-racial-oppression/?mobile=nc.

62. Despite the perception of race as separate from sexuality, LGBT rights are nonetheless invoked using the language of racial civil rights. Following the passage of Proposition 8 in November 2008, which banned same-sex marriage in the state of California, the US mass media compared LGBT rights with the civil rights of African Americans. On December 16, 2008, the mainstream LGBT magazine the *Advocate* posed the following question on its cover, "Is Gay the New Black?"

63. While this essay focuses on the ways in which the mainstream marriage equality discourse constitutes an implicitly white homonationalist subject, it is necessary to note that many queer migrants of color participate in marriage (both heterosexual and same-sex marriage) for the purpose of obtaining legal residency or citizenship. I am not arguing that queer migrants of color are completely excluded from the dominant institution of marriage. Instead, I argue that the broader political discourse of marriage equality relies on racialized notions of (white) queer citizenship that exclude queer migrants of color while making invisible the racialized and gendered labor necessary to uphold the social institution of the hetero- and homonormative nuclear family.

64. The notable exception is, of course, Puar's discussion of the emergence of the homonationalist subject in *Terrorist Assemblages*.

65. Duggan, "The New Homonormativity."

66. Although beyond the scope of this essay, it is worth mentioning that homonormativity does not require the referent of heteronormativity to function. Thus, homonormativity is less a mirror of heteronormativity; instead, it functions independently as a hegemonic normalizing discourse. Thank you to Aren Z. Aizura for bringing this to my attention.

67. Berlant and Warner, "Sex in Public," 313. Within contemporary US queer politics, homonormativity has replaced heteronormativity as the familial model of belonging to the nation. Scholars such as Judith Butler have critiqued how LGBT political organizations such as the Human Rights Campaign reify marriage as the only legitimate (and state-sanctioned) form of queer belonging. See Butler, "Is Kinship?"; Bailey, Kandaswamy, and Richardson, "Is Gay Marriage Racist?"

68. Muñoz's discussion of the performance of racial and ethnic affect has been crucial to the development of my argument. Muñoz critiques the popular view of Latino/a affect as excessive. In contrast, Muñoz describes how the performance of Latino/a affect, or "feeling brown," demonstrates the affective lack or impoverishment of whiteness. Muñoz argues that this white normative affect, what he terms "national affect," is implicitly associated with citizenship in the United States. See Muñoz, "Feeling Brown."

69. Ahmed argues, "Heteronormativity functions as a form of public comfort by allowing bodies to extend into spaces that have already taken their shape" (*The Cultural Politics*, 148).

70. Following Puar's introduction of the term "homonationalism," critiques of the imbrication of racialized nationalism and imperialism within queer politics have multiplied. Puar's analysis of homonationalism belongs to a larger body of queer of color and queer diaspora / queer studies scholarship, including Eng, *The Feeling of Kinship*; Manalansan, *Global Divas*; Gopinath, *Impossible Desires*; Muñoz, *Disidentifications*; Ferguson, *Aberrations in Black*.

71. Thank you to Chandan Reddy for suggesting the term "queer vernacular" to describe the various queer counterdiscourses to homonationalism.

72. For example, during the week of National Coming Out Day (October 11, 2009), the group Queer Kids of Queer Parents Against Gay Marriage published an online manifesto titled "Resist the Gay Marriage Agenda!" As adults raised within queer families, bloggers Katie Miles and Jane Kaufman argued against the neoliberal logic of gay marriage activists, noting, "It's that sneaky thing about late liberal capitalism: its promise of formal rights over real restructuring, of citizenship for those who can participate in the state's economic plan over economic justice for all." Another example of this antiassimilationist queer political culture is the group Queers Against Assimilation (QAA). On October 11, 2009, the day of the National Equality March on Washington, QAA threw black and pink glitter paint grenades at the Human Rights Commission (HRC) headquarters building and issued a manifesto critiquing the HRC's political agenda. Calling their attack on the HRC "glamdalism," Queers Against Assimilation criticized the HRC fund-raising gala held the night before, at which President Obama spoke. QAA described HRC as "a few wealthy elites who are in bed with corporate sponsors who proliferate militarism, heteronormativity, and capitalist exploitation." The actions and statements of Queers Against Assimilation, Queer Kids of Queer Parents Against Gay Marriage, and other queer cultural critics suggest that queer opposition to homonormativity and homonationalism is multifaceted, drawing on critiques of racism, militarism, incarceration, police violence, neoliberalism, and anti-immigrant discrimination.

73. In contrast, queer of color and multiracial radical queer organizations such as SUSPECT, FIERCE, (the former) Queers for Economic Justice, the Audre Lorde Project, and the Sylvia Rivera Law Project integrate economic and racial justice issues into their political campaigns. Although this organization closed in 2014, Queers for Economic

Justice's welfare rights campaign, Welfare Warriors, "organize[d] low-income LGBT people on public assistance to fight for a more humane, just and inclusive welfare system." Welfare rights campaigns inherently address the politics of racialized and gendered labor, particularly domestic and affective labor, in relation to the neoliberal state. See also SUSPECT; Audre Lorde Project; FIERCE; Sylvia Rivera Law Project. While taking note of queer studies scholars' critiques of the tendency to position a priori queer of color subjects and queer of color political organizing as inherently transgressive, it is also necessary to imagine and create queer political cultures that envision issues such as welfare rights, the policing and incarceration of trans and gender nonconforming people, US imperialism, migration, and racialized / gendered labor as fundamentally intertwined with justice for queer and trans people of color. See Puar's critique of intersectionality and the positioning of the queer of color subject as inherently transgressive in *Terrorist Assemblages*, 23–24.

74. Gonzalves, "Unashamed to Be So Beautiful," 273.

Chapter 4. The Queer Cyborg in Gigi Otálvaro-Hormillosa's *Cosmic Blood*

1. Marcuse, *Counter-revolution*, 82.

2. "Bindlestiff Studio," March 1, 2003, www.bindlestiff.org.

3. Anzaldúa, *Borderlands*, 99. Although the framework of postcoloniality has been used to describe the Philippines, the argument could be made that the Philippines exists in a neocolonial relationship with the United States due to the continued influence of the United States on Philippine state policy.

4. Muñoz, *Cruising Utopia*, 1.

5. Muñoz draws on Agamben's notion of "potentiality" to critique what he terms the "gay pragmatism" of contemporary LGBT politics. For Muñoz, "The not-quite-conscious is the realm of potentiality that must be called on, and insisted on, if we are ever to look beyond the pragmatic sphere of the here and now, the hollow nature of the present. Thus, I wish to argue that queerness is not quite here; it is, in the language of Italian philosopher Giorgio Agamben, a potentiality" (ibid., 21).

6. Ibid.

7. Here I refer to the imperialist practice of representing Filipina/o bodies as native, savage, and racial Others, particularly in relation to the US nation. An often-cited historical example of the representation of the savage Filipina/o body is the 1904 St. Louis World's Fair, which displayed Philippine indigenous villages, complete with Filipina/o inhabitants. Drawing on Foucault in *Discipline and Punish*, Rafael discusses ethnological photographs of indigenous Filipinos as another example of the "compulsory visibility" of Filipina/o bodies under US colonialism (*White Love*, 78). Of these photographs, Rafael notes, "In studying and, especially, looking at such photographs, we come into association with imperialist ways of looking and so feel unwittingly implicated in their workings" (ibid., 6, 77).

8. Muñoz, *Cruising Utopia*, 1.

9. Muñoz discusses hope as "both a critical affect and a methodology" (ibid., 4).

10. Ibid. Muñoz argues that "queerness is utopian, and there is something queer about the utopian. Fredric Jameson described the utopian as the oddball or the manic. Indeed, to live inside straight time and ask for, desire, and imagine another time and place is to represent and perform a desire that is both utopian and queer. To participate in such an endeavor is not to imagine an isolated future for the individual but instead to describe a collective futurity, a notion of futurity that functions as a historical materialist critique" (ibid., 26).

11. Pratt introduced the concept of the "contact zone" to describe "the relations among colonizers and colonized . . . not in terms of separateness or apartheid, but in terms of copresence, interaction, interlocking understandings and practices, often within radically asymmetrical relations of power" (*Imperial Eyes*, 7).

12. Muñoz describes the relationship between postcoloniality and queerness: "Thus to perform queerness is to constantly disidentify; to constantly find oneself thriving on sites where meaning does not properly 'line up.' This is equally true of hybridity, another modality where meaning or identifications do not properly line up. The postcolonial hybrid is a subject whose identity practices are structured around an ambivalent relationship to the signs of empire and the signs of 'Native,' a subject who occupies a space between the West and the rest" (*Disidentifications*, 84).

13. Devil Bunny, January 1, 2004, www.devilbunny.org.

14. Vasconcelos's notion of *mestizaje* was integral to the Mexican nationalist project of the early twentieth century. In positioning the mestizo as the ideal national subject, the indigenous element of this hereditary mix was implicitly negated. Indigenous scholars have critiqued Anzaldúa's use of the notion of *mestizaje* for this reason. See Vasconcelos, *The Cosmic Race / La Raza Cósmica*.

15. Forbes cited in Anzaldúa, *Borderlands*, 99.

16. Ibid., 102.

17. As Alarcón, Kaplan, and Moallem remark in their introduction, "Notions such as country, homeland, region, locality, and ethnicity and their construction through racialization, sexualization, and the genderization of female corporeality become crucial sites of inquiry and investigation" (*Between Woman and Nation*, 14, emphasis mine).

18. Arrizón responds to critiques that Anzaldúa's citation of Vasconcelos reproduces an implicitly masculinist narrative of *mestizaje*, noting, "Given that Anzaldúa's mestizaje carries a polyvalent mode, in which the reclamation of the feminist and queer subject rejects Vasconcelos' implicit heterosexism and ethnonationalism, it is understandable why she did not engage analytically with Vasconcelos" (*Queering Mestizaje*, 8).

19. See my discussion of how nationalist movements in the Philippines use Andres Bonifacio, not Jose Rizal, as a national hero. See Ileto, *Filipinos and Their Revolution*, 185.

20. Rafael, *White Love*, 165.

21. Ibid., 166.

22. Arrizón, *Queering Mestizaje*, 127.

23. Ibid., 1.

24. Pratt, *Imperial Eyes*, 7, cited in Arrizón, *Queering Mestizaje*, 2.

25. Butler, *Parable of the Sower*, cited in Otálvaro-Hormillosa, *Cosmic Blood*, 68.

26. The phrase "God is change . . . Change is God" is a central tenet of the belief system upon which the collective Earthseed is founded in Butler's novel *Parable of the Sower*.

27. Tadiar, *Fantasy Production*, 104.

28. Chicago Surrealist Group, cited in Kelley, *Freedom Dreams*, 5.

29. Ibid., 31.

30. Ibid.

31. Ibid., 193.

32. Chow, *The Protestant Ethnic*; Muñoz, *Disidentifications*.

33. Anzaldúa, *Borderlands*, 102.

34. Haraway, *Modestwitness@Second_Millenium.Femaleman© Meets_Oncomouse™*, 265.

35. Halberstam, *In a Queer Time and Place*, 6.

36. Muñoz, *Cruising Utopia*, 5.

37. Ibid., 1.

Conclusion

1. James Byrd Jr. was an African American man who was killed by white supremacists in Jasper, Texas, on June 7, 1998. He was dragged behind a truck until he hit a culvert and his arm and head were severed. Matthew Shepard was a college student at the University of Wyoming who was beaten and left to die in Laramie, Wyoming, on October 12, 1998. Their deaths brought national attention to federal hate crimes legislation, leading to the 2009 Matthew Shepard and James Byrd Jr. Hate Crimes Prevention Act.

2. Lorde, "A Litany for Survival," 31.

3. The term "Latinx" has emerged as a term that encompasses a broader understanding of gender and sexuality than the term "Latina" or "Latino."

4. Laurence La-Fontaine Stokes, "Queer Puerto Ricans and the Burden of Violence," *Latino USA*, June 21, 2016, http://latinousa.org/2016/06/21/opinion-queer-puerto-ricans-burden-violence/.

5. "Undocumented Victims of Orlando Shooting Face Unique Challenges," *New American Media*, June 17, 2016, http://newamericamedia.org/2016/06/undocumented-victims-of-orlando-shooting-face-unique-challenges.php; Letitia Stein and Fiona Ortiz, "Hispanics Shaken by Heavy Toll at Orlando Club Massacre," Reuters, https://www.reuters.com/article/us-florida-shooting-latinos/hispanics-shaken-by-heavy-toll-at-orlando-club-massacre-idUSKCN0YZ2GH.

6. Isaac, *American Tropics*, xxv.

7. Pante, "Kentex Factory."

8. Javier Arbona, "Queer Boricua Geopolitics and the Pulse Shooting," http://javier .faculty.ucdavis.edu/2016/06/25/queer-boricua-geopolitics-and-the-pulse-shooting/.

9. Haritaworn, Kuntsman, and Posocco, "Introduction," 3.

10. La-Fontaine Stokes, "Queer Puerto Ricans"; Arbona, "Queer Boricua Geopolitics"; Juana Maria Rodriguez, "LGBT Clubs Let's Affirm Queer Latinidad, Let's Affirm This," *NBC News*, June 16, 2016, https://www.nbcnews.com/storyline /orlando-nightclub-massacre/voices-lgbt-clubs-let-us-embrace-queer-latinidad -let-s-n593191; Miriam Zoila Perez, "When the One Place That Feels Like Home Is Invaded," *Colorlines*, June 13, 2016, https://www.colorlines.com/articles/when-one -place-feels-home-invaded; Guillermo Rebollo-Gil, "As It Concerns the Ones We've Lost," *Empty Lots*, June 14, 2016, http://patternofthething.blogspot.com/2016/06 /as-it-regards-ones-weve-lost.html; Justin Torres, "In Praise of Latin Night at the Queer Club," *Washington Post*, June 13, 2016, https://www.washingtonpost.com /opinions/in-praise-of-latin-night-at-the-queer-club/2016/06/13/e841867e-317b -11e6-95c0-2a6873031302_story.html?utm_term=.f22eae73a7b7.

11. In contrast to Latinx writers such as Lawrence La-Fontaine Stokes and Guillermo Rebollo-Gil, who connected the Pulse shooting to the history of US empire in Puerto Rico, mainstream media sites such as *Slate* failed to make such a connection. Although Christina Cauterucci, the author of a piece on the Pulse shooting in *Slate*, notes that many of the victims were Puerto Rican, she fails to note this significance, except to state that "Puerto Ricans are U.S. citizens" ("Sadly, Injustices for Queer and Immigrant Murder Victims Don't End with Death," *Slate*, June 14, 2016, http://www .slate.com/blogs/outward/2016/06/14/after_a_shooting_like_orlando_s_pulse_ queer_and_immigrant_victims_suffer.html).

12. Tessa Berenson, "Donald Trump Pushes for Muslim Ban after Orlando Shooting" *Time*, June 13, 2016, http://time.com/4366912/donald-trump-orlando-shooting -muslim-ban/.

13. Kaplan, *The Anarchy of Empire*, 1.

14. Isaac, *American Tropics*, xviii. In 2018 the FX anthology television series *American Crime Story* focused on Andrew Cunanan in *The Assassination of Gianni Versace*. Darren Criss, a half-Filipino American actor, was chosen to play Cunanan, partially because of his Filipino heritage. Michael Schneider, "Darren Criss on Not Whitewashing Half-Filipino Andrew Cunanan in 'Versace,'" *IndieWire*, January 19, 2018, http:// www.indiewire.com/2018/01/darren-criss-versace-american-crime-story-andrew -cunanan-nina-jacobson-brad-simpson-podcast-1201919191/.

15. David Lloyd discusses the implicit resistance to anticolonial movements inherent in critiques of nationalism in Global North scholarship ("Nationalisms against the State," 174). The notable exceptions to my critique of queer studies are the subfields of queer of color and queer globalization studies. See my discussion in the introduction of this book.

16. See my discussion of the representation of the Filipina/o American *balikbayan* within popular Philippine discourse in chapter 1.

17. Alexander, "Not Just (Any) Body"; Eng, *Racial Castration*; Ferguson, *Aberrations in Black.*

18. Muñoz describes the relationship between queer futurity and desire: "This maneuver, a turn to the past for the purpose of critiquing the present, is propelled by a desire for futurity. Queer futurity does not underplay desire. In fact it is all about desire, desire for both larger semiabstractions such as a better world or freedom but also, more immediately, better relations within the social that include better sex and more pleasure" (*Cruising Utopia*, 30).

19. In chapter 4 I discuss Robin Kelley's engagement with surrealism in relation to the cyborg as a utopian figure for an alternative future.

20. Joseph Scott Pemberton was convicted of homicide in the death of Jennifer Laude in 2014. "Marine Convicted of Killing Filipino Transgender Woman," December 1, 2015, http://www.cbsnews.com/news/marine-joseph-scott-pemberton-homicide-killing-filipino-transgender/.

21. "Action and Rally in Response to the Killing of Jennifer Laude," Facebook, https://www.facebook.com/events/349241425253980/.

22. Shane Ortega gained fame as one of the first openly trans men to serve in the US military and has become a symbol for the movement to include transgender individuals in the military. May 28, 2015, http://www.advocate.com/politics/transgender/2015/05/28/poised-perfection-sgt-shane-ortega-puts-face-transgender-military-ba.

23. This protest is obviously not the first occurrence of queer anti-imperialist organizing among Filipina/o American activists. The existence of a queer caucus within the Filipina/o diasporic political organization BAYAN USA attests to this. However, the building of coalitions between organizations focused primarily on US queer politics, such as the Audre Lorde Project and the Anti-Violence Project, with the explicitly anti-imperialist organization BAYAN USA is worth noting as a key political moment.

24. Chávez, *Queer Migration Politics*, 8, 9; Muñoz, *Cruising Utopia*, 21. Here I draw on Chávez's discussion of coalitional moments as "moments that expose a queer temporality." Thus, coalitional moments create both a space and a time of possibility for an alternative envisioning of both the present and the future. I consciously draw on Chávez's notion of a coalitional moment even as I recognize that Chávez is largely critical of the utopian impulse, particularly in relation to Muñoz's work on queer utopias. Despite this difference, I find both Chávez's notion of coalitional moment and Muñoz's theorization of queer utopias to be useful for theorizing forms of queer Filipina/o diaspora.

25. Gonzalez and Rodriguez, "Filipina.com," 218.

26. Stanley and Smith, *Captive Genders*, 4.

Bibliography

Aguilar, Delia. *Toward a Nationalist Feminism*. Quezon City: Giraffe Books, 1998.

Ahmed, Sara. *The Cultural Politics of Emotion*. New York: Routledge, 2004.

Aizura, Aren Z. "The Romance of the Amazing Scalpel: 'Race,' Labour and Affect in Thai Gender Reassignment Clinics." In *Queer Bangkok*, edited by Peter A. Jackson. Hong Kong: Hong Kong University Press, 2011.

Alexander, Jacqui M. "Imperial Desire / Sexual Utopias: White Gay Capital and Transnational Tourism." In *Talking Visions: Multicultural Feminism in a Transnational Age*, edited by Ella Shohat, 281–95. Cambridge, MA: MIT Press, 1998.

———. "Not Just (Any) Body Can Be a Citizen: The Politics of Law, Sexuality and Postcoloniality in Trinidad and Tobago and the Bahamas." *Feminist Review* 48 (1994): 5–23.

Allday, Erin. "Newsom Was Central to Same-Sex Marriage Saga." *San Francisco Chronicle*, November 6, 2008. http://www.sfgate.com/cgi-bin/article.cgi?f=/c/a/2008/11/05/MN1B13S3D3.DTL.

Anderson, Benedict. "Exodus." *Critical Inquiry* 20, no. 2 (1994): 314–27.

Anthias, Floya, and Nira Yuval-Davis. *Racialized Boundaries: Race, Nation, Gender, Colour and Class and the Anti-racist Struggle*. New York: Routledge, 1992.

Anzaldúa, Gloria. *Borderlands / La Frontera: The New Mestiza*. San Francisco: Aunt Lute Books, 1999.

Anzaldúa, Gloria, and Cherríe Moraga. *This Bridge Called My Back: Writings by Radical Women of Color*. New York: Kitchen Table, Women of Color Press, 1983.

Arrizón, Alicia. *Queering Mestizaje: Transculturation and Performance*. Ann Arbor: University of Michigan Press, 2006.

Associated Press. "Marine Convicted of Killing Filipino Transgender Woman." *CBS News*, December 1, 2015. http://www.cbsnews.com/news/marine-joseph-scott -pemberton-homicide-killing-filipino-transgender/.

———. "Philippines Agrees to 10-Year Pact Allowing US Military Presence." *Guardian*, April 27, 2014. http://www.theguardian.com/world/2014/apr/27/philippines-us -military-presence-china-dispute.

Bailey, Marlon M., Priya Kandaswamy, and Matt Richardson. "Is Gay Marriage Racist?" In *That's Revolting! Queer Strategies for Resisting Assimilation*, edited by Mattilda Bernstein Sycamore, 87–93. San Francisco: Counterpoint Press, 2008.

Balce, Nerissa. *Body Parts of Empire: Visual Abjection, Filipino Images, and the American Archive*. Ann Arbor: University of Michigan Press, 2016.

———. "The Filipina's Breast: Savagery, Docility, and the Erotics of the American Empire." *Social Text* 87, no. 24 (2006): 89–110.

Baron, Steve. "List of How Many Homes Each Cable Network Is in as of February 2015." *TV by the Numbers*, February 22, 2015. http://tvbythenumbers.zap2it.com /2015/02/22/list-of-how-many-homes-each-cable-network-is-in-as-of-february -2015/366230/.

Barry, Kathleen. *The Prostitution of Sexuality*. New York: New York University Press, 1995.

Bartolome, Tina. *Balikbayan Confessions*. 2006.

Berlant, Lauren, and Elizabeth Freeman. "Queer Nationality." *Boundary 2* 19, no. 1 (1992): 149–80.

Berlant, Lauren, and Michael Warner. "Sex in Public." *Critical Inquiry* 24, no. 2 (1998): 547–66.

Brenneman, Christine. "Mail Order Brides Engage SF with Their Unusual Brand of Campy, Goofy Fun." *MetroActive Arts*, October 19, 1998.

Burns, Lucy Mae San Pablo. *Puro Arte: Filipinos on the Stages of Empire*. New York: New York University Press, 2012.

———. "Your Terno's Draggin': Fashioning Filipino American Performance." *Women and Performance: A Journal of Feminist Theory* 21, no. 2 (2011): 199–217.

Butler, Judith. "Is Kinship Always Already Homosexual?" *Differences: A Journal of Feminist Cultural Studies* 13, no. 1 (2002): 14–44.

Butler, Octavia. *Parable of the Sower*. New York: Warner Books, 1993.

Campomanes, Oscar. "The New Nation's Forgotten and Forgetful Citizens: Unrepresentability and Unassimilability in Filipino American Postcolonials." *Hitting Critical Mass, a Journal of Asian American Cultural Criticism* 2, no. 2 (1995): 145–200.

Candido, Romeo. *Ang Pamana / The Inheritance*. 2006.

Caronan, Faye. *Legitimizing Empire: Filipino American and U.S. Puerto Rican Cultural Critique*. Champaign: University of Illinois Press, 2015.

Chang, Grace. *Disposable Domestics: Immigrant Women Workers in the Global Economy*. Cambridge, MA: South End Press, 2000.

Chapkis, Wendy. *Live Sex Acts: Women Performing Erotic Labor*. New York: Routledge, 1997.

Chávez, Karma R. *Queer Migration Politics: Activist Rhetoric and Coalitional Possibilities.* Urbana: University of Illinois Press, 2013.

Cheah, Pheng. "Introduction Part II." In *Cosmopolitics: Thinking and Feeling beyond the Nation,* edited by Pheng Cheah and Bruce Robbins. Minneapolis: University of Minnesota Press, 1998.

Chow, Rey. *The Protestant Ethnic and the Spirit of Capitalism.* New York: Columbia University Press, 2002.

Choy, Catherine Ceniza. "Towards Trans-Pacific Social Justice: Women and Protest in Filipino American History." *Journal of Asian American Studies* 8, no. 3 (2006): 293–307.

Chuh, Kandace. *Imagine Otherwise: On Asian Americanist Critique.* Durham, NC: Duke University Press, 2003.

Clifford, James. *Routes: Travel and Translation in the Late 20th Century.* Cambridge, MA: Harvard University Press, 1997.

Constantino, Renato, and Letizia R. Constantino. *The Philippines: A Past Revisited.* Quezon City: Tala Pub. Services, 1975.

Cruz, Denise. *Transpacific Femininities: The Making of the Modern Filipina.* Durham, NC: Duke University Press, 2012.

Cvetkovich, Ann. *An Archive of Feelings: Trauma, Sexuality, and Lesbian Public Cultures.* Durham, NC: Duke University Press, 2003.

Diaz, Robert. "Failed Returns: The Queer Balikbayan in R. Zamora Linmark's *Leche* and Gil Portes' *Miguel/Michelle.*" In *Global Asian American Popular Cultures,* edited by Shilpa Dave, LeiLani Nishime, and Tasha Oren, 335–50. New York: New York University Press, 2016.

———. "The Limits of *Bakla* and Gay: Feminist Readings of *My Husband's Lover, Vice Ganda,* and *Charice Pempengco.*" *Signs* 40, no. 3 (2015): 721–45.

Dines, Gail. *Pornland: How the Porn Industry Has Hijacked Our Sexuality.* Boston: Beacon Press, 2010.

———. *Pornland: How the Porn Industry Has Hijacked Our Sexuality.* DVD. Media Education Foundation Collection. 2014. http://www.kanopystreaming.com/node/127015.

Doezema, Jo. "Forced to Choose: Beyond the Voluntary v. Forced Prostitution Dichotomy." In *Global Sex Workers: Rights, Resistance, and Redefinition,* edited by Kamala Kempadoo and Jo Doezema, 34–50. New York: Routledge, 1998.

———. "Ouch! Western Feminists' 'Wounded Attachment' to the 'Third World Prostitute.'" *Feminist Review,* no. 67 (2001): 16–38.

Duggan, Lisa. "Making It Perfectly Queer." *Socialist Review* 22, no. 1 (1992): 11–31.

———. "The New Homonormativity: The Sexual Politics of Neoliberalism." In *Materializing Democracy: Towards a Revitalized Cultural Politics,* edited by Russ Castronovo and Dana D. Nelson, 175–94. Durham, NC: Duke University Press, 2002.

Eilperin, Juliet. "Transgender in the Military: A Pentagon in Transition Weighs Its Policy." *Washington Post,* April 9, 2015. https://www.washingtonpost.com/politics /transgender-in-the-military-a-pentagon-in-transition-weighs-its-policy/2015 /04/09/ee0ca39e-cf0d-11e4-8c54-ffb5ba6f2f69_story.html.

Elliott, Stephan. *The Adventures of Priscilla, Queen of the Desert*. DVD. Alice Springs, Australia: PolyGram Filmed Entertainment, 1994.

Eng, David. *Racial Castration: Managing Masculinity in Asian America*. Durham, NC: Duke University Press, 2001.

Enloe, Cynthia. *Bananas, Beaches, and Bases: Making Feminist Sense of International Politics*. 2nd ed. Berkeley: University of California Press, 2014.

Espiritu, Yen Le. *Home Bound: Filipino American Lives across Cultures, Communities, and Countries*. Berkeley: University of California Press, 2003.

Fajardo, Kale Bantigue. *Filipino Crosscurrents: Oceanographies of Seafaring, Masculinities, and Globalization*. Minneapolis: University of Minnesota Press, 2011.

———. "Transportation: Translating Filipino and Filipino American Tomboy Masculinities through Global Migration and Seafaring." *GLQ* 14, no. 2–3 (2008): 404–24.

Farrow, Kenyon. "Black Working Class Gays Left Out of National Gay Rights Agenda." *Grio*, October 12, 2009. http://www.thegrio.com/2009/10/when-obama-delivered -his-gay.php.

Ferguson, Roderick A. *Aberrations in Black: Toward a Queer of Color Critique*. Minneapolis: University of Minnesota Press, 2004.

Flores, Patrick D. "The Dissemination of Nora Aunor." In *Geopolitics of the Visible: Essays on Philippine Film Cultures*, edited by Roland B. Tolentino, 77–95. Quezon City: Ateneo de Manila University Press, 2000.

Foucault, Michel. *Discipline and Punish: The Birth of the Prison*. New York: Vintage Books, 1979.

Francisco-Menchavez, Valerie. *The Labor of Care: Filipina Migrants and Transnational Families in the Digital Age*. Champaign: University of Illinois Press, 2018.

Frasier. Season 2, Episode 10. First broadcast November 29, 1994, by NBC. Directed by Andy Ackerman and written by David Lloyd.

Garcia, J. Neil C. *Philippine Gay Culture: The Last Thirty Years Binabae to Bakla, Silahis to MSM*. Diliman, Quezon City: University of the Philippines Press, 1996.

———. *Slip/Pages: Essays in Philippine Gay Criticism (1991–1996)*. Manila: De La Salle University Press, 1998.

Garcia, J. Neil C., and Danton Remoto. *Ladlad: An Anthology of Philippine Gay Writing*. Pasig City, Philippines: Anvil Publishing, 1994.

Gonzalez, Vernadette. *Securing Paradise: Tourism and Militarism in Hawai'i and the Philippines*. Durham, NC: Duke University Press, 2013.

Gonzalez, Vernadette, and Robyn Rodriguez. "Filipina.com: Wives, Workers, and Whores on the Cyberfrontier." In *Asian America.Net: Ethnicity, Nationalism, and Cyberspace*, edited by Rachel C. Lee and Sau-ling Cynthia Wong, 215–34. London: Routledge, 2003.

Gonzalves, Theodore. *The Day the Dancers Stayed: Performing in the Filipina/o American Diaspora*. Philadelphia: Temple University Press, 2009.

———. "'The Show Must Go On': Production Notes on the Pilipino Cultural Night." *Critical Mass: A Journal of Asian American Cultural Criticism* 2, no. 2 (1995): 129–44.

———. "'Unashamed to Be So Beautiful': An Interview with Celine Salazar Parreñas." In *Countervisions: Asian American Film Criticism*, edited by Darrell Y. Hamamoto and Sandra Liu, 263–74. Philadelphia: Temple University Press, 2000.

Gopinath, Gayatri. *Impossible Desires: Queer Diasporas and South Asian Public Cultures.* Durham, NC: Duke University Press, 2005.

Griggers, Camilla, and Sari Raissa Lluch Dalena. *Memories of a Forgotten War.* Video recording. New York: Third World Newsreel, 2001.

Gross, Michael Joseph. "Gay Is the New Black." *Advocate*, December 16, 2008. http://www.advocate.com/news/2008/11/16/gay-new-black.

Guerrero, Amado. *Philippine Society and Revolution.* Hong Kong: Ta Kung Pao, 1971.

Guevarra, Anna Romina. *Marketing Dreams, Manufacturing Heroes: The Transnational Labor Brokering of Filipino Workers.* New Brunswick, NJ: Rutgers University Press, 2010.

Halberstam, Jack. *In a Queer Time and Place: Transgender Bodies, Subcultural Lives.* New York: New York University Press, 2005.

Hall, Stuart. *New Ethnicities.* London: Routledge, 1996.

Hanna, Karen Buenavista. "A Call for Healing: Transphobia, Homophobia, and Historical Trauma in Filipina/o/x American Activist Organizations." *Hypatia* 32, no. 3 (2017): 696–714.

Haraway, Donna. "A Cyborg Manifesto: Science, Technology, and Socialist-Feminism in the Late Twentieth Century." In *Simians, Cyborgs and Women: The Reinvention of Nature*, 149–81. New York: Routledge, 1991.

———. *Modestwitness@Second_Millenium.Femaleman©Meets_Oncomouse™.* New York: Routledge, 1997.

Hardt, Michael. "Affective Labor." *Boundary 2* 26, no. 2 (1999): 89–100.

Haritaworn, Jin. "Loyal Repetitions of the Nation: Gay Assimilation and the 'War on Terror.'" *DarkMatter* 3 (2008). http://www.darkmatter101.org/site/2008/05/02/loyal-repetitions-of-the-nation-gay-assimilation-and-the-war-on-terror/.

Haritaworn, Jin, Adi Kuntsman, and Sylvia Posocco. "Introduction: 'Queer Necropolitics.'" In *Queer Necropolitics*, edited by Jin Haritaworn, Adi Kuntsman, and Sylvia Posocco. New York: Routledge, 2104.

Hau, Caroline. *On the Subject of the Nation: Filipino Writings from the Margins 1981 to 2004.* Quezon City: Ateneo de Manila University Press, 2004.

Hennessy, Rosemary. *Profit and Pleasure: Sexual Identities in Late Capitalism.* New York: Routledge, 2000.

Hochschild, Arlie Russell. *The Managed Heart: Commercialization of Human Feeling.* Berkeley: University of California Press, 1983.

Hua, Julietta. *Trafficking Women's Human Rights.* Minneapolis: University of Minnesota Press, 2011.

Hunter, Margaret. "The Persistent Problem of Colorism: Skin Tone, Status, and Inequality." *Sociology Compass* 1, no. 1 (2007): 237–54.

Ileto, Reynaldo. *Filipinos and Their Revolution: Event, Discourse, and Historiography.* Manila: Ateneo de Manila University Press, 1998.

———. "Outlines of a Non-linear Emplotment of Philippine History." In *Reflections on Development in Southeast Asia*, edited by Lim Teck Gnee, 130–59. Singapore: Institute of Southeast Asian Studies, 1998.

Isaac, Allan Punzalan. *American Tropics: Articulating Filipino America*. Minneapolis: University of Minnesota Press, 2006.

———. "In a Precarious Time and Place: The Refusal to Wallow and Other Migratory Temporal Investments in Care Divas, the Musical." *Journal of Asian American Studies* 19, no. 1 (2016): 5–24.

Kaplan, Amy. *The Anarchy of Empire in the Making of U.S. Culture*. Cambridge, MA: Harvard University Press, 2005.

Kaplan, Caren, and Inderpal Grewal. "Transnational Feminist Cultural Studies: Beyond the Marxism/Poststructuralism/Feminism Divides." In *Between Woman and Nation: Nationalisms, Transnational Feminisms, and the State*, edited by Caren Kaplan, Norma Alarcon, and Minoo Moallen, 349–64. Durham, NC: Duke University Press, 1999.

Kares, Faith R. "Practicing 'Enlightened Capitalism': 'Fil-Am' Heroes, NGO Activism, and the Reconstitution of Class Difference in the Philippines." *Philippine Studies: Historical and Ethnographic Viewpoints* 62, no. 2 (2014): 175–204.

Kelley, Robin. *Freedom Dreams*. Boston, MA: Beacon Press, 2002.

Kempadoo, Kamala. "Women of Color and the Global Sex Trade: Transnational Feminist Perspectives." *Meridians* 1, no. 2 (2001): 28–51.

Kidron, Beeban. *To Wong Foo, Thanks for Everything! Julie Newmar*. 1995.

Krehely, Jeff, and Aisha Moodie-Mills. "Gay Newspaper Editorial on Trayvon Martin's Death Ignores Reality of Racial Oppression." *ThinkProgress*. http://thinkprogress .org/lgbt/2012/04/10/461681/gay-newspaper-editorial-on-trayvon-martins-death -ignores-reality-of-racial-oppression/?mobile=nc.

Lalu, Gabriel Pabico. "Over 400 Killed in a Month in Drug War." *Philippine Daily Inquirer*, September 26, 2018. https://newsinfo.inquirer.net/1036460/drug-war-death-toll -now-at-4854-govt?utm_expid=.XqNwTug2W6nwDVUSgFJXed.1.

Lloyd, David. "Nationalisms against the State." In *The Politics of Culture in the Shadow of Capital*, edited by Lisa Lowe and David Lloyd, 173–97. Durham, NC: Duke University Press, 1997.

Lorde, Audre. "A Litany for Survival." In *Black Unicorn: Poems*. New York: Norton, 1995.

Louie, Andrea. *Chineseness across Borders: Renegotiating Chinese Identities in China and the United States*. Durham, NC: Duke University Press, 2004.

Lowe, Lisa. *Immigrant Acts: On Asian American Cultural Politics*. Durham, NC: Duke University Press, 1996.

Maglipon, Jo-Ann Q. *Primed: Selected Stories, 1972–1992*. Pasig City, Philippines: Anvil Publishing, 1993.

Mail Order Brides / M.O.B. *Always a Bridesmaid, Never a Bride*. Video recording. San Francisco Bay Area: Mail Order Brides / M.O.B., 2005.

Manalansan, Martin F., IV. *Global Divas: Filipino Gay Men in the Diaspora*. Durham, NC: Duke University Press, 2003.

———. "Queering the Chain of Care Paradigm." *Scholar and Feminist Online* 6, no. 3 (2008). http://www.barnard.edu/sfonline/immigration/manalansan_01.htm.

———. "Wayward Erotics: Mediating Queer Diasporic Return." In *Media, Erotics and Transnational Asia*. Edited by Purnima Mankekar and Louisa Schein, 33–52. Durham, NC: Duke University Press, 2012.

Marcuse, Herbert. *Counter-revolution and Revolt*. Boston: Beacon Press, 1972.

Mariano, L. Joyce Zapanta. "Doing Good in Filipino Diaspora: Philanthropy, Remittances, and Homeland Returns." *Journal of Asian American Studies* 20, no. 2 (2017): 219–44.

Mendoza, S. Lily. "A Different Breed of Filipino Balikbayans: The Ambiguities of (Re-)turning." In *Positively No Filipinos Allowed: Building Communities and Discourse*, edited by Antonio T. Tiongson Jr., Edgardo V. Gutierrez, and Ricardo V. Gutierrez, 199–214. Philadelphia: Temple University Press, 2006.

Mendoza, Victor Roman. *Metroimperial Intimacies: Fantasy, Racial-Sexual Governance, and the Philippines in U.S. Imperialism, 1899–1913*. Durham, NC: Duke University Press, 2015.

Mitchell, Nick. "Marriage and Military: Missing the Point of Queer Advancement." *New America Media: EthnoBlog*. 2009. http://ethnoblog.newamericamedia.org/2009/10/marriage-and-military-missing-the-point-of-queer-advancement.php.

Mohanty, Chandra Talpade. "Under Western Eyes: Feminist Scholarship and Colonial Discourses." *Feminist Review*, no. 30 (1988): 61–88.

———. "Women Workers and Capitalist Scripts: Ideologies of Domination, Common Interests, and the Politics of Solidarity." In *Feminist Genealogies, Colonial Legacies, Democratic Futures*, edited by Jaqui M. Alexander and Chandra Mohanty, 3–29. New York: Routledge, 1995.

Morel, Pierre. *Taken*. 2009.

Muñoz, José Esteban. "The Autoethnographic Performance: Reading Richard Fung's Queer Hybridity." *Screen* 36, no. 2 (1995): 83–99.

———. *Cruising Utopia: The Then and There of Queer Futurity*. New York: New York University Press, 2009.

———. *Disidentifications: Queers of Color and the Performance of Politics*. Minneapolis: University of Minnesota Press, 1999.

Naber, Nadine. *Arab America: Gender, Cultural Politics, and Activism*. New York: New York University Press, 2012.

National Heroes. (Re)Creation. 2006. Pilipino Cultural Night, University of California at Berkeley.

Nichols, Mike. *The Birdcage*. 1996.

Nobile, Joseph. *Closer to Home*. DVD. Elbion Film Productions, 1994.

Otálvaro-Hormillosa, Gigi. *Cosmic Blood*. Bindlestiff Studio, San Francisco, March 1, 2003.

Pante, Biel. "Kentex Factory and the Economy Death Trap." Rappler.com, May 21, 2015. http://www.rappler.com/move-ph/ispeak/93879-kentex-death-trap-economy.

Parker, Andrew, Mary Russo, Doris Sommer, and Patricia Yaeger. *Nationalisms and Sexualities*. New York: Routledge, 1992.

Parreñas, Rhacel Salazar. "Benevolent Paternalism and Migrant Women: The Case of Migrant Filipina Entertainers in Japan." *Gender Kenkyu (Journal of Gender Studies)* 10 (2007): 1–17.

——. *Children of Global Migration: Transnational Families and Gendered Woes*. Palo Alto, CA: Stanford University Press, 2005.

——. "Homeward Bound: The Circular Migration of Entertainers between Japan and the Philippines." *Global Networks* 10, no. 3 (2010): 301–23.

——. *Servants of Globalization: Women, Migration, and Domestic Work*. Stanford, CA: Stanford University Press, 2001.

Pido, Eric. "Balikbayan Paranoia: Tourism Development in Manila and the Anxiety of Return." In *Southeast Asian Diaspora in the United States: Memories & Visions Yesterday, Today, & Tomorrow*, edited by Jonathan X. H. Lee, 31–46. Cambridge: Cambridge Scholars Publishing, 2014.

Pierce, Linda M. "Not Just My Closet: Exposing Familial, Cultural, and Imperial Skeletons." In *Pinay Power: Theorizing Peminist Critical Theory*, edited by Melinda De Jesus, 31–44. New York: Routledge, 2005.

Ponce, Martin Joseph. *Beyond the Nation: Diasporic Filipino Literature and Queer Reading*. New York: New York University Press, 2012.

Pratt, Mary Louise. *Imperial Eyes: Travel Writing and Transculturation*. London: Routledge, 1992.

Puar, Jasbir K. *Terrorist Assemblages: Homonationalism in Queer Times*. Durham, NC: Duke University Press, 2007.

Quintos, Rory. *Anak*. 2000.

Rafael, Vicente. *White Love and Other Events in Filipino History*. Durham, NC: Duke University Press, 2000.

Raymundo, Sarah. "In the Womb of the Global Economy: Anak and the Construction of Transnational Imaginaries." *Positions* 19, no. 2 (2011): 551–79.

Rebollo-Gil, Guillermo. "As It Concerns the Ones We've Lost." Empty Lots. June 14, 2016. http://patternofthething.blogspot.com/2016/06/as-it-regards-ones-weve-lost.html.

Riggs, Marlon. *Tongues Untied*. DVD. Signifyin' Works, 1989.

Rivera, Rachel. *Sin City Diary*. VHS. New York: Women Make Movies, 1992.

Robertson, Pamela. "The Kinda Comedy That Imitates Me: Mae West's Identification with the Feminist Camp." *Cinema Journal* 32, no. 2 (1993): 57–72.

——. "What Makes the Feminist Camp?" In *Camp: Queer Aesthetics and the Performing Subject*, edited by Fabio Cleto, 266–82. Ann Arbor: University of Michigan Press, 1999.

Rodriguez, Dylan. "A Million Deaths? Genocide and the 'Filipino American' Condition of Possibility." In *Positively No Filipinos Allowed: Building Communities and Discourse*, edited by Antonio Tiongson, Ricardo Gutierrez, and Edgardo Gutierrez, 145–61. Philadelphia: Temple University Press, 2006.

———. *Suspended Apocalypse: White Supremacy, Genocide, and the Filipino American Condition*. Minneapolis: University of Minnesota Press, 2010.

Rodriguez, Robyn Magalit. *Migrants for Export: How the Philippine State Brokers Labor to the World*. Minneapolis: University of Minnesota Press, 2010.

Rondilla, Joanne L., and Paul Spickard. *Is Lighter Better? Skin-Tone Discrimination among Asian Americans*. Lanham, MD: Rowman and Littlefield Publishers, 2007.

San Juan, E., Jr. *After Postcolonialism: Remapping Philippines–United States Confrontations*. Lanham, MD: Rowman and Littlefield Publishers, 2000.

See, Sarita. *The Decolonized Eye: Filipino American Art and Performance*. Minneapolis: University of Minnesota Press, 2009.

Sevilla, Lolan, and Aimee Espiritu. *The Bakla Show*. Bindlestiff Studio, San Francisco, January 25, 2007.

Shahani, Lila Ramos. "Human Trafficking and Its Intricate Web." *GMA News Online*, January 28, 2013. http://www.gmanetwork.com/news/story/291688/opinion/human-trafficking-and-its-intricate-web.

Shahshahani, Azadeh. "The Philippine President Is Waging a Ruthless War on Drugs—and the U.S. Is Complicit." *In These Times*, October 2, 2018. http://inthesetimes.com/article/21500/peoples-tribunal-philippines-rodrigo-duterte-drug-war-executions-repression.

Shimizu, Celine Parreñas. *The Hypersexuality of Race: Performing Asian/American Women on Screen and Scene*. Durham, NC: Duke University Press, 2007.

Smith, Andrea. "Queer Theory and Native Studies: The Heteronormativity of Settler Colonialism." *GLQ: A Journal of Lesbian and Gay Studies* 16, no. 1–2 (2010): 41–68.

Soriano, Zelda. *Kung Saan Ako Pupunta*. N.p.: Artista at Manunulat ng Sambayanan, 1993.

Soto, Sandra K. "Where in the Transnational World Are US Women of Color?" In *Women's Studies for the Future: Foundations, Interrogations, Politics*, edited by Elizabeth Lapovsky Kennedy and Agatha Beins, 111–24. New Brunswick, NJ: Rutgers University Press, 2005.

Stanley, Eric A., and Nat Smith. *Captive Genders: Trans Embodiment and the Prison Industrial Complex*. Oakland, CA: AK Press, 2015.

Suzara, Aimee. *Pagbabalik/Return*. La Pena Cultural Center, Berkeley, June 14, 2007.

Suzuki, Nobue. "'Japayuki,' or, Spectacles for the Transnational Middle Class." *Positions* 19, no. 2 (2011): 439–62.

Tadiar, Neferti. *Fantasy-Production: Sexual Economies and Other Philippine Consequences for the New World Order*. Hong Kong: Hong Kong University Press, 2004.

———. *Things Fall Away: Philippine Historical Experience and the Makings of Globalization*. Durham, NC: Duke University Press, 2009.

Tolentino, Roland B. "Bodies, Letters, Catalogs: Filipinas in Transnational Space." In *Transnational Asia Pacific: Gender, Culture, and the Public Sphere*, edited by Shirley

Lim, Larry E. Smith, and Wimal Dissanayake, 43–68. Champaign: University of Illinois Press, 1999.

Toribio, Helen C. "We Are Revolution: A Reflective History of the Union of Democratic Filipinos (KDP)." *Amerasia Journal* 24, no. 2 (1998): 155–77.

Torres, Justin. "In Praise of Latin Night at the Queer Club." *Washington Post*, June 13, 2016. https://www.washingtonpost.com/opinions/in-praise-of-latin-night-at-the-queer-club/2016/06/13/e841867e-317b-11e6-95c0-2a6873031302_story.html?utm_term=.f22eae73a7b7.

Tungohan, Ethel. "The Transformative and Radical Feminism of Grassroots Migrant Women's Movement(s) in Canada." *Canadian Journal of Political Science* 50, no. 2 (2017): 479–94.

Vasconcelos, José. *The Cosmic Race / La Raza Cósmica: A Bilingual Edition with an Introduction and Notes.* Translated by Didier T. Jaén. Los Angeles: Pace Publications, 1979.

Velasco, Gina. "Negotiating Legacies: The 'Traffic in Women' and the Politics of Filipina/o American Feminist Solidarity." In *Asian American Feminisms and Women of Color Politics*, edited by Lynn Fujiwara and Shireen Roshanravan. Seattle: University of Washington Press, 2018.

Vergara, Benito. *Pinoy Capital: The Filipino Nation in Daly City.* Philadelphia: Temple University Press, 2008.

Villegas, Mark. "Currents of Militarization, Flows of Hip Hop: Expanding Geographies of Filipino American Culture." *Journal of Asian American Studies* 19, no. 1 (2016): 25–46.

Viola, Michael Joseph. "Toward a Filipino Critical Pedagogy: Exposure Programs to the Philippines and the Politicization of Melissa Roxas." *Journal of Asian American Studies* 17, no. 1 (2014): 1–30.

Visweswaran, Kamala. *Fictions of Feminist Ethnography.* Minneapolis: University of Minnesota Press, 1994.

Weeks, Kathi. "Life within and against Work: Affective Labor, Feminist Critique, and Post-Fordist Politics." *Ephemera* 7, no. 1 (2007): 233–49.

Yuval-Davis, Nira, and Floya Anthias. "The Citizenship Debate: Women, Ethnic Processes and the State." *Feminist Review* 39 (1991): 58–68.

Index

GINA K. VELASCO is an assistant professor in the Women, Gender, and Sexuality Studies Program at Gettysburg College.

THE ASIAN AMERICAN EXPERIENCE

The University of Illinois Press
is a founding member of the
Association of University Presses.

University of Illinois Press
1325 South Oak Street
Champaign, IL 61820-6903
www.press.uillinois.edu